FROM OCEAN LINER
TO CRUISE SHIP

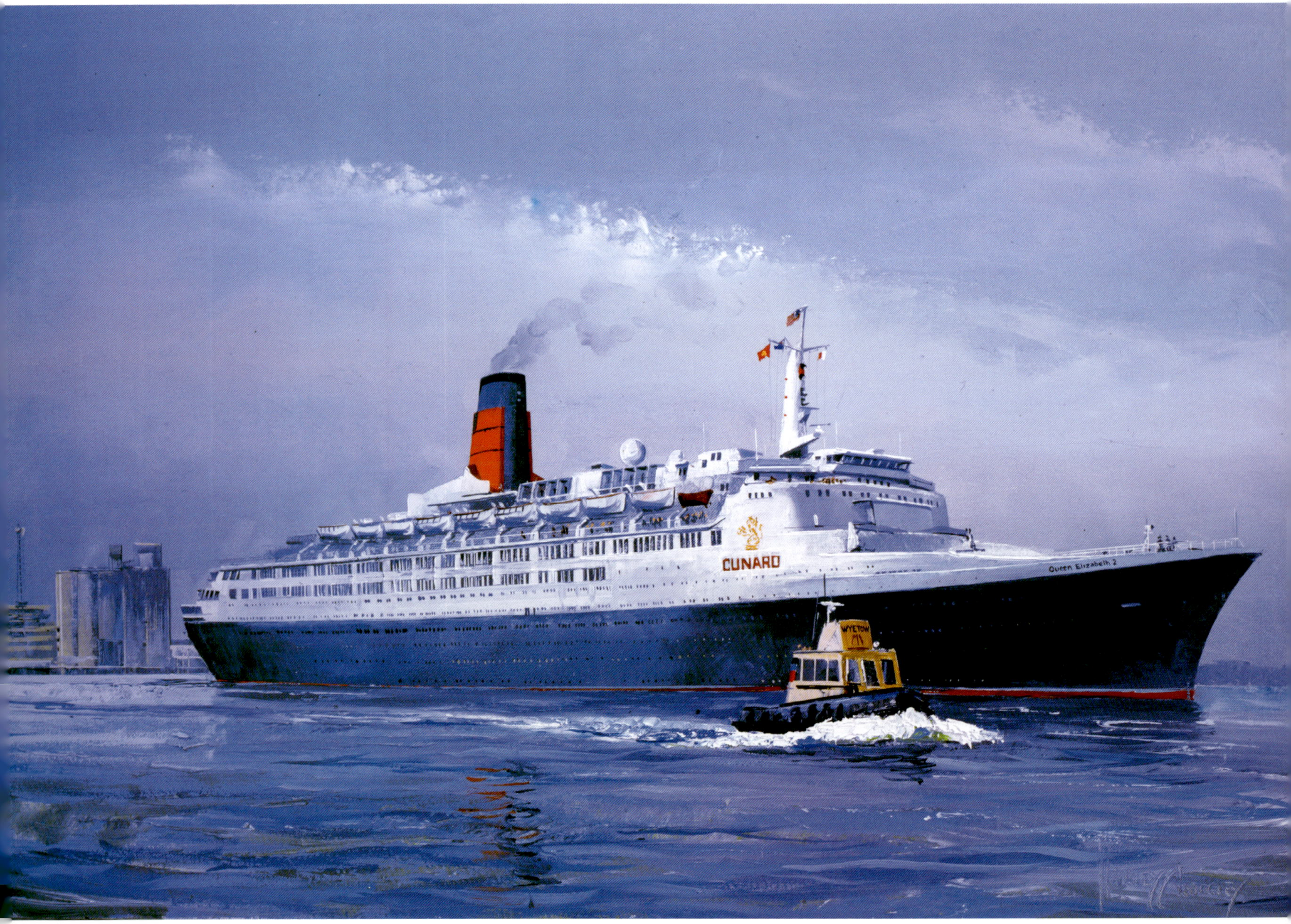

Queen Elizabeth 2 leaving Southampton

FROM OCEAN LINER
TO CRUISE SHIP

The Marine Art of
HARLEY CROSSLEY

AMBERLEY

This book is dedicated to my wife, Barbara,
also a ship enthusiast, without whose total commitment, assistance
and unfailing sense of humour in the face of adversity
it would never have been completed.

ACKNOWLEDGEMENT

My grateful thanks to Mike Lindsay and Campbell McCutcheon, who willingly gave me access to their libraries of photographs and kindly allowed me to reproduce some of them in this book.

First published 2010

Amberley Publishing Plc
Cirencester Road, Chalford,
Stroud, Gloucestershire, GL6 8PE

www.amberley-books.com

ISBN 978 1 84868 926 8

British Library Cataloguing in Publication Data.
A catalogue record for this book is available from the British Library.

Typeset in 10pt on 13pt Sabon.
Typesetting by Amberley Publishing.
Printed in the UK.

CONTENTS

STAGES IN THE PAINTING OF KAISER WILHELM DER GROSSE

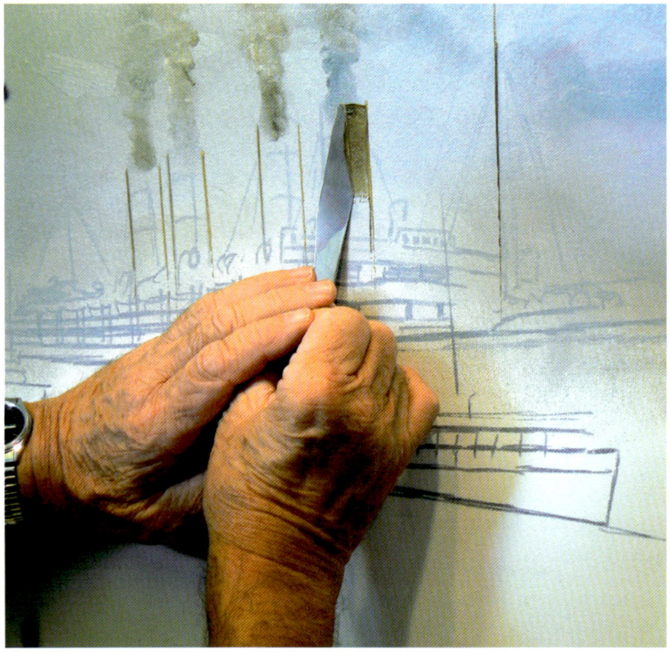

Using the large knife to drag the paint across the forward funnel

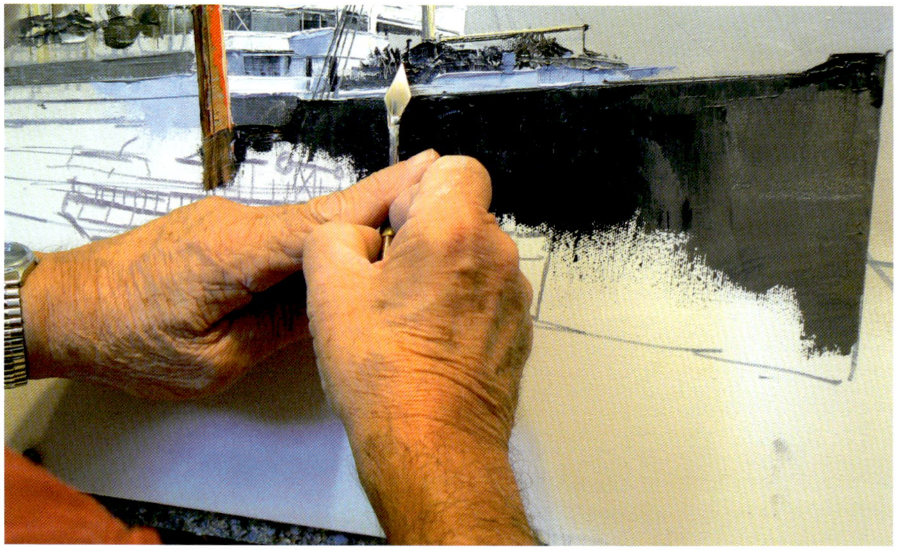

Using the tip of the small knife to scratch into the paint

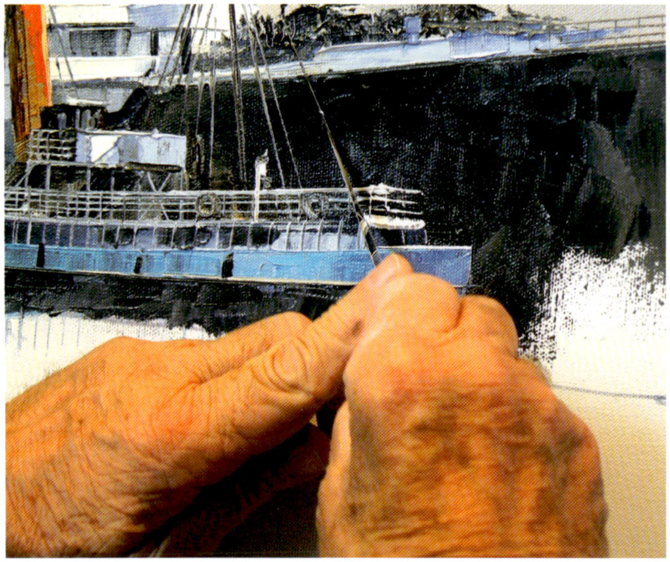

Using the edge of the blade of the large knife to 'draw' the rigging

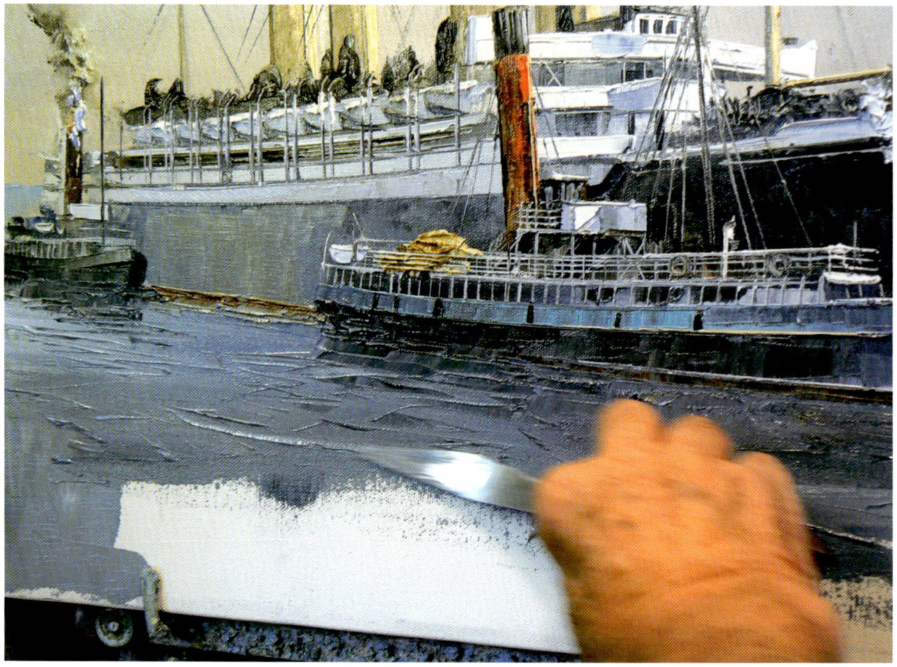

Dragging the blade of the large knife to paint the sea

PREFACE

Harley Crossley was born in Southampton and spent much of his early life close to the busy docks. He grew up within sight of the ocean liners arriving and departing on their regular line passages to destinations around the world. Every week, from his bedroom window, he would see the tall funnels of the Cunard, Union Castle, Royal Mail and other ships as they loaded or unloaded their cargo and passengers in the docks.

Accustomed to the dull grey of the ships during the war, he was fascinated to see the brightness of the funnels as they were repainted in their company colours when it was over. The billowing steam from the approaching boat trains coupled with the resounding whistles of the magnificent ocean liners stirred his imagination with visions of exotic destinations.

Living through the heyday of transatlantic travel by ocean liners, it is no wonder that Harley developed a deep love for these giants of the sea. As a teenager in 1950, he witnessed the last of the four-funnelled passenger liners, the *Aquitania*, leaving the Southampton New Docks on her way to the scrap yard.

His first job as a messenger in Southampton Docks found Harley spending his lunch breaks sketching the ships, frequently selling them to members of the ships' crews. He worked in the new Ocean Terminal, which was opened in 1950 to cope with the amount of passengers flocking to cross the Atlantic Ocean on the luxury liners: an exciting era for anyone with an interest in ships.

Sadly, the development of the jet airliner led to the demise of these giants of the oceans as seaborne passenger numbers dwindled in favour of the new excitement of travelling by air. Many famous ships struggled to remain viable by cruising for the first time. Destinations previously unthought of were visited as companies fought to stay in business and keep the magnificent liners afloat. Many people thought that this would be the end of large passenger ships, truly the end of an era of luxury travel.

Nowadays, although line passages are almost unheard of, cruising is big business and cruise ships have brought about a rebirth of travelling by sea. Vessels of unbelievable size now visit exotic destinations around the world – but purely as a holiday voyage. Ships are no longer a means of transporting people to a new life in another country, but more like a bus journey with entertainment to pass the time between stops.

As time went by, Harley developed his talent for drawing and painting until he eventually became a professional artist, evolving his technique of painting in oils with knives. Although he also paints landscapes and old city scenes, Harley specialises in paintings of ships, particularly the old ocean liners, which are so evocative of a bygone age.

Over the last fifteen years, Harley has painted all over the world, frequently travelling on board the cruise ships that sail the oceans today, lecturing on art and shipping, and thus providing some of the entertainment which their passengers enjoy. His love of the sea and ships is reflected in the precision and detail of his paintings, some of which are reproduced in this book for your enjoyment.

To view more paintings by Harley Crossley visit the website at www.harley-crossley-studio.co.uk

Harley is always happy to accept commissions and can be contacted through his website.

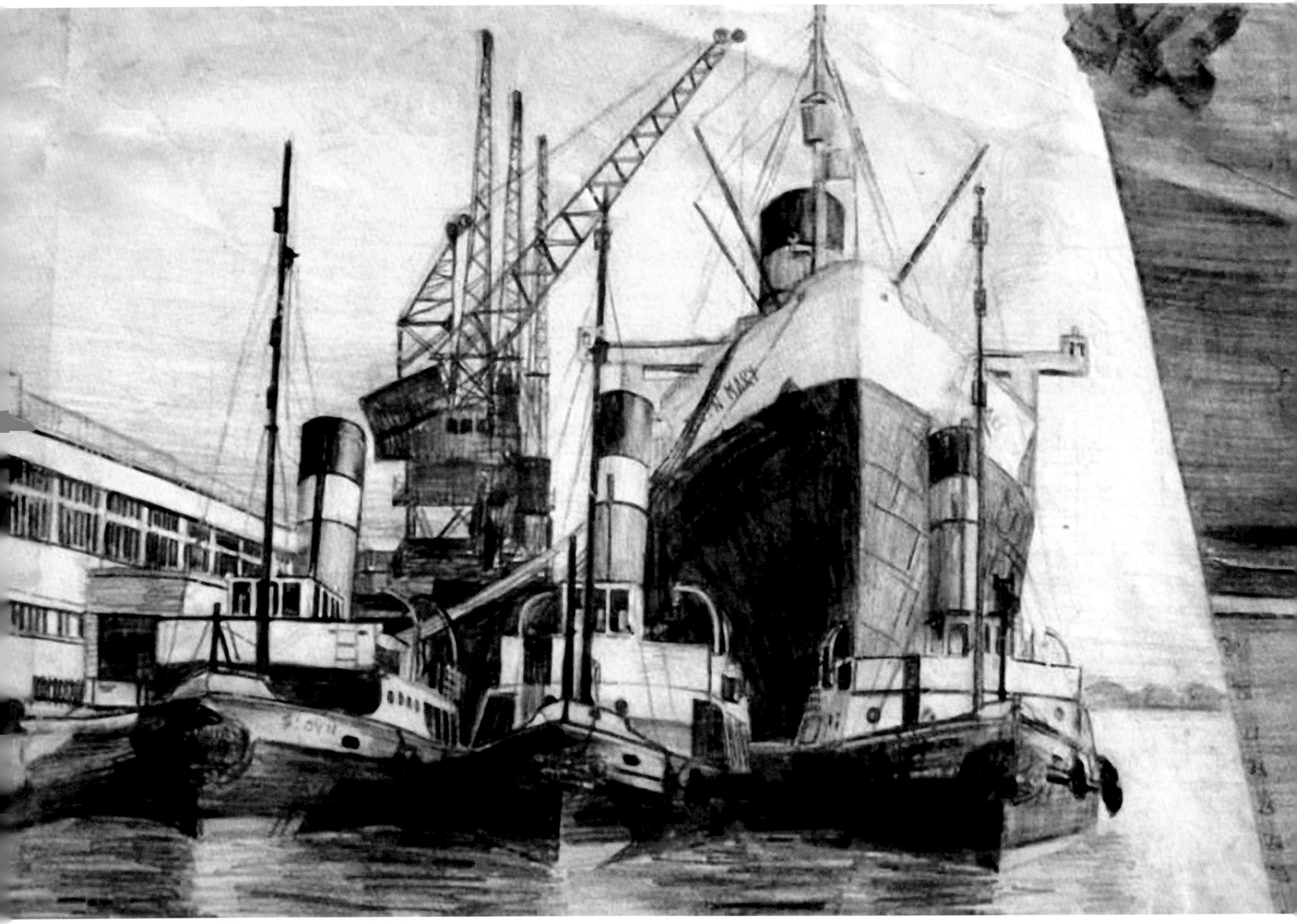

Early sketch – Southampton Docks

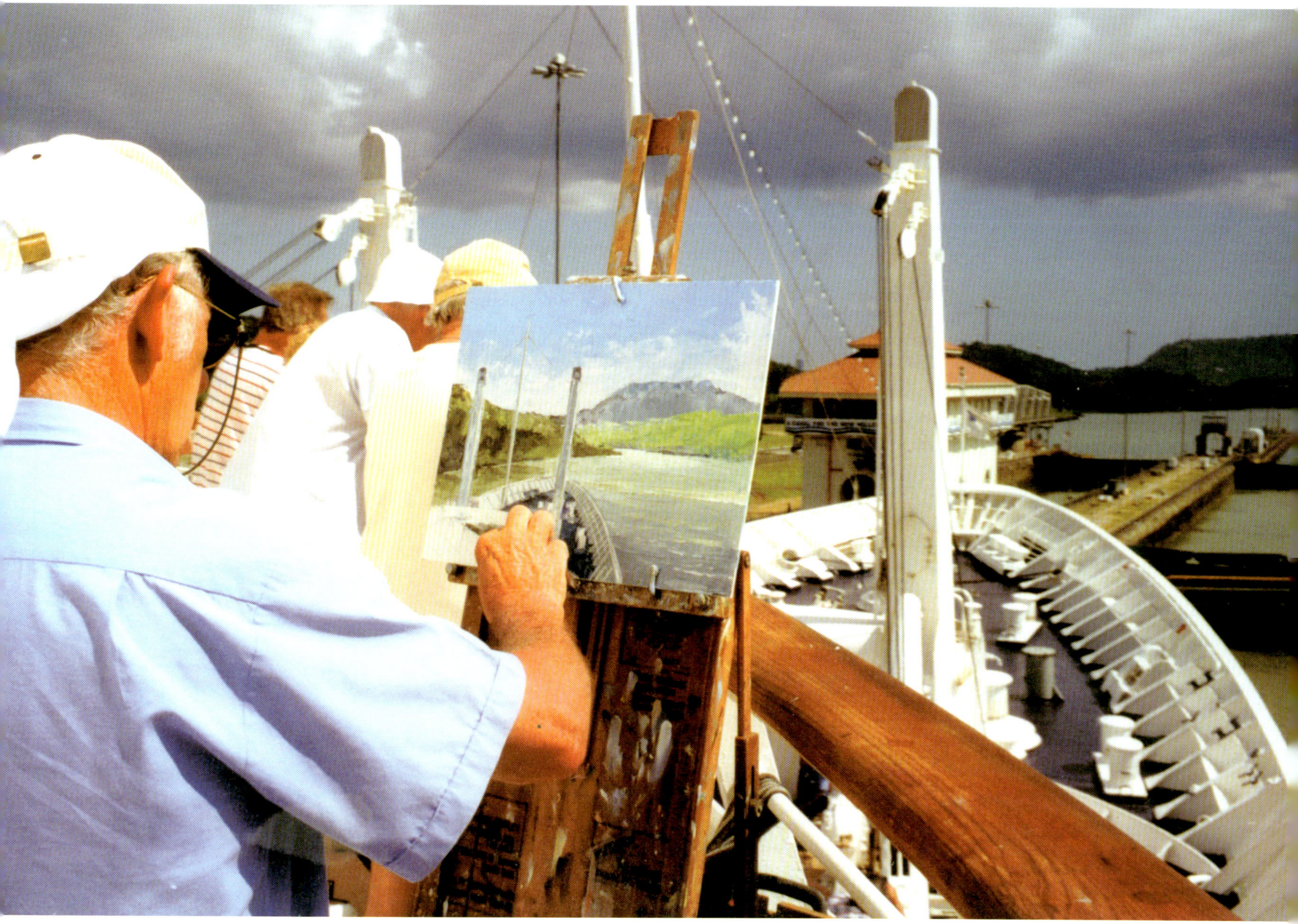

Painting on *Saga Rose* in Panama Canal

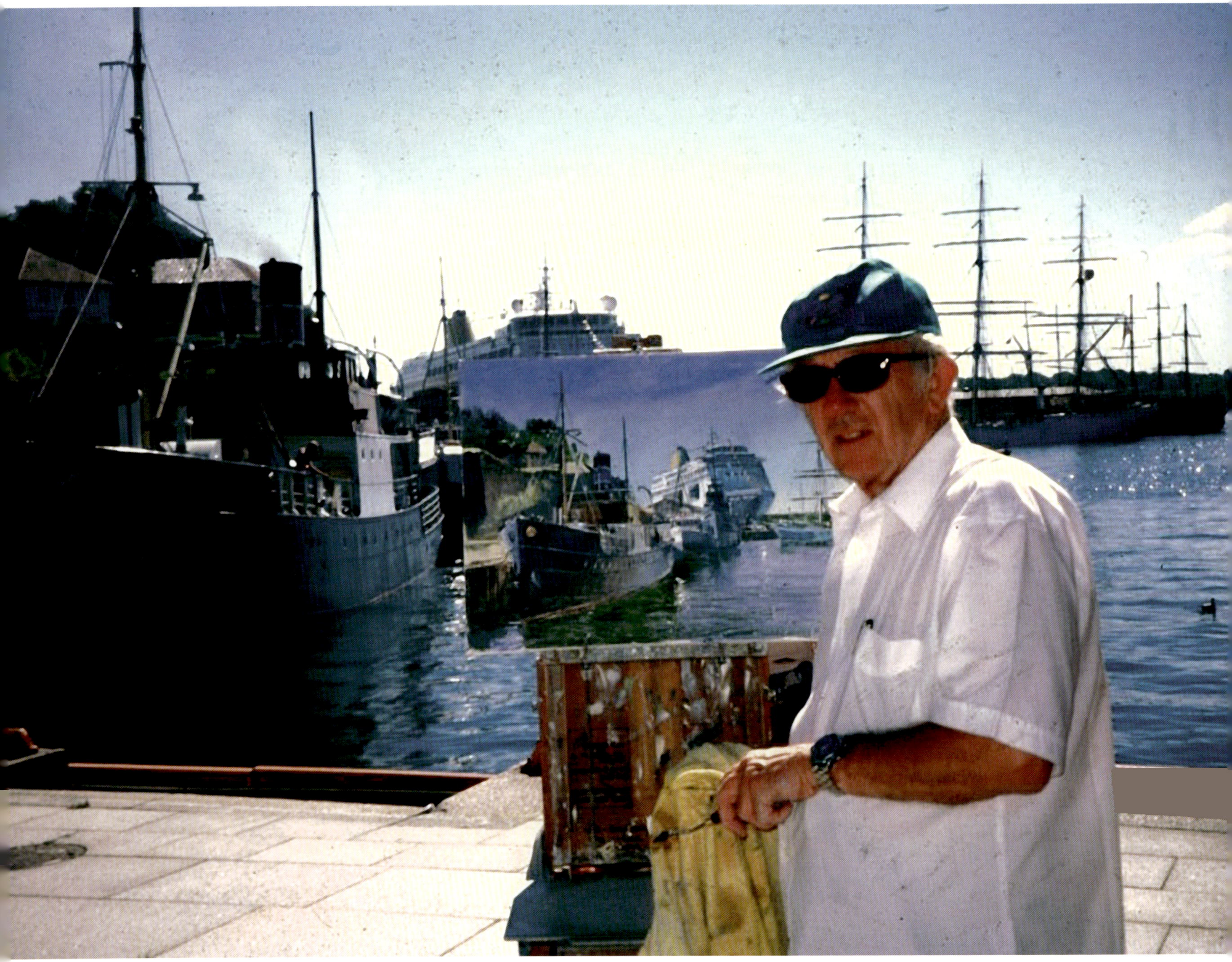

Painting in Oslo

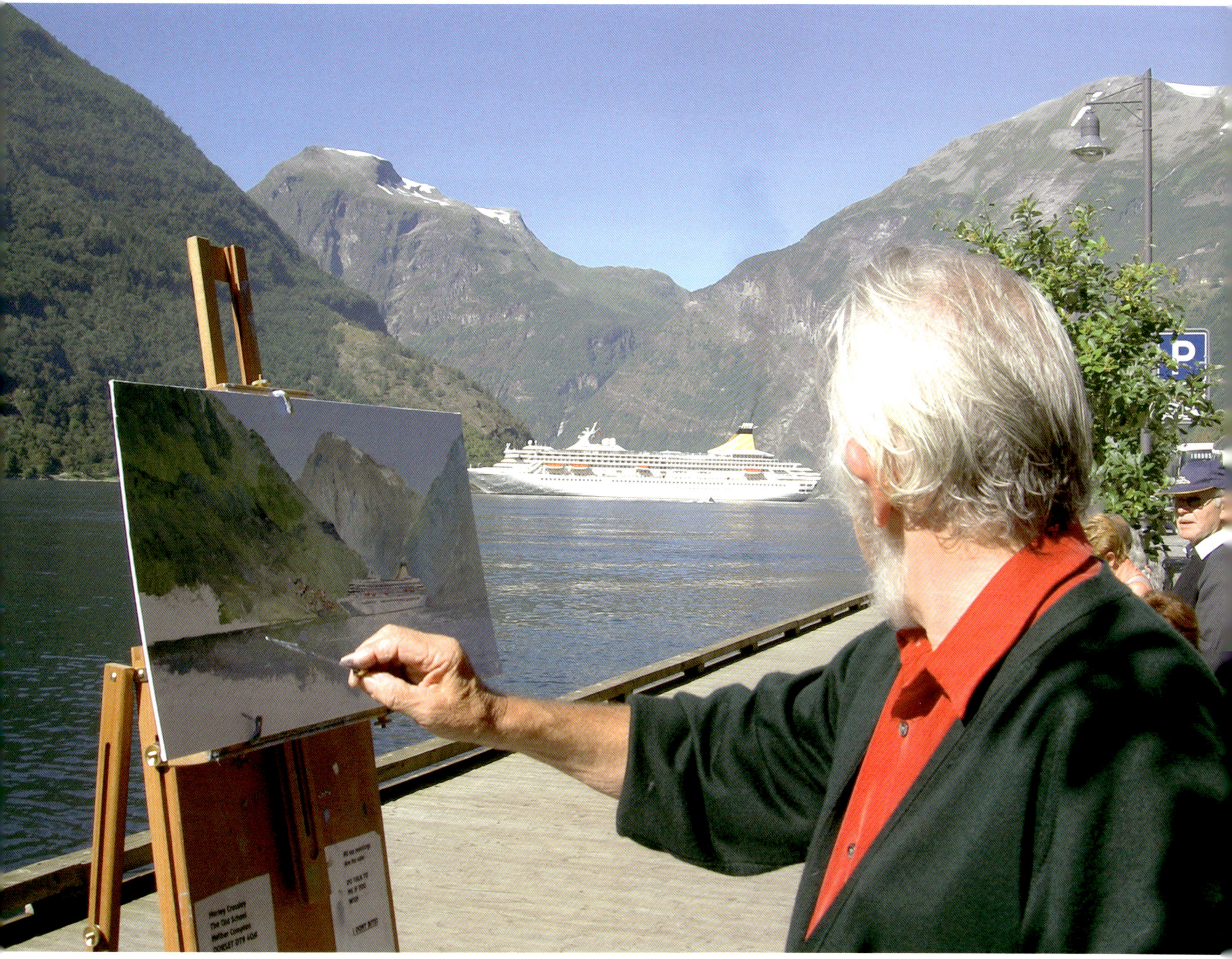

Painting *Artemis* in Norway

SOUTHAMPTON OCEAN DOCK

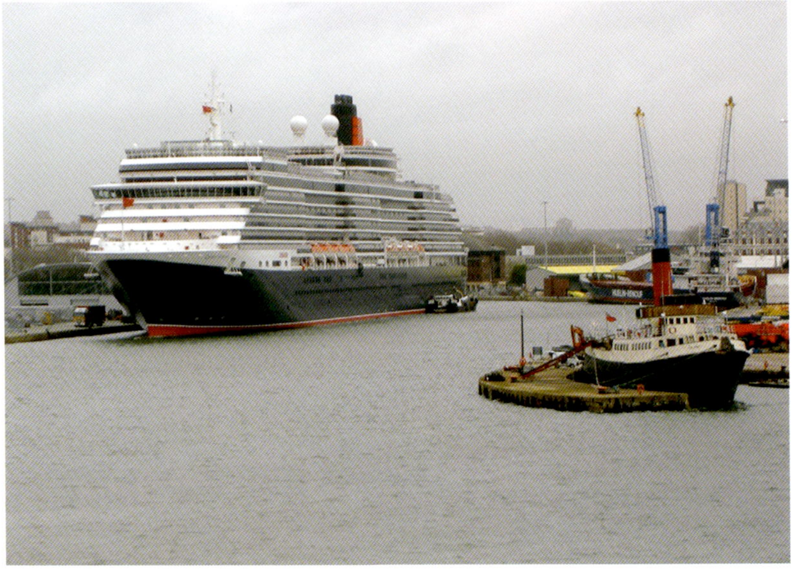

Southampton Ocean Dock, 2010

Construction of what was originally called the White Star Dock began in 1907 when White Star Line transferred their large liner service to New York from Liverpool to Southampton.

A large new dock would be required when White Star introduced the first of the three new Olympic-class ships, which would be the first ships of over 40,000 grt in the world.

By June 1911, work was advanced enough for the new *Olympic* to sail from 44 berth on her maiden voyage to New York.

With a total quayside length of 3,800 feet, the dock covered an area of 15½ acres and provided an additional five berths to the port. It was the first dock in Southampton to be fitted with all electric quayside cranes. With 40 feet of water at the lowest tides, the world's largest liners were always able to berth in the dock at any time.

The name of the dock was changed to Ocean Dock in 1922. It became the UK terminal for the Cunard and White Star's largest passenger liners, with ships from the fleets of America, France, Germany and Holland regularly using the dock on UK calls.

After the Second World War, plans were made to modernise the entire docks in Southampton, including the building of the famous Ocean Terminal. Berths 43 and 44 were cleared for this terminal, which was opened by the Prime Minister Clement Attlee in July 1950.

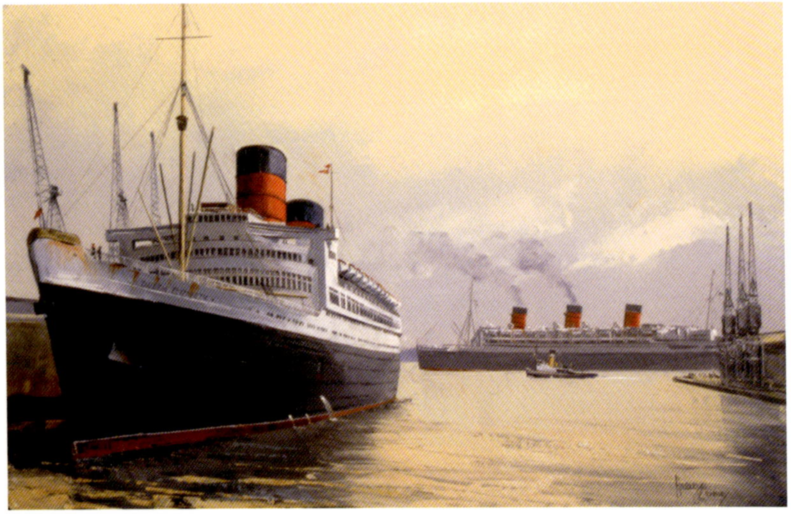

Queen Elizabeth and *Queen Mary*

This Art Deco-style building was 1,297 feet long with two railway platforms at the lower level for the boat trains, which carried railway passengers to the liners. The ground floor of the terminal building was used for freight and stores, with magnificent reception areas for passengers on the first floor. There were three pairs of telescopic gangways used to connect the ships with the upper level of the building. RMS *Queen Elizabeth* was the first ship to use the new Ocean Terminal the day after the opening ceremony.

With the increased popularity of air travel, passenger numbers on liners declined, and sadly, in 1983, the Ocean Terminal building was demolished. The dock area was relegated to use for ship layups, scrap metal and grain exports.

In 2009, a new 300-metre-long Ocean Terminal was completed at 46/47 berth for the cruise ships of the giant Carnival group. *Oceana*, one of P&O's cruise ships, was the first vessel to use the new terminal in May 2009. Once again, the dock is being used by large passenger ships.

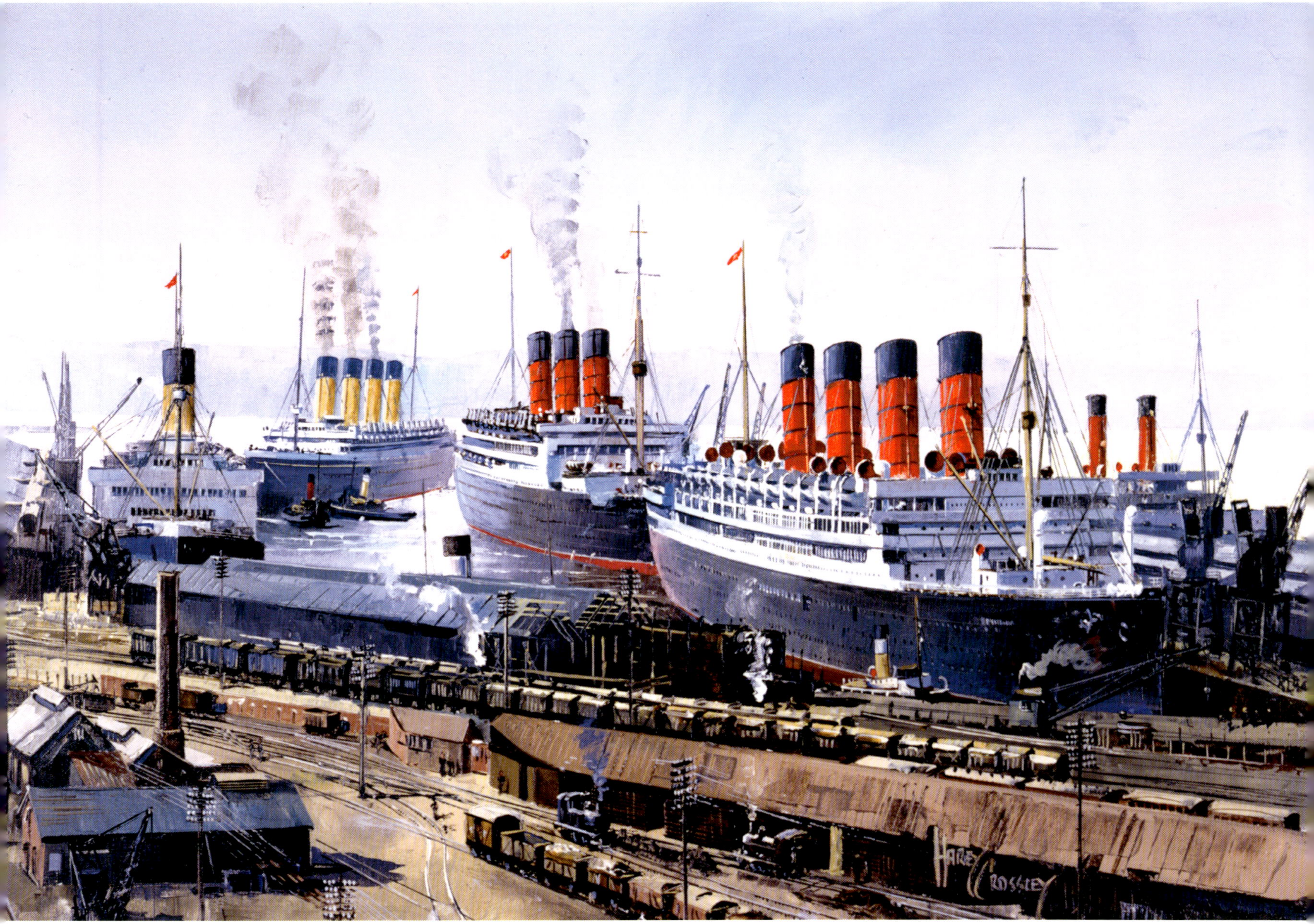

Southampton Ocean Dock. *Homeric* (left), *Olympic* (sailing), *Berengaria*, *Aquitania* and a Union Castle vessel

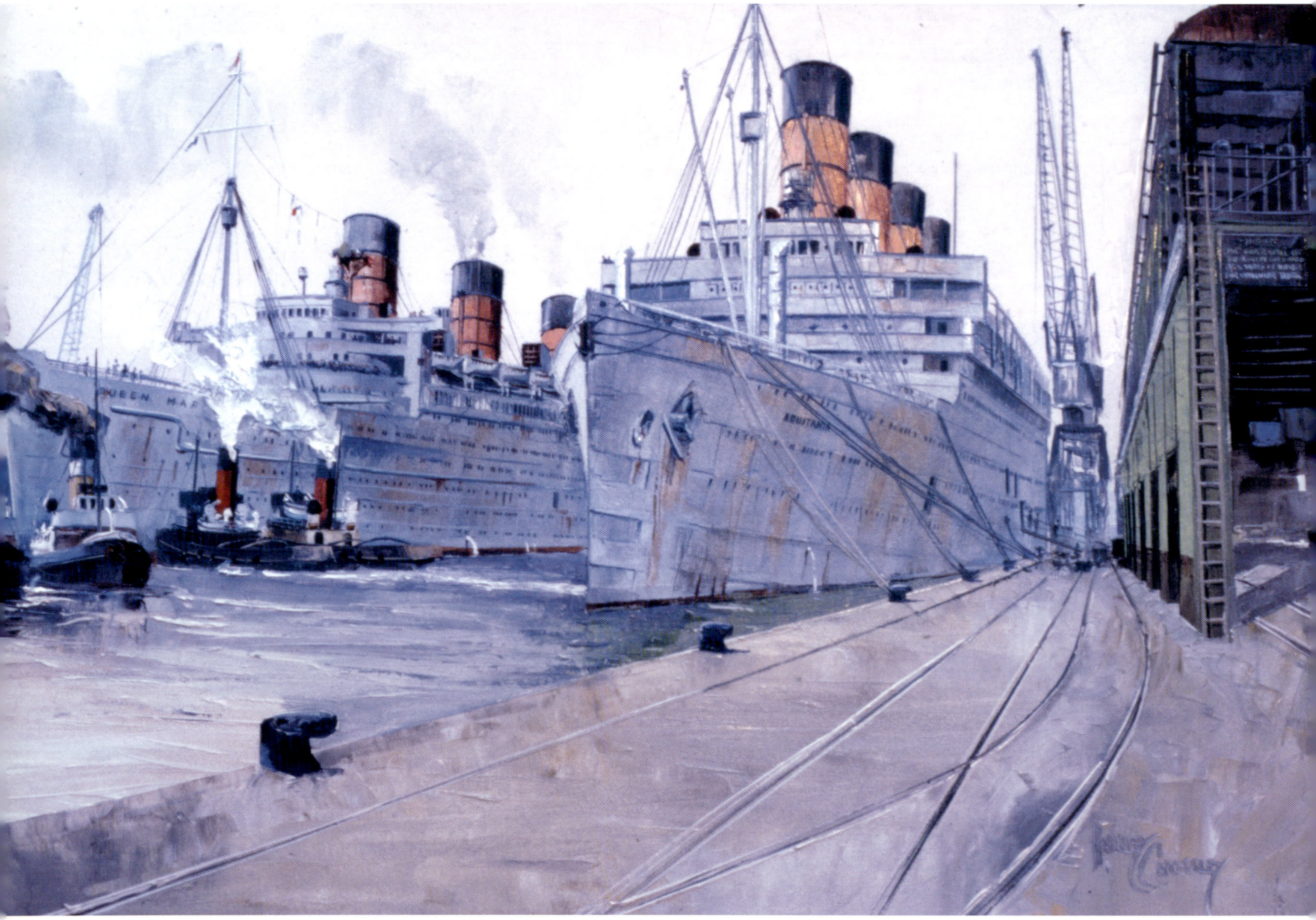

Queen Mary and *Aquitania* in Ocean Dock, 1945

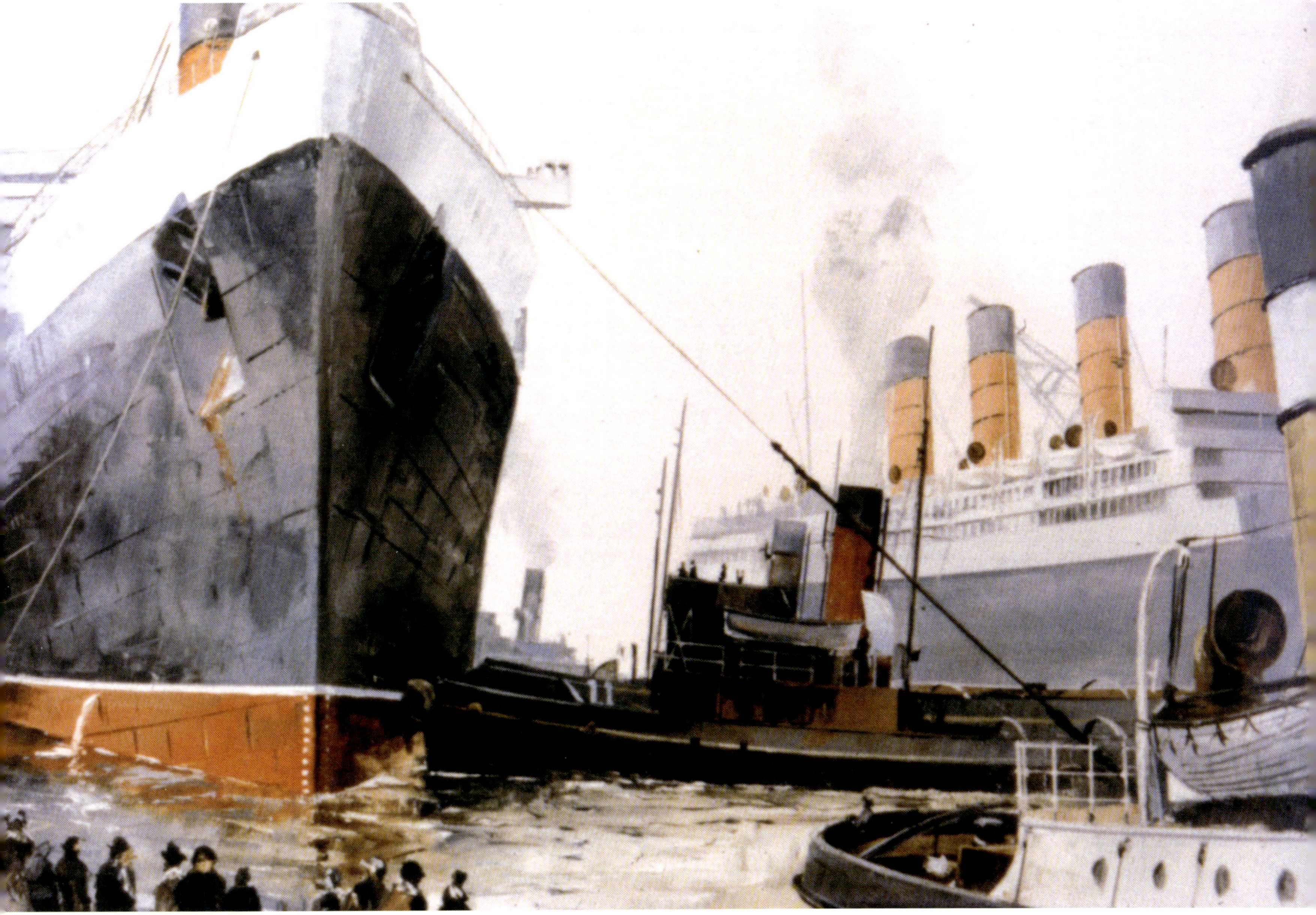

First arrival of *Queen Mary* into Ocean Dock, 1936 (unfinished painting)

KAISER WILHELM DER GROSSE

655 feet x 66 feet 14,349 grt

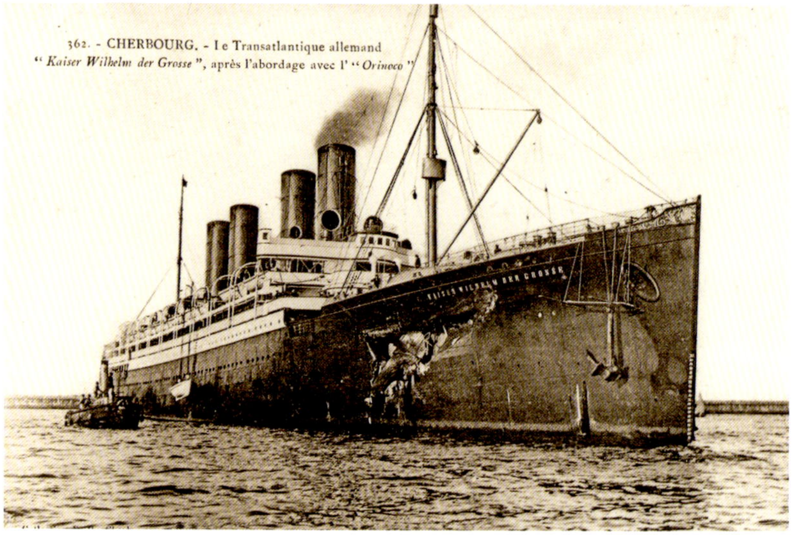

Kaiser Wilhelm der Grosse after having been rammed by *Orinoco* (C. McCutcheon)

Built by the Vulcan shipyard in Stettin for North German Lloyd, *Kaiser Wilhelm der Grosse* was launched in May 1897, the first four-funnelled transatlantic passenger liner and the world's largest ship until 1899.

Powered by two sets of four-cylinder triple-expansion engines with steam supplied by twelve double-ended boilers consuming 250 tons of coal per day, she made her maiden voyage from Bremerhaven to New York in September 1897.

In November, she became the first German ship to win the Blue Riband for the fastest eastbound crossing of the Atlantic, at a speed of 22.35 knots. Four months later, she made a record-breaking voyage westbound from the Needles in the Isle of Wight to Sandy Hook, New York in 5 days, 20 hours, an average speed of 22.29 knots, winning the Blue Riband from the Cunard ship *Lucania*.

Not only was *Kaiser Wilhelm der Grosse* the first German ship to hold the coveted Blue Riband, she was also the first non-British ship in forty years to do so. She was the first commercial ship to have a Marconi wireless telegraphy system fitted in 1900.

Within months of her record-breaking crossing, she became the most popular ship sailing the route. North German Lloyd were soon carrying 24 per cent of all passengers crossing the Atlantic, and for the first time, the company carried more First and Second Class passengers than Cunard.

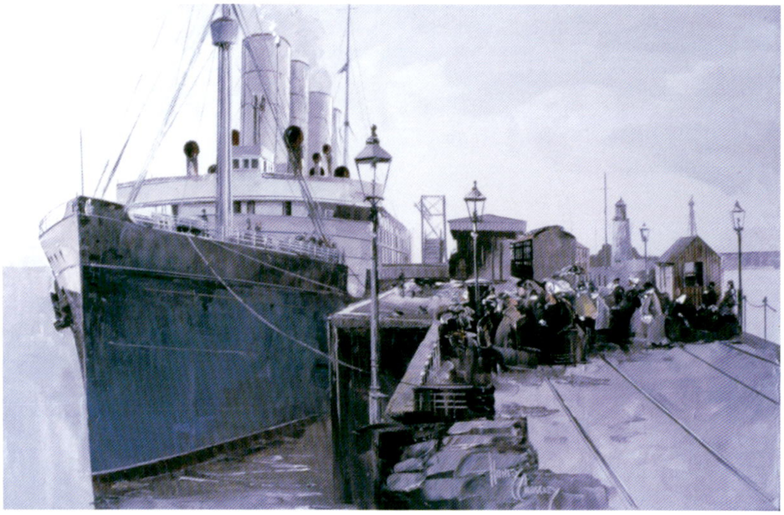

Kaiser Wilhelm der Grosse at Prince of Wales Pier, Dover

In November 1906, she tore a hole 70 feet by 26 feet in her hull when she collided with the British steamer *Orinoco* off Cherbourg. Five passengers were killed in the incident, and the German ship was later found to be at fault for the accident.

At the beginning of the First World War, she was taken over by the German Navy, converted into an auxiliary cruiser and fitted with six 4-inch guns. She then sank three ships in the North Atlantic. However, the big drawback to using such a ship as a cruiser was her enormous fuel consumption, and this led to her demise.

On 26 August 1914, whilst the ship was bunkering off Rio del Oro in Spanish West Africa, she was intercepted by the elderly British cadet training cruiser HMS *Highflyer*. The German captain refused to leave the anchorage, and the British cruiser opened fire.

After a duel lasting for ninety minutes, *Kaiser Wilhelm der Grosse* ran out of ammunition. The German version of events says that the crew then scuttled the ship, but the British insist that they sank her with gunfire.

She was the first passenger ship to be sunk in the First World War.

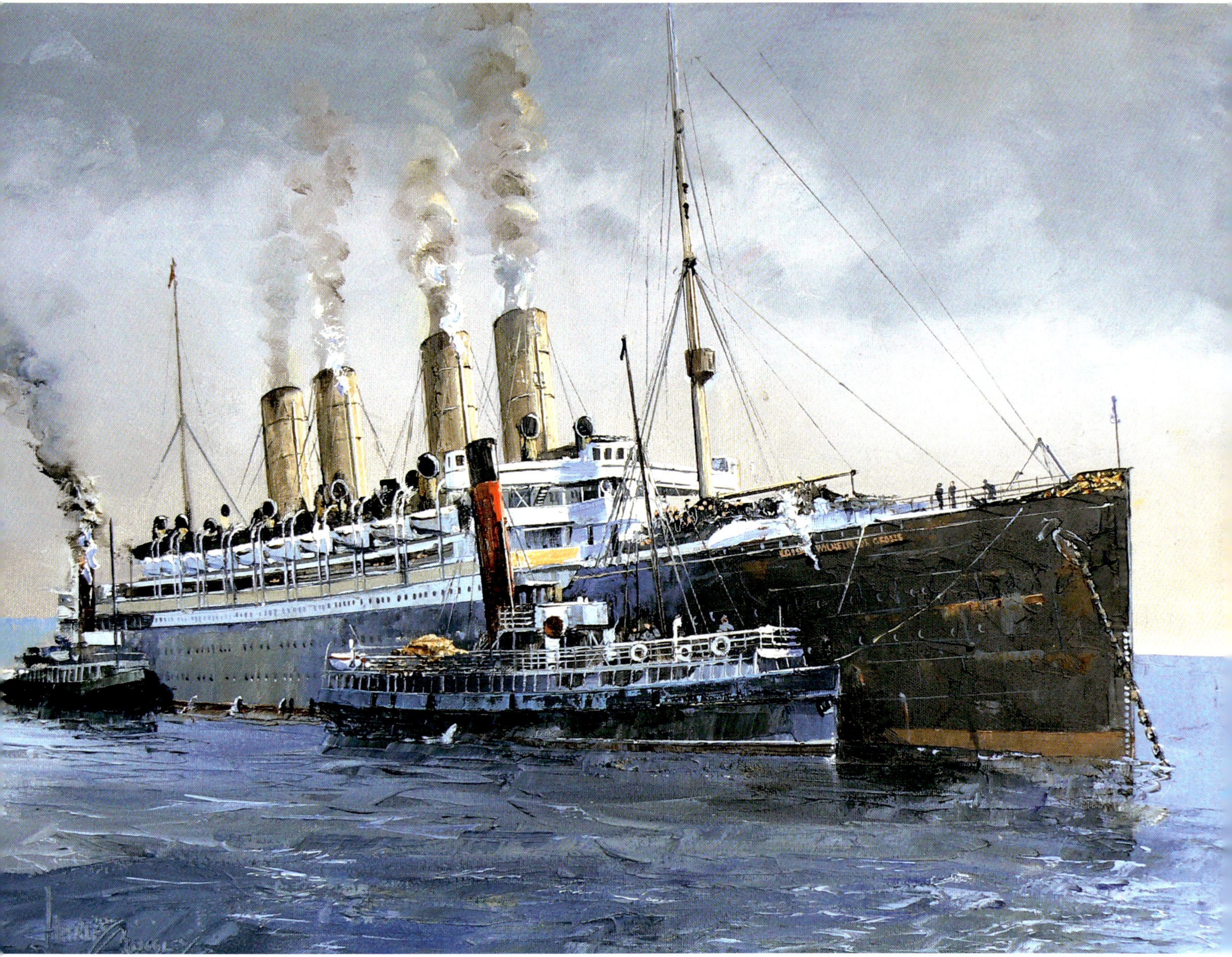

Kaiser Wilhelm der Grosse offloading mail at Plymouth

LUSITANIA

787 feet x 87 feet 31,550 grt

When White Star Line was bought by the American IMM Company in 1902, the concerned British Government offered the Cunard Company a low-interest loan of £2,600,000 to construct two giant express liners. Conditions were attached to the loan, one being that they should remain British, and that they should incorporate certain features that would be useful to the Admiralty in the event of war.

Designed to break the dominance of the record-breaking German liners, the two ships were the *Lusitania* and the *Mauretania*.

Built by John Brown on Clydebank for Cunard, *Lusitania* represented a giant step forward in marine engineering. She was the first British-built four-funnelled liner, the largest ship in the world when built and also the first four-screw turbine-powered ship.

She was launched on 7 June 1906 by Lady Inverclyde, watched by thousands of people, before moving to her fitting-out berth.

During her speed runs on her trials in July 1907, she averaged 26.45 knots, well above the 24.5 knots called for in her mail contract.

On 7 September 1907, *Lusitania* left Liverpool for New York on her maiden voyage, carrying 2,200 passengers. On her second crossing to New York, she took the Blue Riband with an average speed of 23.99 knots, crossing the Atlantic in 4 days, 19 hours, 52 minutes: the first time the crossing had been made in fewer than five days.

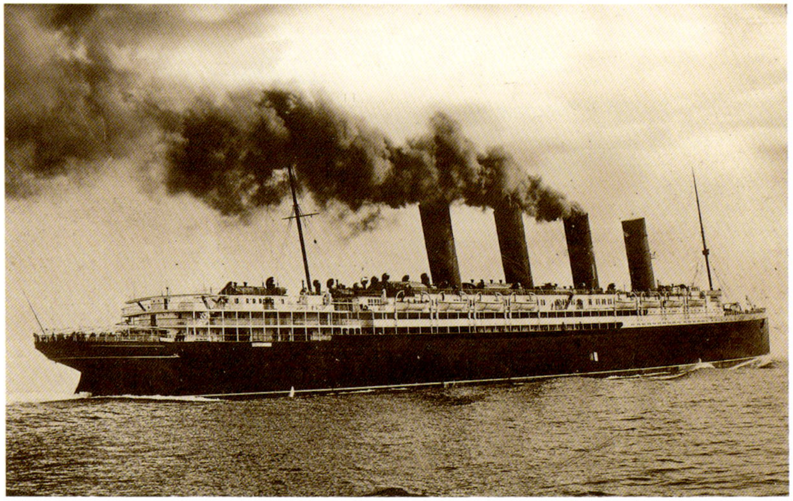

Lusitania on trials

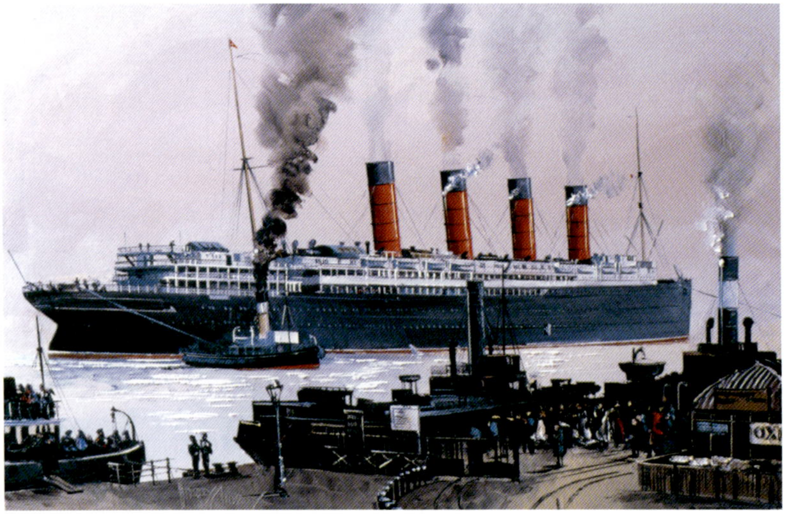

Lusitania at Liverpool

In September 1909, she began calling at Fishguard in South Wales on her homeward voyages to Liverpool. This sped up the delivery of mails and also the journey for passengers who were travelling on to London and the Continent.

Although originally built for possible use by the Admiralty during hostilities, *Lusitania* was not requisitioned by the Admiralty at the start of the First World War because of her size and fuel consumption. Instead, in November 1914, she began a monthly service to New York with six of her twenty-five boilers closed down as an economy measure. This reduced her speed to 21 knots.

She left New York on 1 May 1915 on what was to be her final voyage. The German Government had declared the waters around Great Britain and Ireland a war zone. Prior to her sailing, the German Embassy in New York had published a warning in a newspaper reminding passengers of the danger they would face if they sailed on the ship.

She was torpedoed by the German submarine U20 off the Old Head of Kinsale, Ireland, at 2.15 p.m. on 7 May. Weather conditions were good, and the ship was in sight of land at the time. The torpedo hit the starboard side of the ship, and there was a secondary explosion, possibly caused by exploding coal dust.

Lusitania sank in twenty minutes with the loss of 1,198 lives.

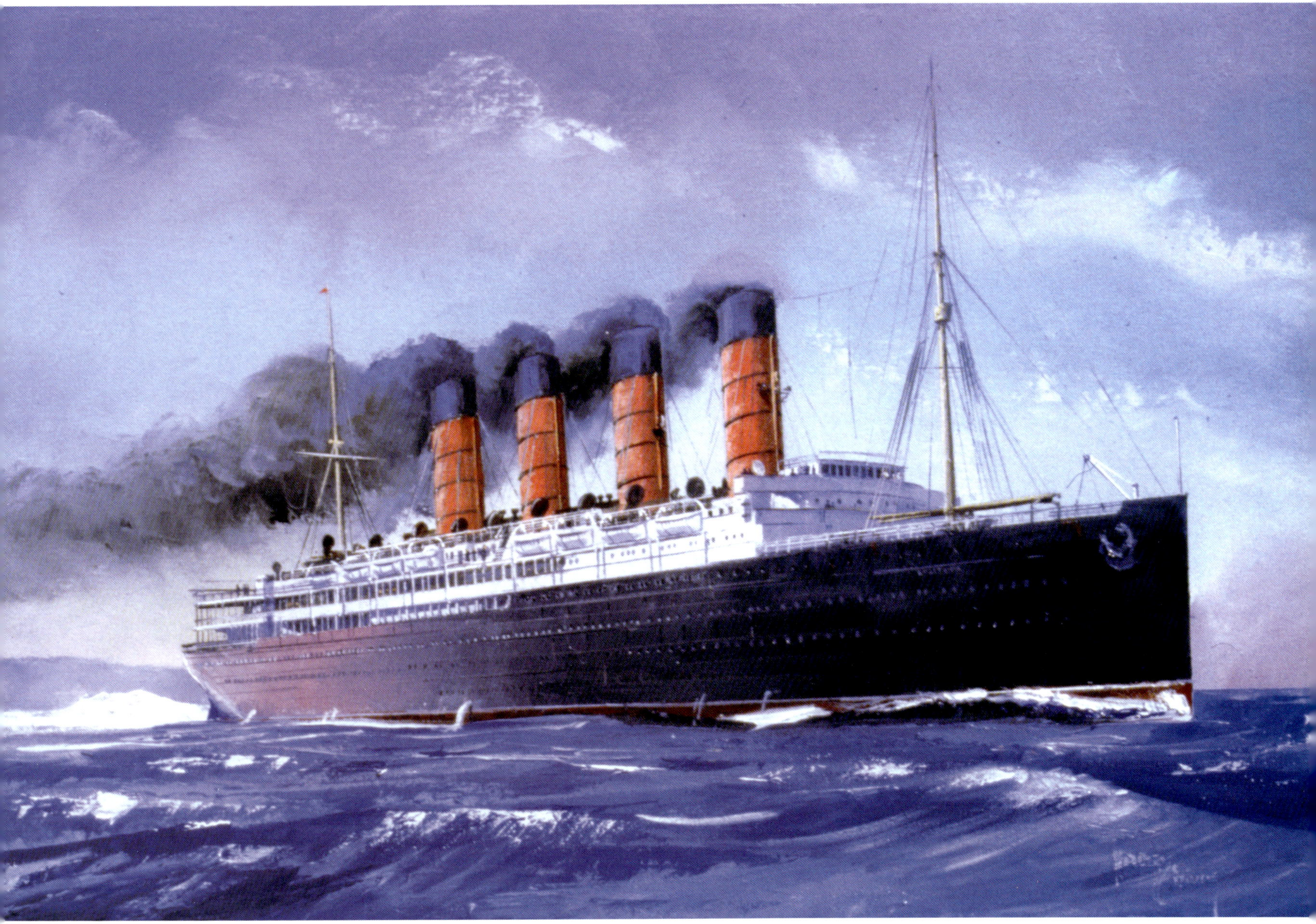

Lusitania at Speed

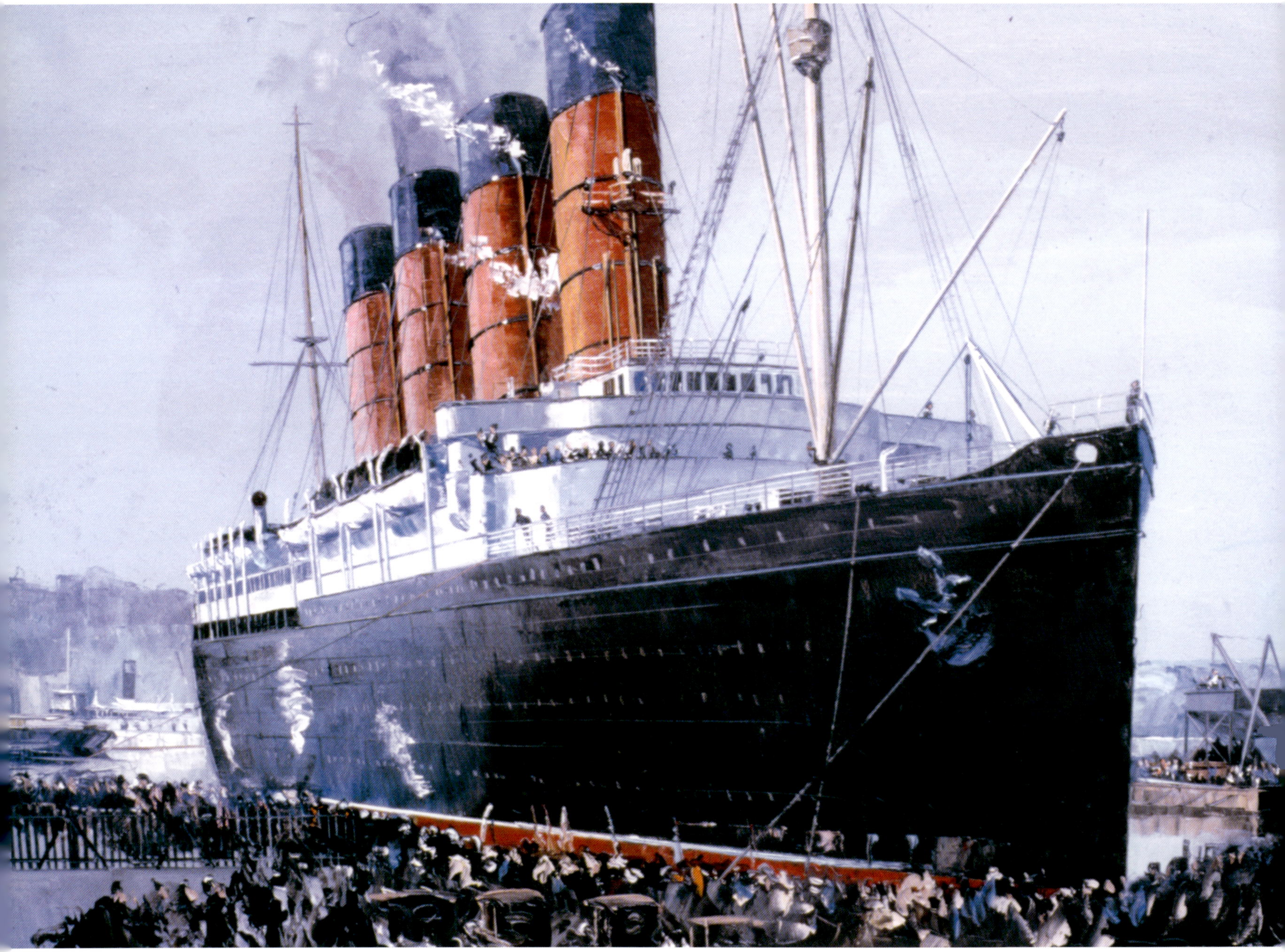

Above: Lusitania, Arrival at New York

Opposite: Lusitania Sinking, 7 May 1915

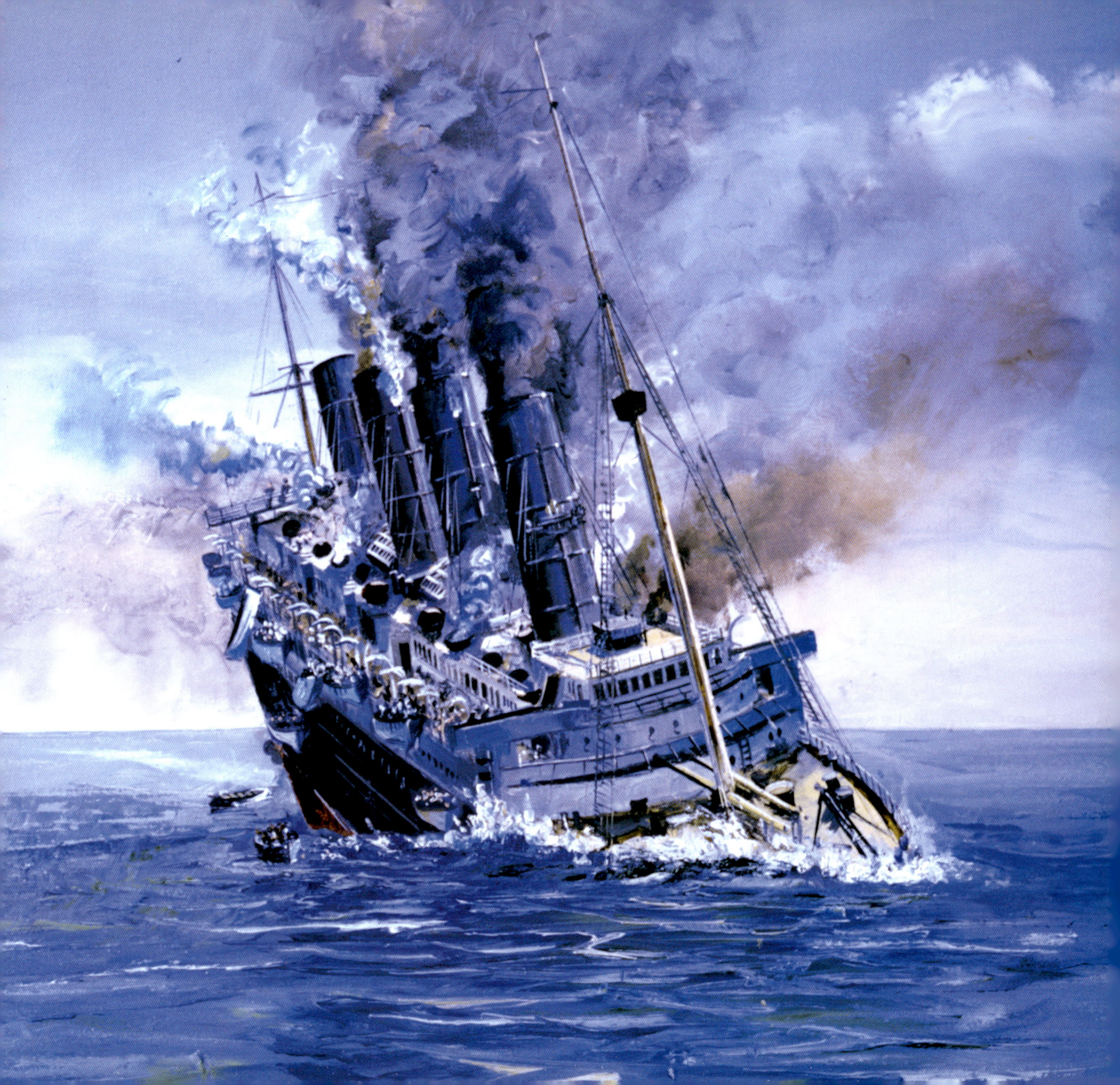

MAURETANIA

790 feet x 88 feet 31,938 grt

Built for Cunard in the north-east of England on the River Tyne at the yard of Swan Hunter & Wigham Richardson, *Mauretania*'s keel was laid in August 1904.

Like her near sister ship *Lusitania*, she was part funded by a low-interest loan from the British Government and an annual subsidy towards the running costs. Two new covered slipways were built at the yard, one with a glass roof, and a 140-ton floating crane, named *Titan*, was purchased from Germany, to help with the fitting out of the ship.

Mauretania was launched on the Tyne by the Dowager Duchess of Roxburghe on 20 September 1906, three months after the launch of the *Lusitania* on the Clyde. The Duchess arrived at the yard in her Rolls-Royce Silver Ghost motor car and proceeded to drive through the funnels, which had been laid on their sides especially to facilitate this publicity event.

Fitted with four giant direct-drive Parsons turbines developing 78,000 shp, the ship achieved a speed of 27.36 knots during her official trials from Liverpool in the Irish Sea in November 1907. Being three feet longer than *Lusitania*, she was now the largest ship in the world, and she retained this title until 1911.

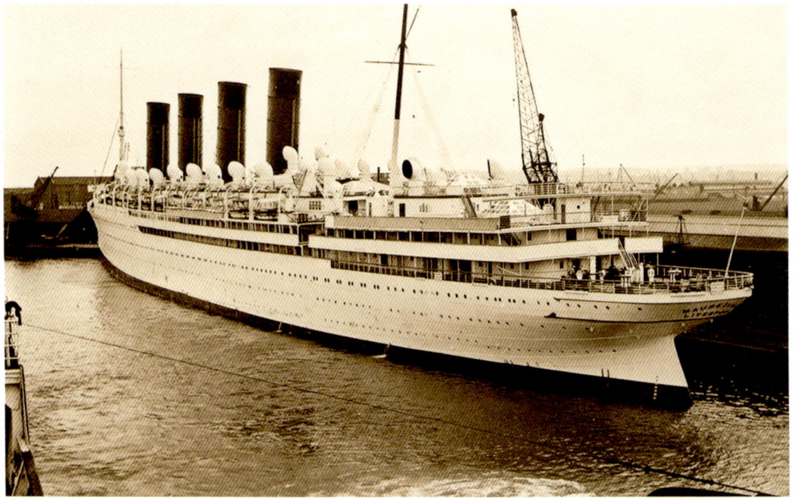

Mauretania (C. McCutcheon)

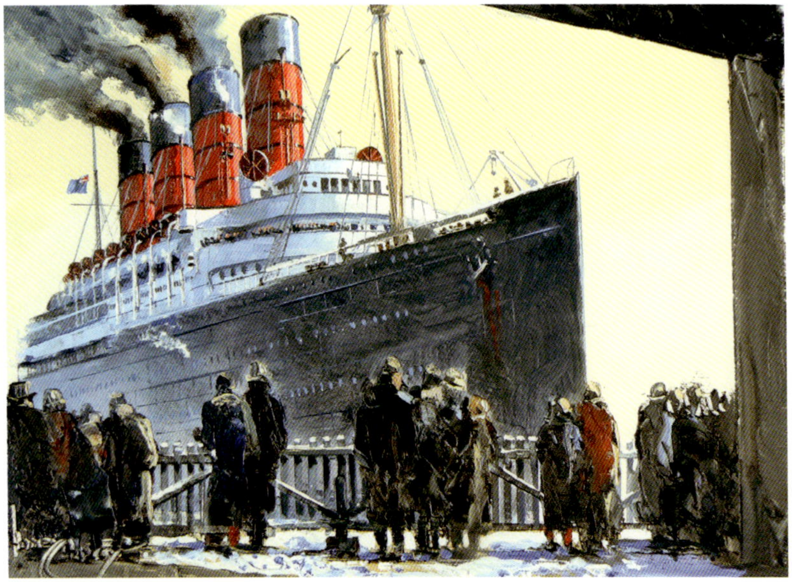

Mauretania in New York

Mauretania left on her maiden voyage from Liverpool to New York on 16 November, and on her return, she broke the record for the fastest eastward crossing of the Atlantic, with a speed of 23.69 knots. In September 1909, she managed an average speed of 26.06 knots across the Atlantic. This gave her the Blue Riband, which she then held for over twenty years.

At the outbreak of the First World War, it was realised that *Mauretania*, like the *Lusitania*, was unsuitable for use as an auxiliary cruiser as had been originally intended. Instead, from June 1915, she was used as a troop transport and hospital ship until she was laid up in 1917 due to boiler-room damage.

She was subsequently brought back into service for the Admiralty, painted in dazzle camouflage and armed with 6-inch guns, to transport American troops to Europe. Her final voyage as a troopship was with 4,000 Canadians in June 1919. After the war, her home port was changed from Liverpool to Southampton, and she resumed her Atlantic crossings on this route.

In July 1921, *Mauretania* was badly damaged by fire at Southampton. The ship returned to her builders on the Tyne for renovation, during which time she was also converted from coal to oil burning before returning to her Southampton to New York service again in March 1922.

After her winter overhaul in 1930, she returned to service with a white hull, mainly for cruising from New York to the West Indies. She made her final voyage in September 1934 and was then laid up in Southampton until April 1935, when she was sold for scrap. Her fixtures and fittings were sold at auction before she departed on her last voyage to Rosyth for breaking up.

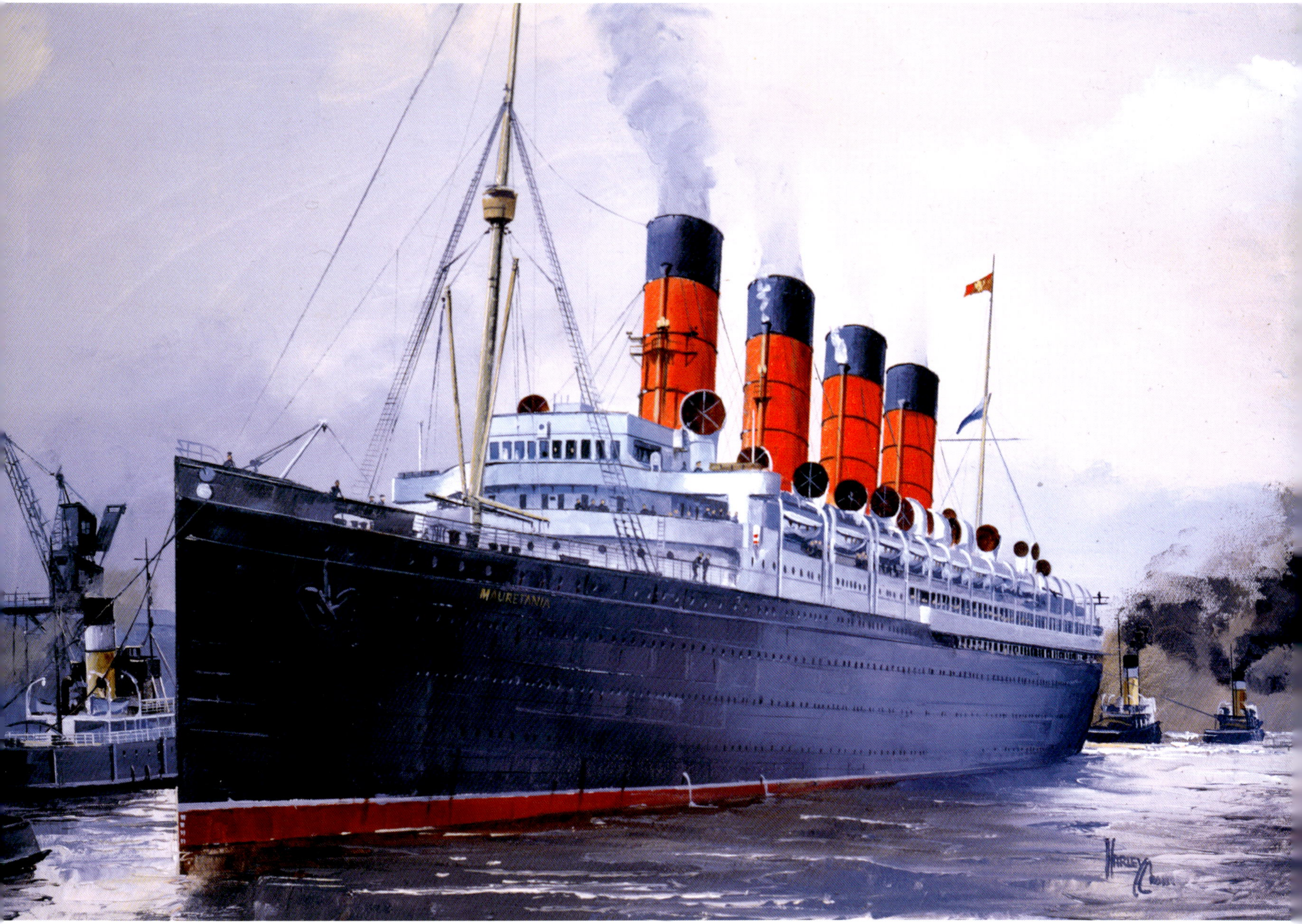

Mauretania at Southampton

OLYMPIC

882 feet x 92 feet 45,324 grt

Built for White Star Line, in December 1908, the keel of *Olympic* was laid on a specially constructed double slipway at the Belfast yard of Harland & Wolff. Three months later, the yard would begin work alongside on her sister ship, *Titanic*. When launched in October 1910, *Olympic* was the largest ship in the world and the first to be built over 40,000 grt.

The white-painted hull of the ship slid into the water without ceremony, as was the custom for White Star Line, watched by company officials. A huge 200-ton German crane was used for her fitting out and a new dry dock was constructed by the Belfast Harbour Commissioners to accommodate the new ships.

Seven months after her launch, *Olympic* left Belfast for her acceptance trials. She then paid a short visit to Liverpool before proceeding south to her home port of Southampton. Although not a record-breaking ship, her interiors were luxurious with many new features, such as the largest Turkish bath and the largest swimming pool afloat.

On 14 June 1911, she left Southampton for her maiden voyage to New York. She was a popular ship from the beginning and always carried good passenger numbers.

On 20 September, leaving Southampton on her fifth voyage, she was involved in a collision with HMS *Hawke* at Spithead near Cowes in the Isle of Wight. Both ships were badly damaged, and *Olympic* had to return to Belfast for repairs before she could resume service.

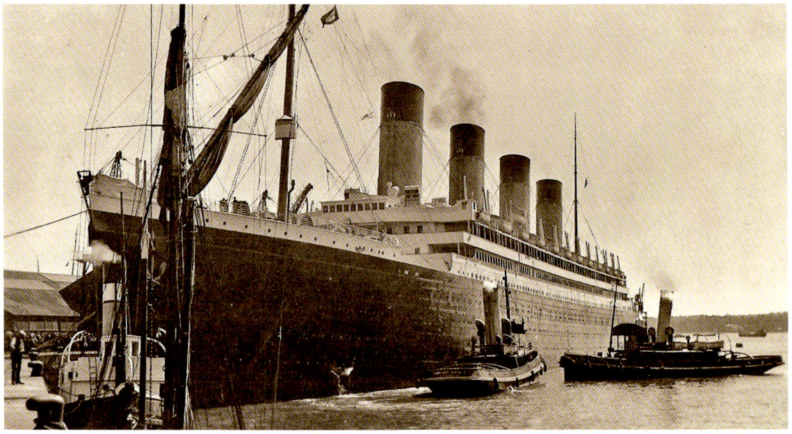

Olympic, Ocean Dock, Southampton

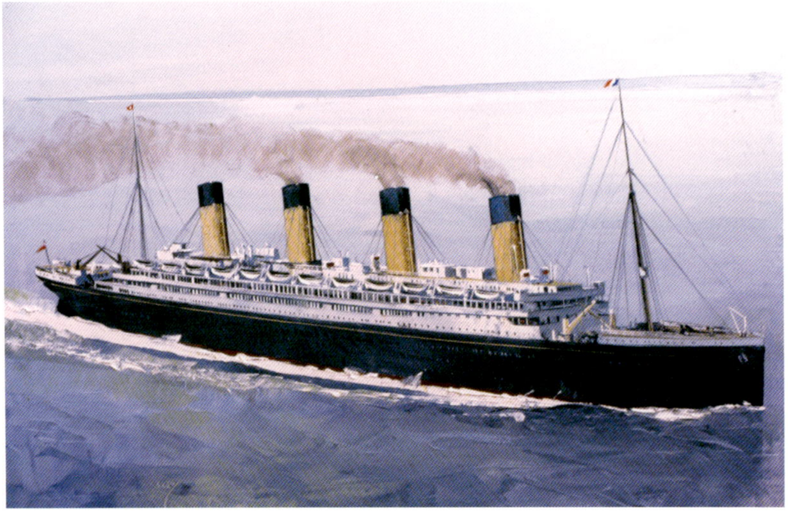

Olympic

She was back in Belfast again in March 1912, this time to repair a broken propeller blade.

After the *Titanic* disaster, some of the crew of *Olympic* mutinied over the provision of suitable extra lifeboats. This delayed her next scheduled sailing for three weeks. As a result of the *Titanic* sinking, the *Olympic* returned to Belfast for extensive modifications, which took six months to complete.

During the First World War, she was used as a troopship, steaming more than 184,000 miles and reputedly carrying over 200,000 troops. Afterwards, she returned to Belfast once more, where she was converted from coal to oil burning at a cost of £500,000, reducing the engine-room staff from 350 to sixty.

In July 1920, she returned to her transatlantic route. Running with *Majestic* and *Homeric*, she maintained a fortnightly service, averaging fifteen round trips annually. Her regular service earned her the affectionate name of Old Reliable.

In 1932, cracks were discovered in one of her crankshafts, and the ship underwent an extensive overhaul and refurbishment.

In May 1934, in poor visibility, she collided with the Nantucket lightship, sinking it, which caused the loss of seven of the lightship crew.

During 1934, Cunard and White Star merged, and upon completion of the new motor ships *Georgic* and *Britannic*, *Olympic* left New York for the last time on 3 April 1935.

In September, she was sold for scrapping in Jarrow on the River Tyne. Demolition continued for two years and was completed when the remains of the hull was towed to Inverkeithing in 1937 for breaking up.

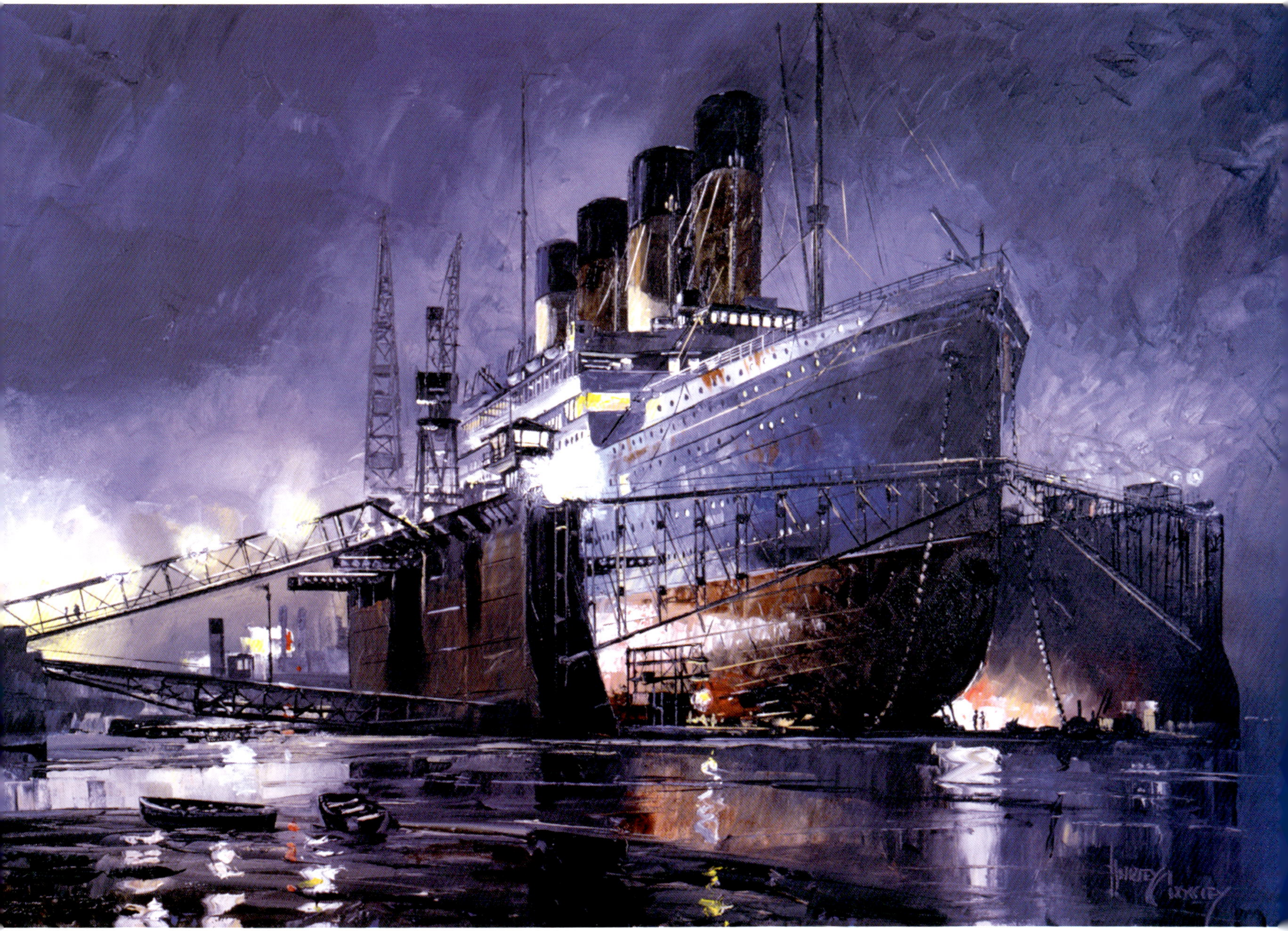

Olympic in Floating Dry Dock, Southampton

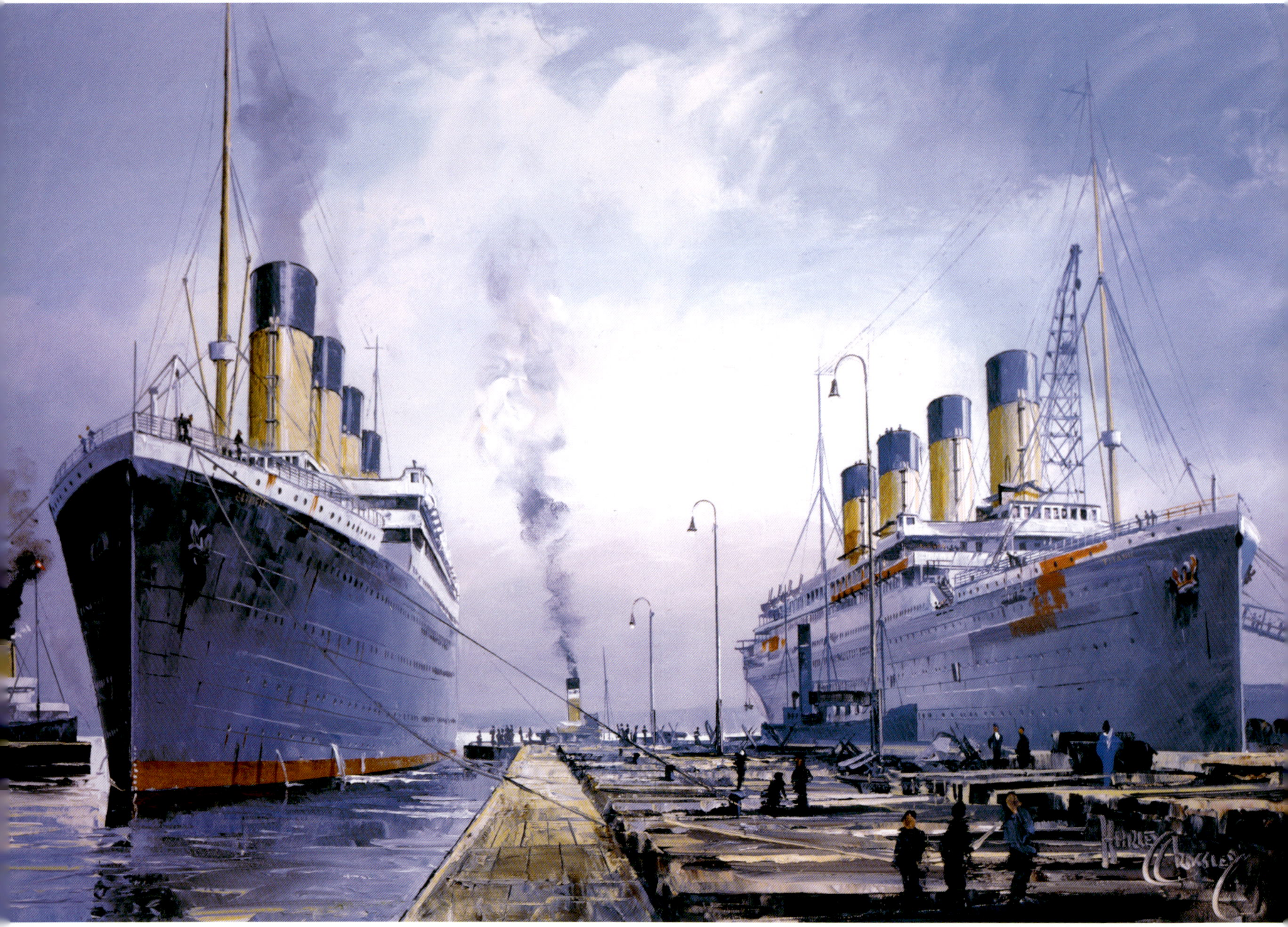

Olympic (left) and *Titanic* in Belfast

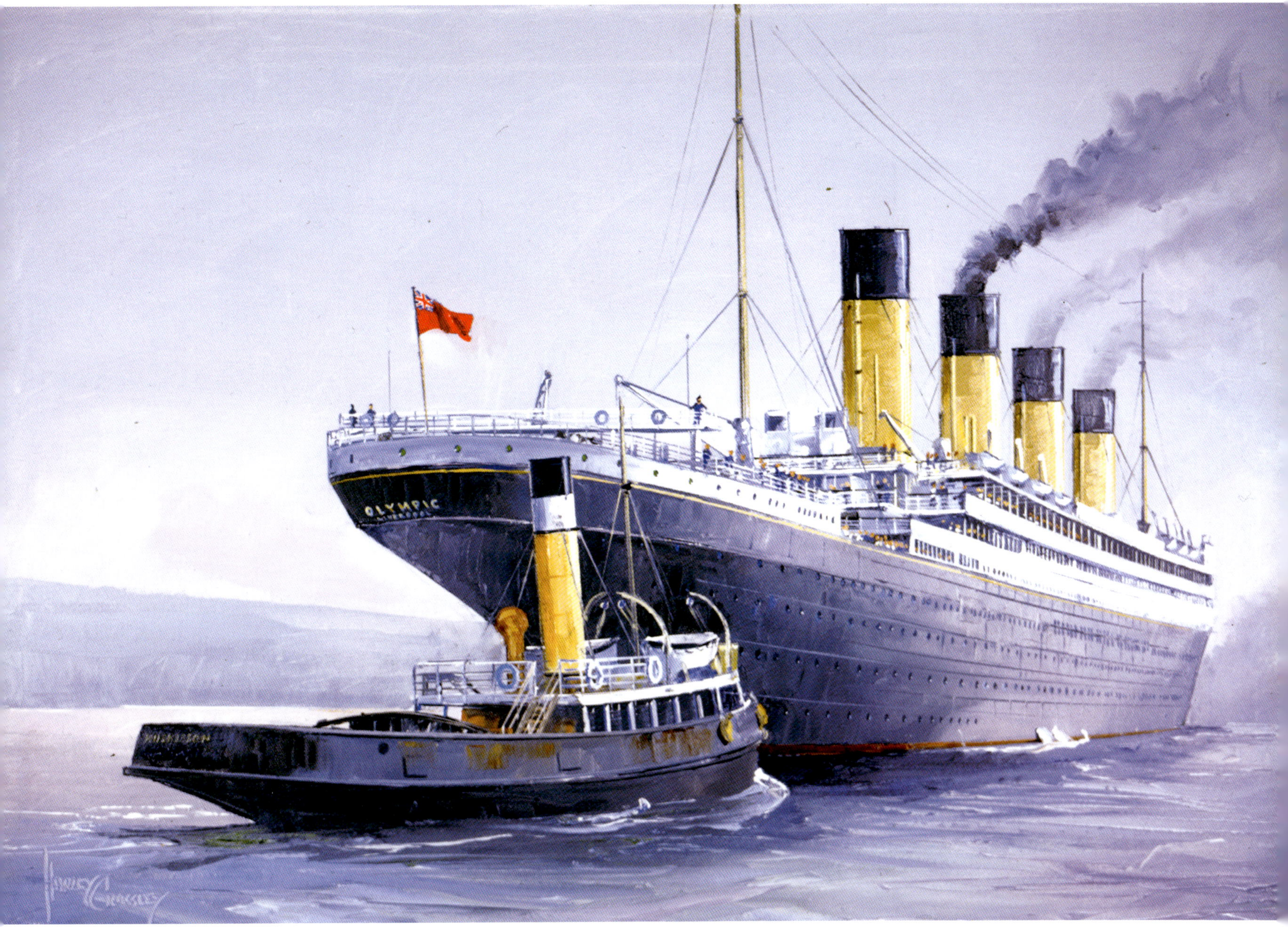

Olympic stern view

TITANIC

883 feet x 92 feet 46,329 grt

Built by Harland & Wolff in Belfast, *Titanic* was the second of three great liners scheduled for the American-controlled White Star Line to compete with the record-breaking Cunard ships and new German transatlantic liners. Launched on 31 May 1911, the same day that her sister ship *Olympic* was accepted into commercial service, she was, at the time, the world's largest ship.

In March 1912, just before *Titanic* left the Belfast yard the A deck forward promenade was closed in and glazed, one of the few visible differences between her and *Olympic*. This was to provide additional shelter from the weather for First Class passengers.

Due to adverse sea conditions, her sea trials scheduled for 1 April had to be delayed until the next day. Finally, after a day of successful trials, *Titanic* left Belfast Lough and sailed for Southampton in the evening of 2 April 1912. Like her sister ship *Olympic*, no expense had been spared to ensure that *Titanic* was luxuriously fitted out with public rooms equal to those in the finest hotels. She also boasted a Turkish bath and gymnasium in addition to the swimming pool, which was 30 feet long and 14 feet wide.

After spending a week in Southampton for final fitting out, storing and bunkering (after the end of a national coal strike), *Titanic* embarked her passengers on the morning of 10 April 1912 and sailed for Cherbourg at noon.

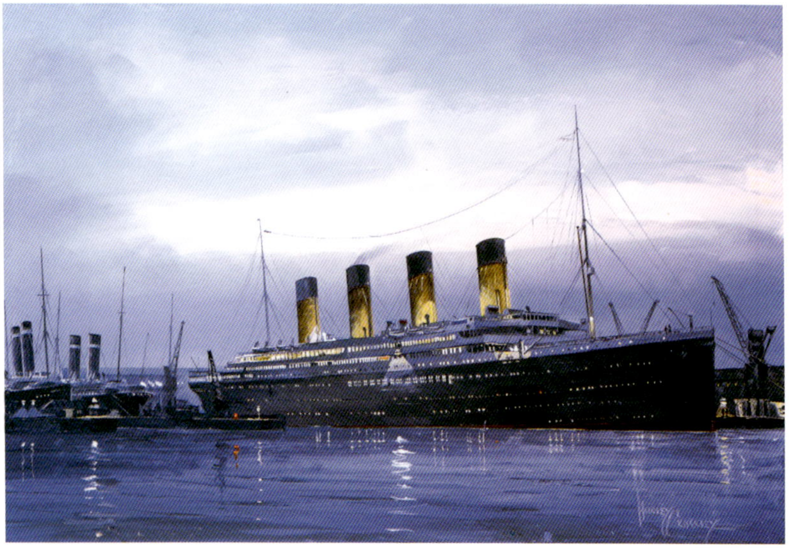

Titanic, eve of departure

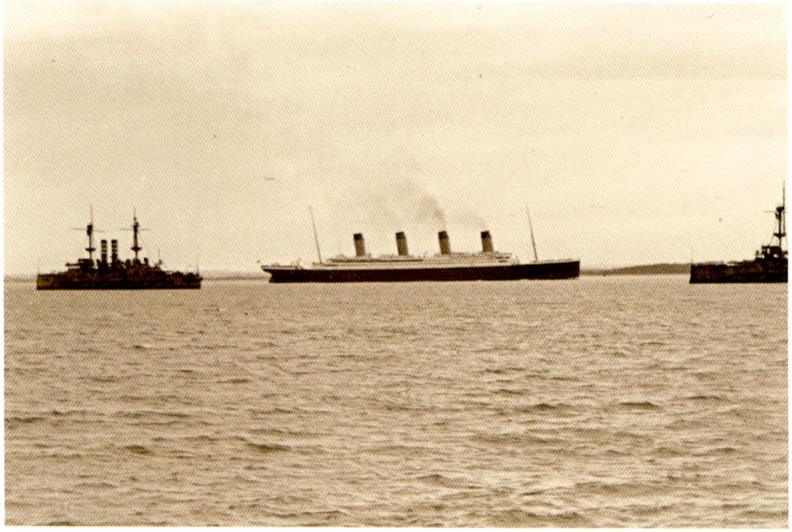

Titanic (C. McCutcheon)

As she passed 38 berth, the American liner *New York* broke from her moorings and her stern drifted outwards. *Titanic* stopped, and when the two ships were only 12 feet apart, the tug *Vulcan* managed to get lines aboard the *New York* and succeed in slowing her drift towards the giant ship. After an hour's delay, she continued her voyage to Cherbourg, where she arrived at 6.30 p.m. Using White Star tenders, she disembarked twenty-two passengers and 274 boarded before she headed for Ireland.

The next day, at 11.30 a.m., she moored off Queenstown (Cobh) and again using tenders took on board 120 passengers and 1,385 sacks of mail. Two hours later, the anchor was raised, and she sailed for New York.

At 9 o'clock on the morning of 14 April, *Titanic* received her first message warning of ice ahead. Despite further warnings received during the day, she pressed on at her full service speed of 21 knots. At 11.40 p.m., in a calm sea and with good visibility, the lookout reported an iceberg directly ahead. The ship struck the berg a glancing blow, which tore a 300-foot gash through six compartments in her side.

Titanic sank at 2.20 a.m. on 15 April 1912 with the loss of 1,513 lives.

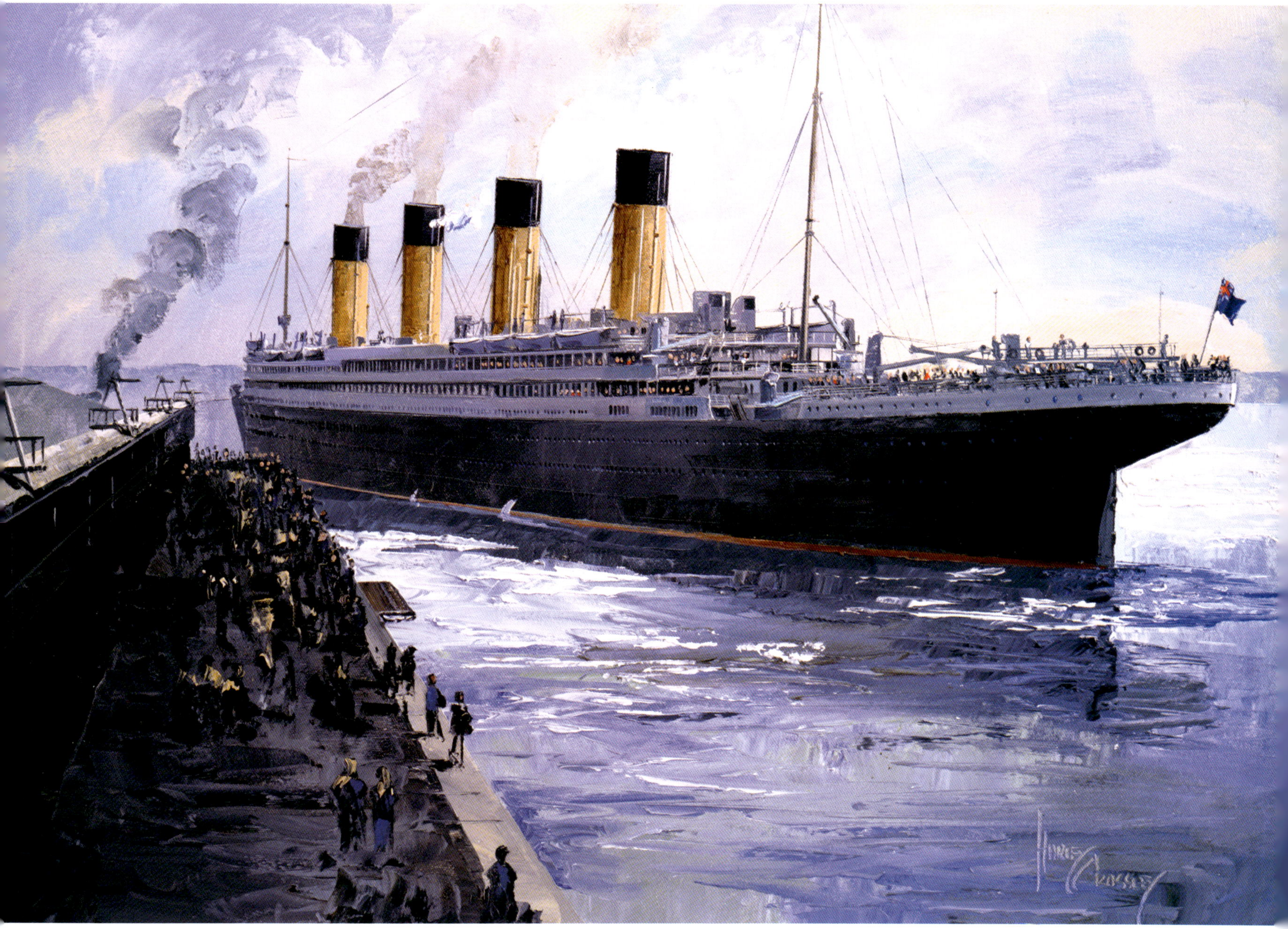

Titanic leaving White Star Dock, Southampton

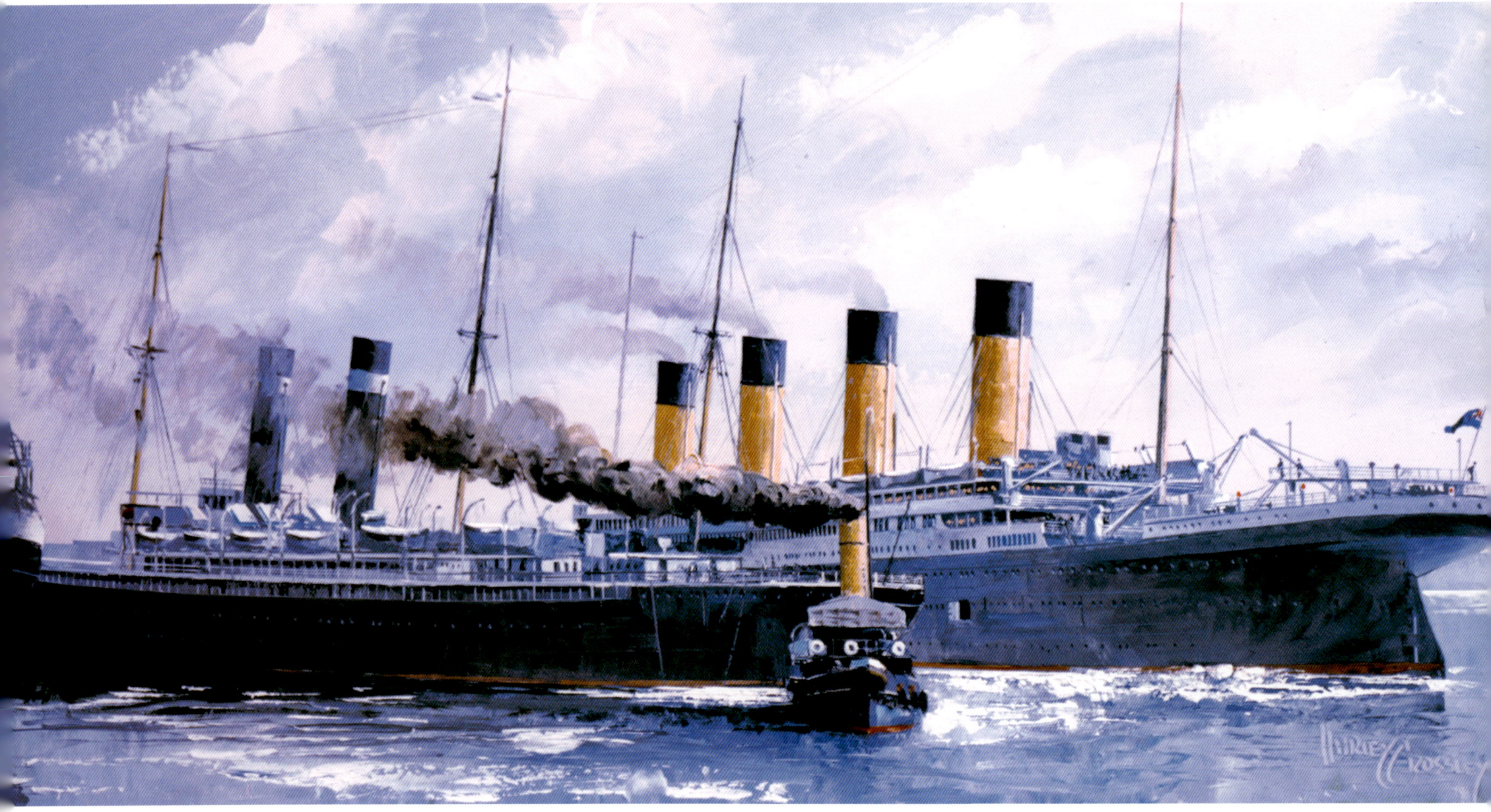

Titanic and *New York* Incident

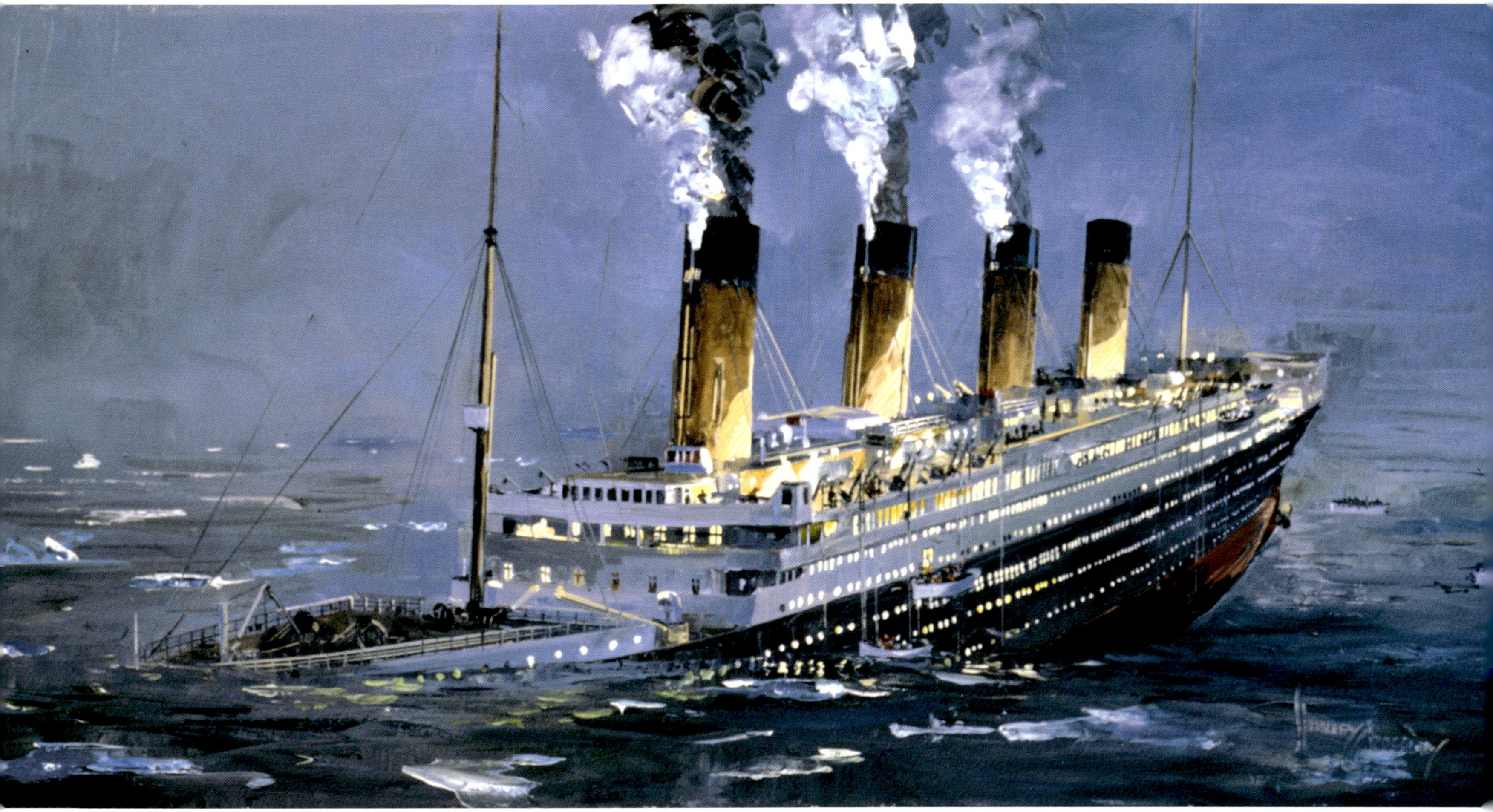

Titanic sinking

AQUITANIA

901 feet x 97 feet 45,647 grt

Aquitania was launched on 21 April 1913 from the shipyard of John Brown on Clydebank. Completed in May 1914, her maiden voyage from Liverpool to New York began on 30 May. Her career spanned thirty-five years, and until the advent of the *Queen Elizabeth 2*, she was the longest-serving Cunard ship. The only giant liner to serve under the white ensign, she was used in both the First and Second World Wars.

Built for a weekly transatlantic service, to run in conjunction with the *Mauretania* and the *Lusitania*, she was the world's largest ship at that time. Designed for luxury, not speed, her fixtures and fittings surpassed anything seen before. Four screws were powered by direct-acting turbines. Steam supplied by twenty-one double-ended coal-fired boilers gave 62,000 shp and a service speed of 23.5 knots.

Requisitioned by the Government at the start of the First World War as an armed merchant cruiser, she was fitted with ten 6-inch guns, and was commissioned into the Royal Navy on 7 August 1914. After colliding with the 9,300-ton cargo vessel *Canadian*, she returned to Liverpool, and at the subsequent court of enquiry, it was decided that *Aquitania* was too large to be used as an armed merchant cruiser. She was decommissioned on 5 September 1914 and subsequently used as a troop transport and hospital ship during the war, although she was laid up throughout most of 1917.

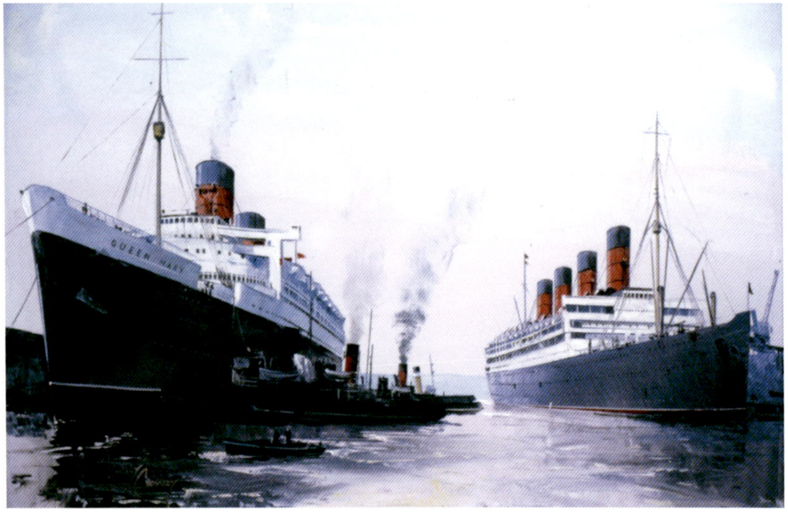

Queen Mary and *Aquitania*, Ocean Dock, Southampton

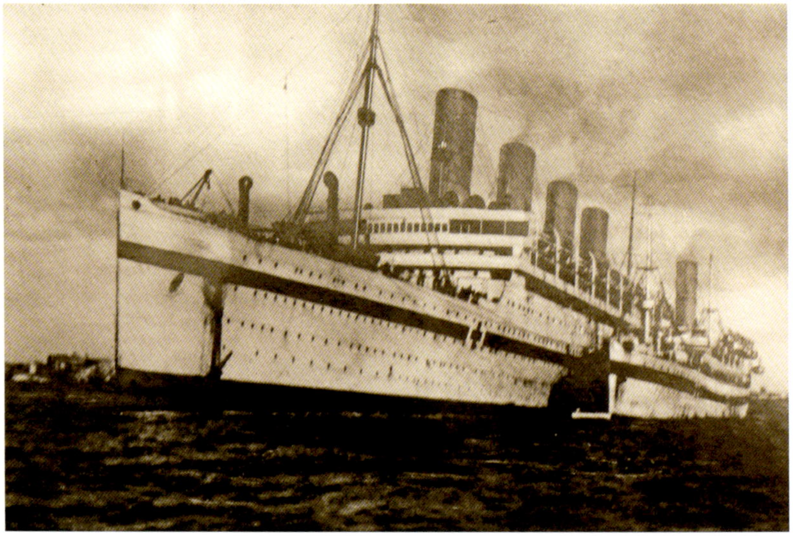

Aquitania (C. McCutcheon)

At the end of the war, she was converted to oil burning during her refit. The work took thirty weeks, after which the ship was based in Southampton. During her first voyage after the conversion, there was an explosion in the engine room that killed a crew member.

In February 1932, she was used for cruising for the first time from New York to the Mediterranean. She was scheduled to be scrapped when the *Queen Elizabeth* was completed, but this did not happen.

In March 1940, she sailed to Australia and was used as a troopship around the world throughout the Second World War.

In 1948, she was chartered by the Canadian Government for twenty-five voyages to carry mainly emigrants to Halifax, Nova Scotia. The years had taken their toll of the ship, which had been scheduled for scrapping some nine years earlier, and in December 1949, the company withdrew her from service.

Her furnishings and equipment were sold at auction, and the ship sold for scrap.

Aquitania sailed to Faslane, Scotland, in February 1950 to be broken up by Metal Industries. She was the last surviving four-funnelled ship.

One of her ship's bells is now in All Saints Cathedral, Halifax, Nova Scotia, and another was placed on the *Queen Elizabeth 2* in 1969.

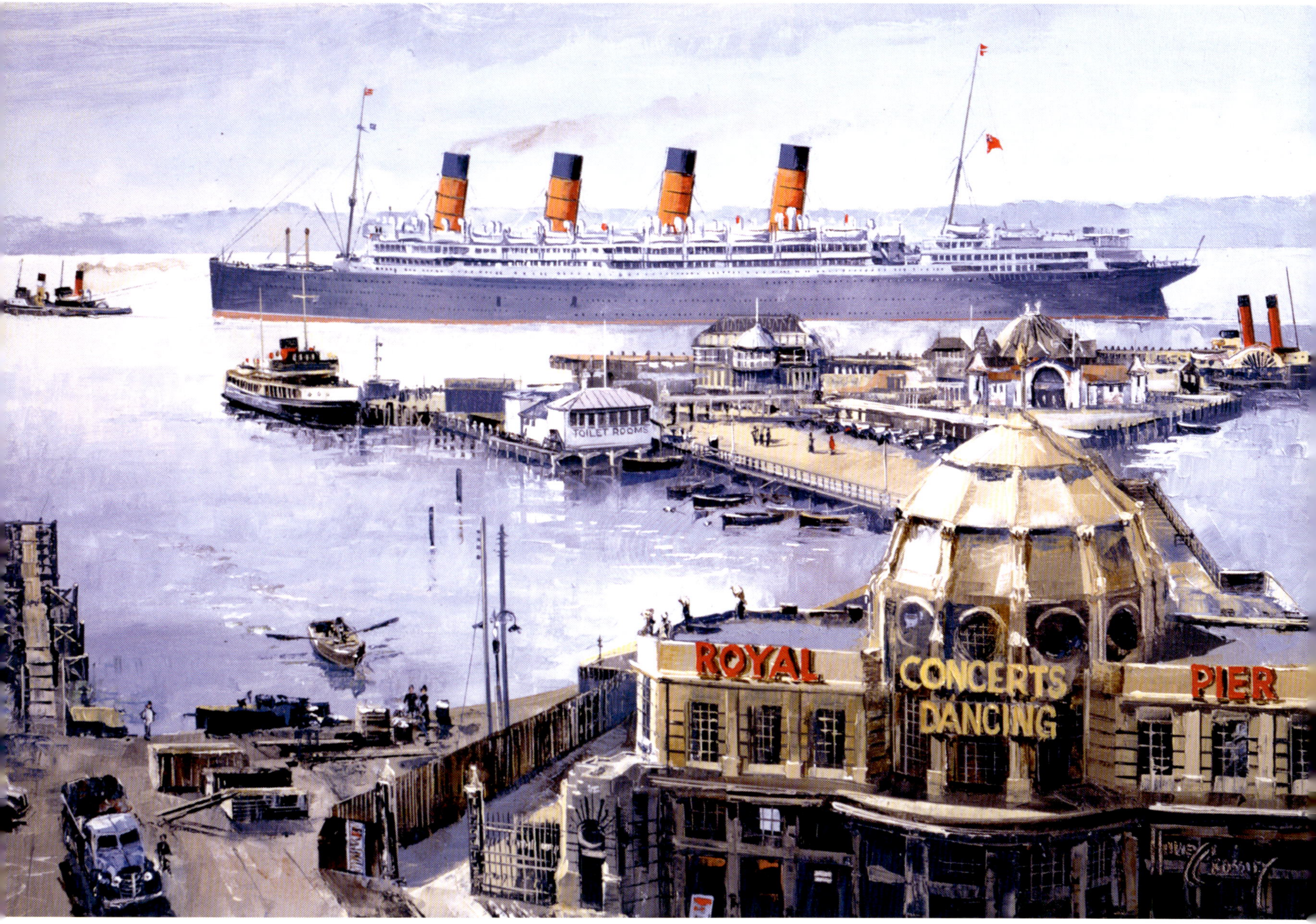

Aquitania passing Royal Pier, Southampton

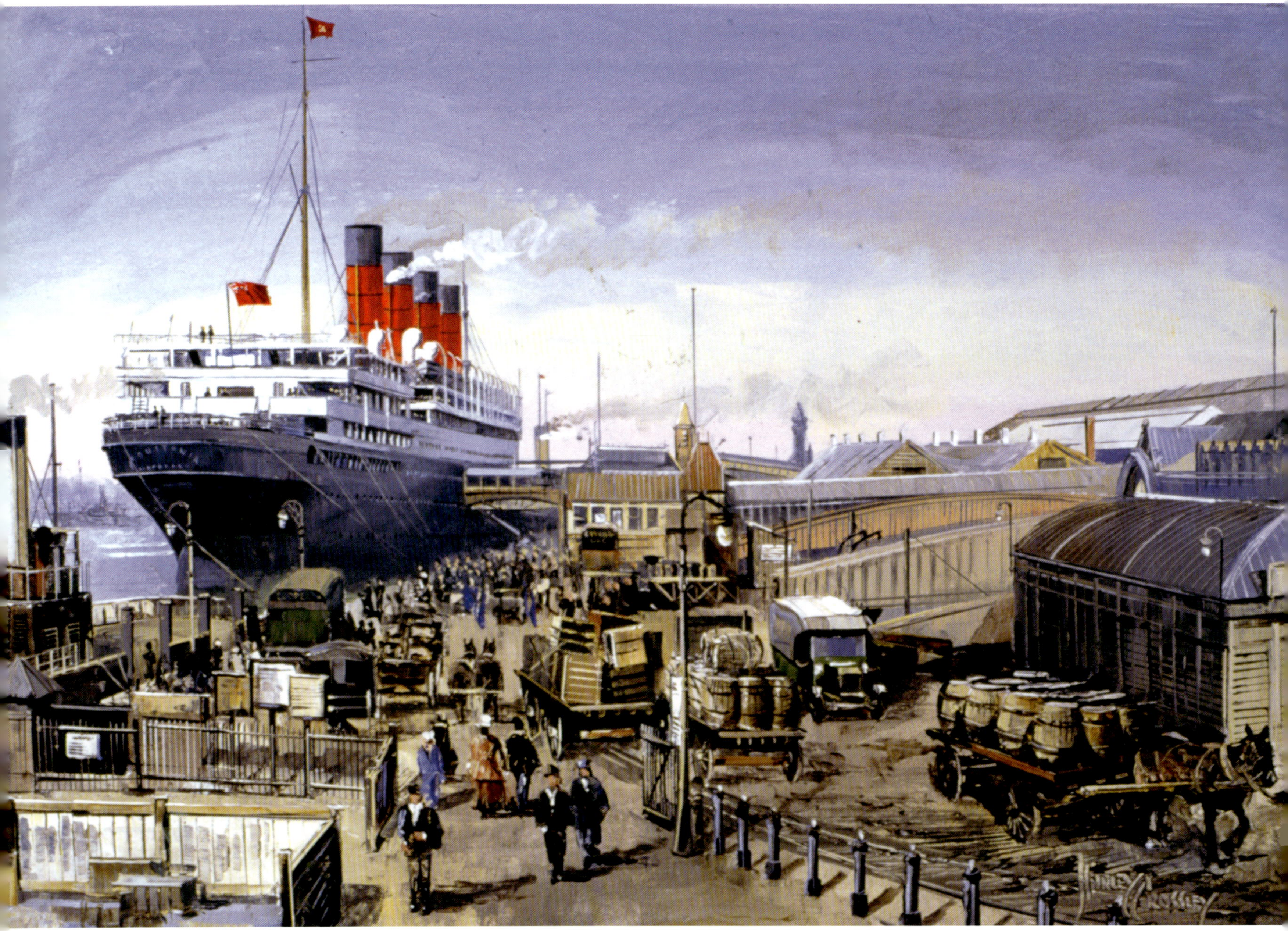

Aquitania at Liverpool Landing Stage

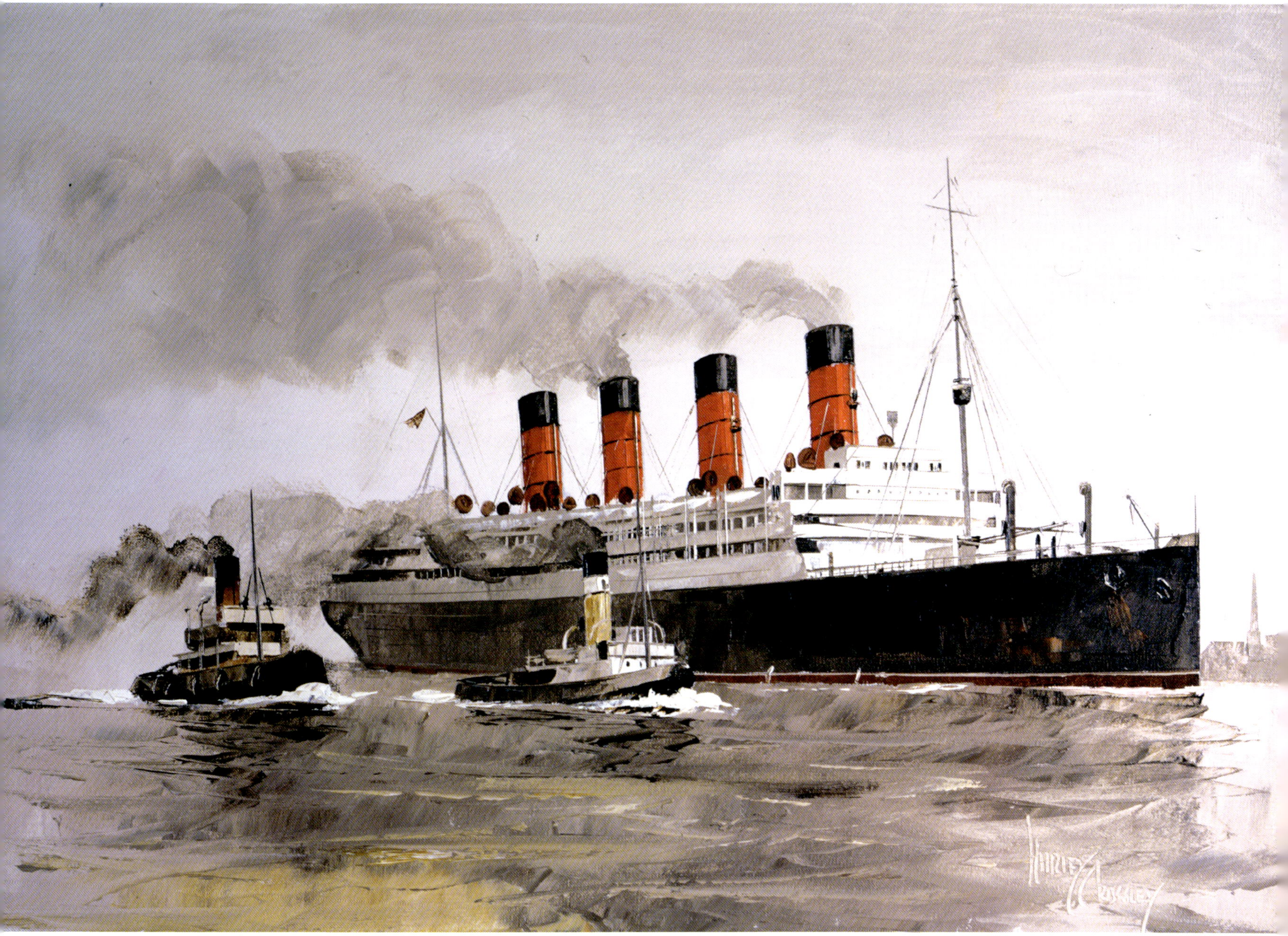

Aquitania, final departure from Southampton

BERENGARIA

909 feet x 98 feet 52,117 grt

Berengaria was built in Hamburg by AG Vulcan and launched by the German Emperor, Kaiser Wilhelm II, on 23 May 1912 as the *Imperator*. When launched, she was the world's largest ship and was to be the first of three almost identical ships built for Hamburg America Line. The others were *Vaterland* and *Bismark*.

Launched five weeks after the *Titanic* tragedy, she was eventually fitted with eighty-three lifeboats and was the first merchant vessel to be fitted with a gyrocompass. She also had a 43,000-candle power searchlight on the foremast for spotting icebergs.

After troublesome trials during which she went aground, a boiler exploded, and her turbines overheated, her delayed maiden voyage to New York finally began on 10 June 1913, calling at Cherbourg and Southampton. The voyage took 6 days, 5 hours, and she carried 2,440 passengers.

The ship suffered from stability problems and was described as being 'deficient in initial stability', a problem which was addressed when the ship was returned to the builders in October. Her funnels were reduced in height by about 9 feet, heavy upper deck fittings were replaced and 2,000 tons of concrete were poured into her double bottom. In her first year of operation, she frequently carried over 3,000 passengers per trip.

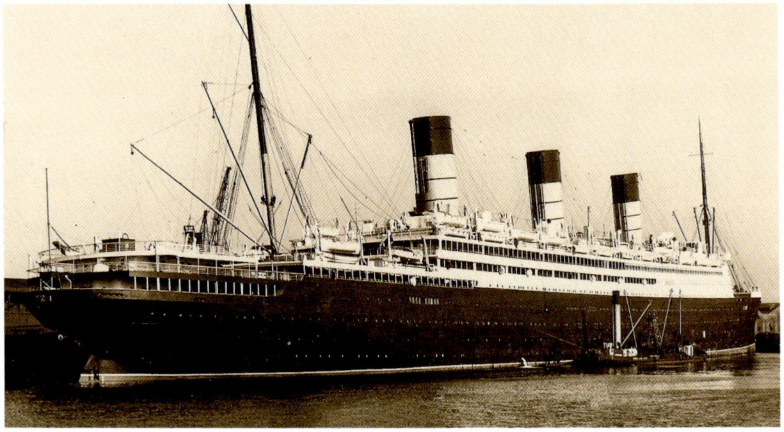

Berengaria in Ocean Dock, Southampton

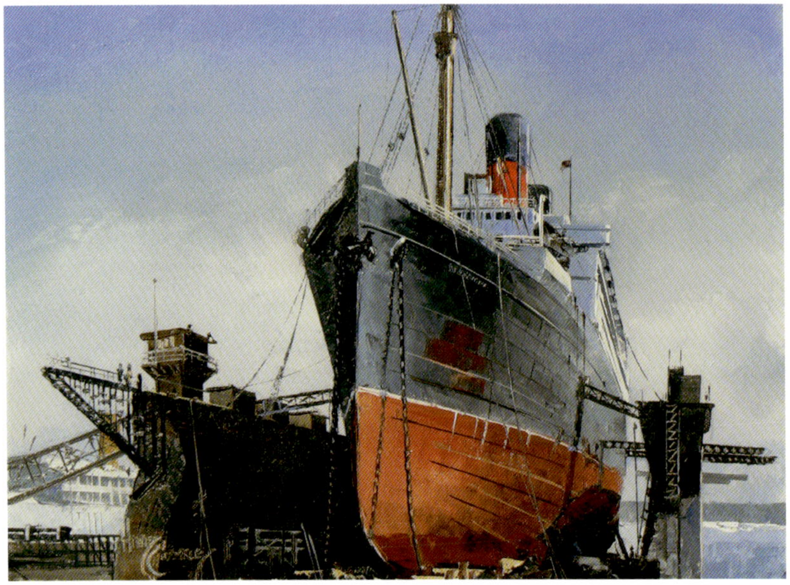

Berengaria in Floating Dry Dock, Southampton

Imperator made six round trips in 1914 before being laid up in Germany for the next four years. Following the end of the war, she was seized by the Americans, renamed USS *Imperator* and was used as a troop ship. She made three voyages from Brest to New York and repatriated 25,000 people. In December 1919, she was allocated to the British by the Allied Control Commission and became RMS *Imperator*, chartered by Cunard Line for the Liverpool to New York service.

In 1921, the ship was in poor condition when she was purchased by Cunard from the commission and renamed *Berengaria*. A six-month refit in the Armstrong Whitworth yard on the Tyne included conversion from coal to oil burning and an increased grt of 52,226. Her refit was completed at Southampton when she entered the Trafalgar Dry Dock (where she had 8 inches clearance) for hull cleaning.

From 1923 to 1934, *Berengaria* sailed from Southampton on Cunard's express Atlantic service with *Mauretania* and *Aquitania*. In March 1938, a fire was discovered on board whilst the ship was in New York. After the fire was extinguished, Lloyds surveyors refused permission for passenger service due to the poor condition of her electrical fittings. She sailed to Southampton empty. After another fire at Southampton, the ship was removed from the sailing list. She was eventually purchased by Sir John Jarvis, MP, for £108,000 and sailed to Jarrow in 1939, where 200 unemployed men began the job of demolishing the ship. However, the Second World War intervened and work ceased. The remains were finally towed to Rosyth in 1946 and broken up.

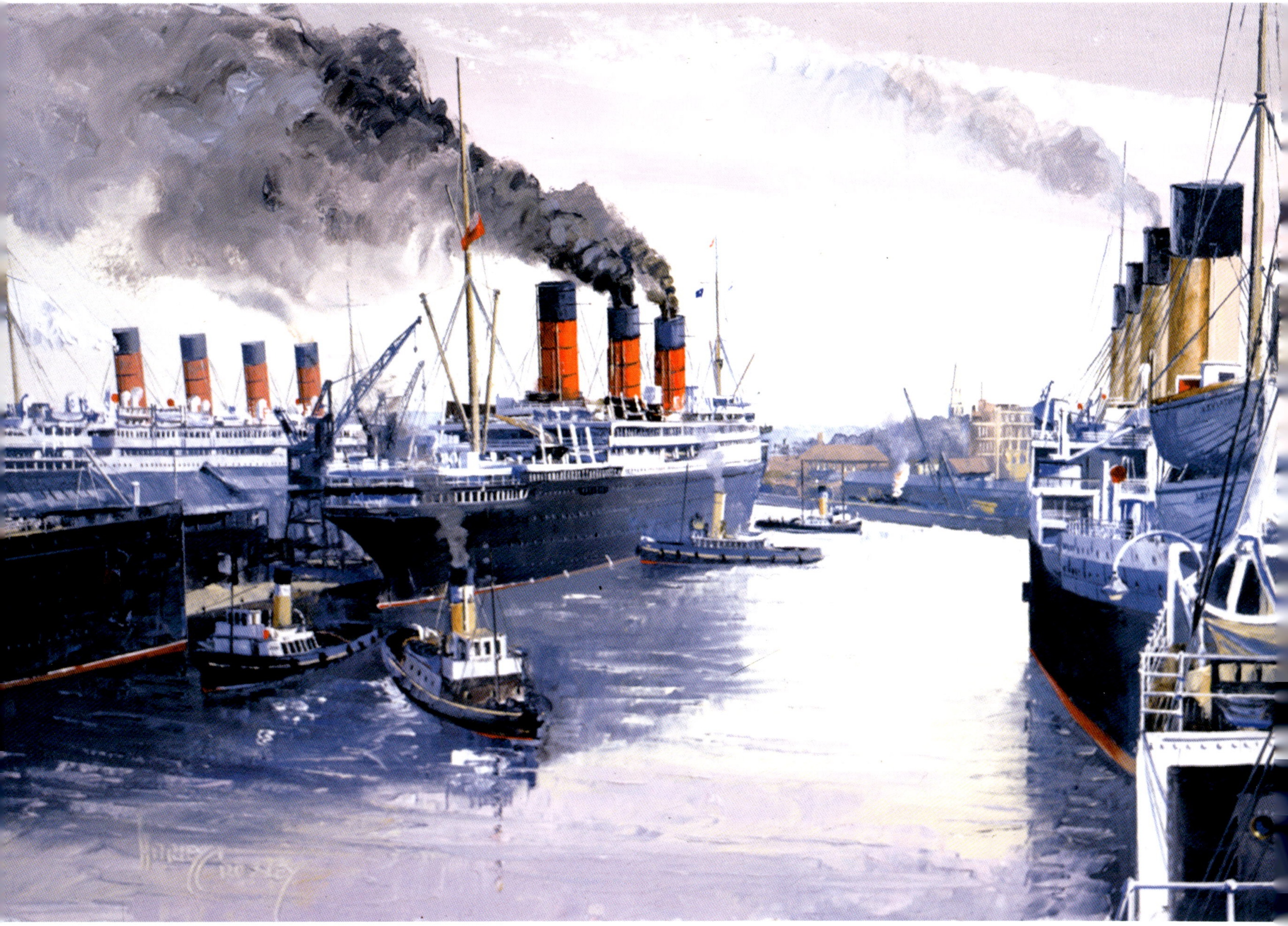

Berengaria in Ocean Dock, Southampton (*Aquitania* on left, *Olympic* on right)

LEVIATHAN

948 feet x 100 feet 54,282 grt

Launched as the *Vaterland* from Blohm & Voss shipyard in Hamburg on 3 April 1913, she was the second of three similar ships built for Hamburg America Line. The launch by Prince Rupert of Bavaria was watched by 40,000 people.

When completed, she was the largest ship to sail under the German flag and also the world's largest ship until 1922.

Of her three funnels, the rear was a dummy used for engine-room ventilation. The divided funnel uptakes were a novel feature of her design, which enabled large public rooms to be built through the centre of the ship. Luxuriously fitted out, she boasted a row of shops, travel bureau and gymnasium, and pool complex. Her First Class cabins had brass bedsteads and marble washstands with hot and cold water, whilst the finest staterooms were fitted with marble baths.

As originally designed, she could carry a total of over 5,000 passengers and crew. Equipped with eighty-three lifeboats and 5,500 lifejackets, she had a bunker capacity of 9,000 tons and room for 12,000 tons of cargo with a designed service speed of 23½ knots.

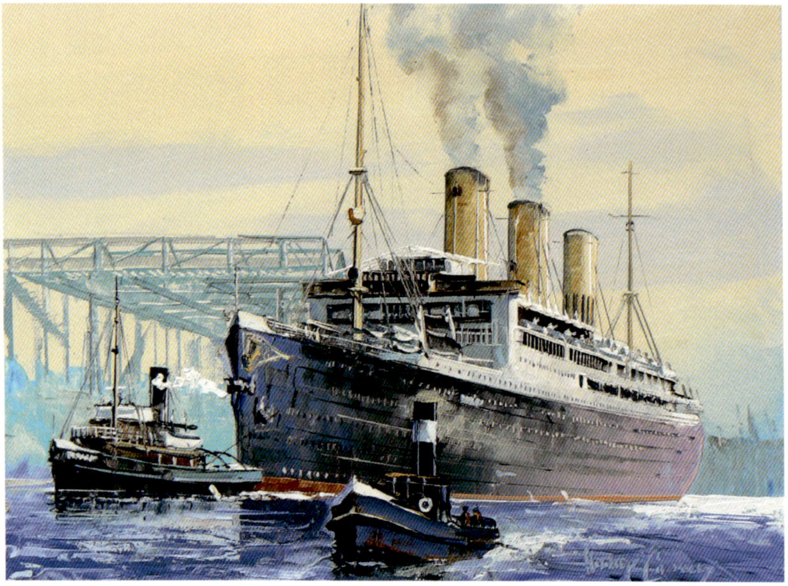

Vaterland in Hamburg

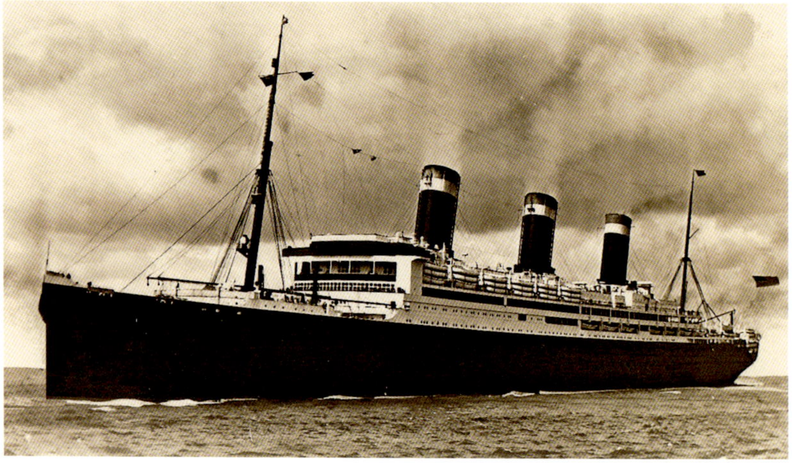

Leviathan

Her maiden voyage was from Cuxhaven to New York in May 1914, and it was here that she was interned in August at the start of the First World War. Threatened with seizure in 1917, the crew sabotaged the engines and boilers prior to the formal seizure of the ship by the Americans on 4 April.

When first moved after her lay up, forty-six tugs were required to assist, as the ship was surrounded by 27 feet of silt. She was converted to a US Navy troop ship and renamed USS *Leviathan*.

After the end of the war in 1919, she carried 14,416 troops across the Atlantic on one voyage, the largest number ever carried on a ship at that time.

In 1919, after her war service, she was laid up in New York, and before work could be started to renovate the ship for passenger service, blueprints had to be produced. This took a team of 100 draughtsmen two years to complete.

After reconstruction, she was re-measured at 59,956 grt and, in 1923, made her first voyage from New York to Southampton for United States Lines as *Leviathan*. She spent most of her life as a 'dry ship' due to the American prohibition laws.

In 1931, by manipulating the measuring regulations, she was re-measured at 48,932 grt, thus reducing her harbour dues.

Leviathan was laid up in 1932 but made four voyages in 1934, before being laid up again in New York. In December 1937, she was sold for scrap.

Her final voyage was in January 1938 from New York to Rosyth in Scotland, where she was broken up.

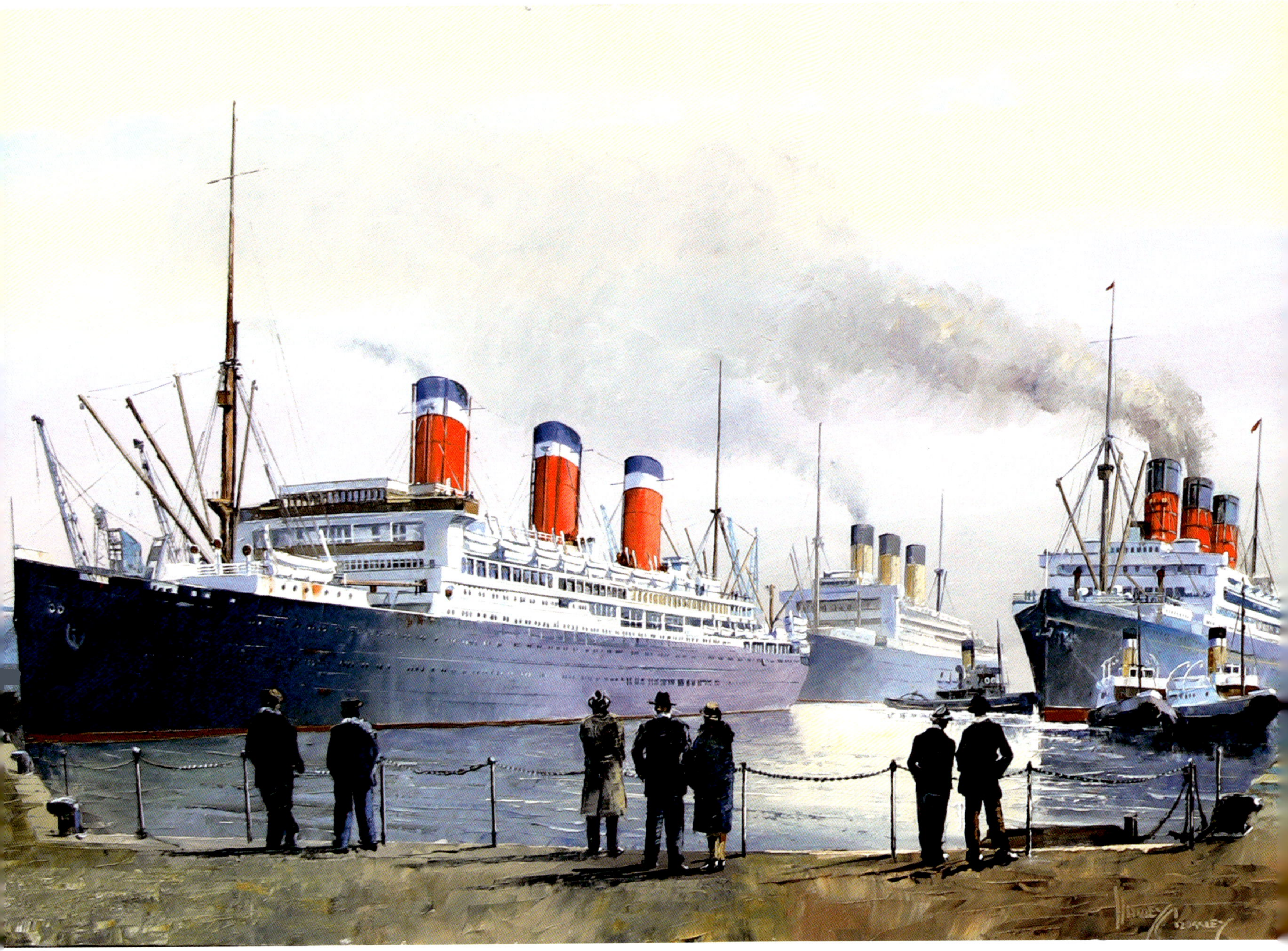

Leviathan, Ocean Dock, Southampton, 27 July 1930, with *Majestic* and *Berengaria* (on right)

MAJESTIC

956 feet x 100 feet 56,551 grt

Built by Blohm & Voss as the *Bismarck* for Hamburg America Line, she was launched on 20 June 1914, equipped with Parsons steam turbines driving four screws to give an operating speed of 23½ knots. She was the same class of ship as the *Imperator* and the *Vaterland*, and together they were known as the Three German Giants.

With the outbreak of the First World War, all work on the ship ceased, and she never sailed under the German flag apart from on her sea trials after the war ended.

In June 1919, after the end of the war, she was handed over to Britain and work continued under British supervision. Completion was delayed due to fire, but in February 1921, she was sold to White Star Line still unfinished. When finally completed in March 1922, she was the largest ship in the world.

She sailed to Liverpool, and after her trials, she was renamed *Majestic* ready to begin her service with White Star Line.

She sailed on her maiden voyage from Southampton to New York on 10 May 1922, nearly eight years after her launch. *Majestic* became one of the most popular ships afloat, and in 1923, she carried more passengers than any other Atlantic liner. She was given the affectionate nickname of the Magic Stick.

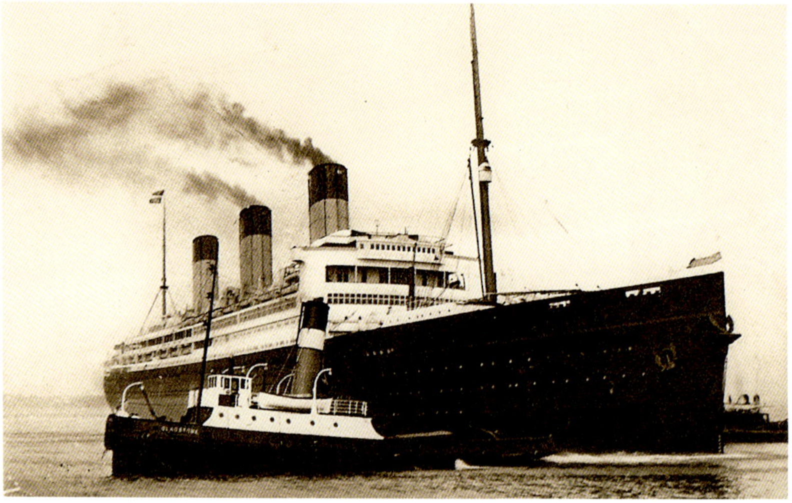

Majestic

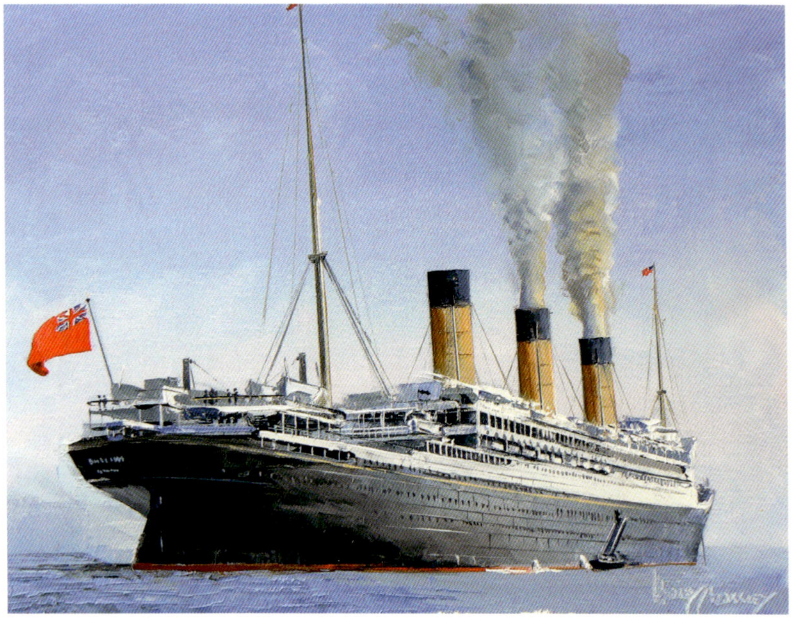

Majestic

Late in 1924, a 100-foot crack was discovered in her superstructure, and she went in for extensive repair and strengthening before returning to service in April 1925.

In 1928, after modernization, she returned to service and once again enjoyed immense popularity until the Depression in the 1930s caused a drop in numbers.

In 1934, she was transferred to the newly formed Cunard White Star Company and continued in service until she was laid up in Southampton before being sold for scrap in May 1936. However, instead of being scrapped, she was converted by Thornycroft in Southampton to a cadet training ship. As equivalent scrap value, the Admiralty sent twenty-four old destroyers to the breaker's yard in her place.

With her masts and funnels shortened so she could fit under the Forth Bridge, she sailed to Rosyth as HMS *Caledonia* on 8 April 1937 to be used as a stationary training ship for 2,000 cadets.

On 29 September 1939, whilst being converted to a troopship, she caught fire and burned out, sinking at her moorings in the Firth of Forth. She was sold for scrap in March 1940 and broken up on the spot, but it wasn't until July 1943 that the remains were raised and towed to Inverkeithing for final scrapping.

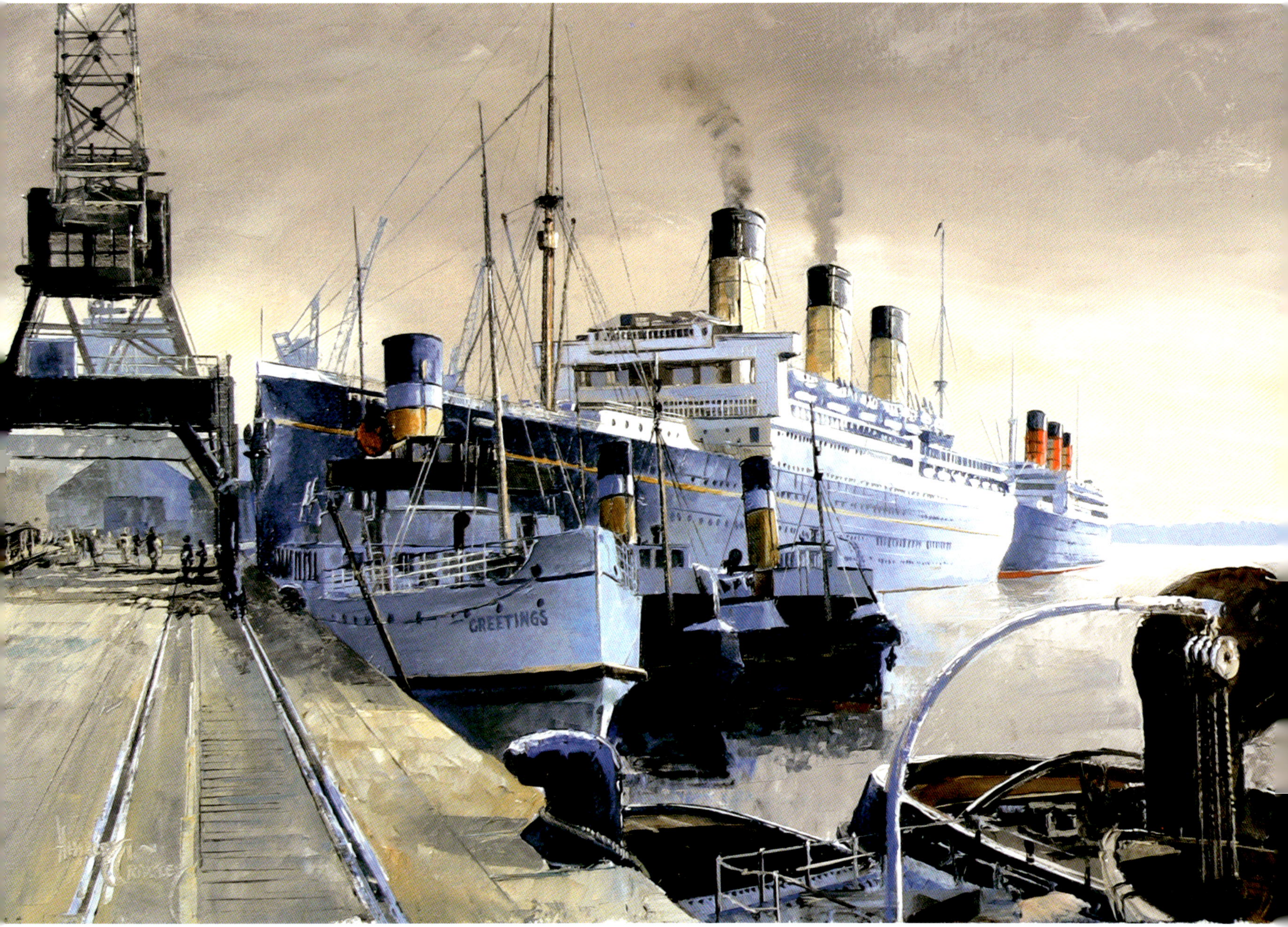

Majestic in Ocean Dock, Southampton

BRITANNIC

903 feet x 94 feet 48,158 grt

Britannic was the last of three almost identical ships built for White Star Line by Harland & Wolff at Belfast. Construction was started on the new ship (which was to be named *Gigantic*) in November 1911, but work was suspended in April 1912 after the *Titanic* disaster.

When work was recommenced, the name was changed to *Britannic* and an extra bulkhead was installed, together with an inner skin that ran for over 60 per cent of the ship's length. Five bulkheads were also extended up to the Bridge deck. Most of the forty-eight open lifeboats fitted were clustered under five huge derricks that could launch boats a distance out from the ship's side, designed to clear the hull in the event of the ship listing.

Britannic was launched on 26 February 1914 at 11.15 a.m. without ceremony in the White Star tradition. In August of that year, work on the ship was disrupted by the declaration of war. *Britannic* was laid up in Belfast Lough for ten months together with *Olympic*.

Due to the increasing number of casualties in the Dardanelles, she was requisitioned in November 1915 by the Admiralty as a hospital ship. Rapidly converted to carry 3,309 casualties and with a total of fifty-eight lifeboats, after trials lasting one day, she left Belfast for Liverpool on 11 December.

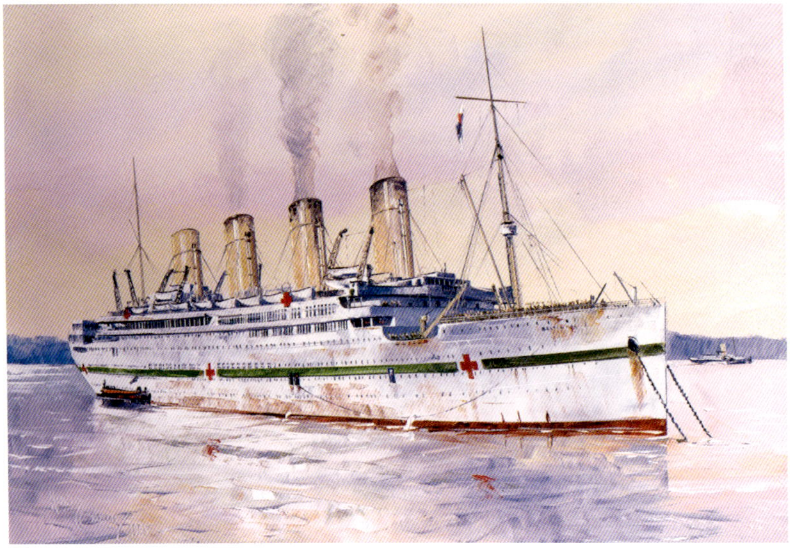

Britannic

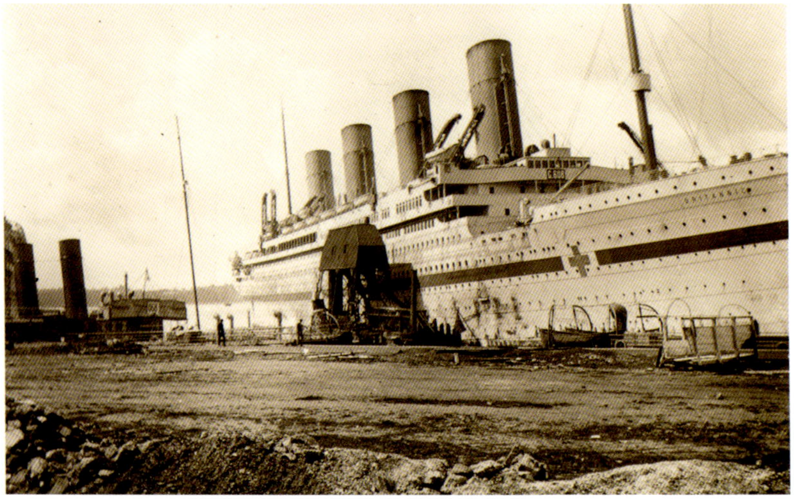

Britannic coaling in Southampton (C. McCutcheon)

She sailed from Liverpool on her maiden voyage to Mudros on 23 December 1915, calling at Naples to refuel ready for the return journey when she would be carrying wounded soldiers. At Mudros, smaller ships transferred casualties from the battlefields to the *Britannic* for the return voyage to Southampton, where she arrived on 9 January 1916.

After three voyages, the ship was discharged from service and White Star were paid £76,000 to cover the cost of refitting her for normal service. She was then laid up in Belfast until August, when she was again taken over for use as a hospital ship.

In September, she once more sailed from Southampton for Naples and Mudros.

Leaving on her sixth voyage on 12 November, she bunkered as usual in Naples before continuing on her way to Mudros to pick up more wounded. On 21 November, as she was passing through the Kea Channel on the last stage of her journey at a speed of 20 knots, she struck a mine that had been laid by German submarine U73 one hour previously. The ship sank in fifty minutes.

A total of 1,134 people were rescued in thirty-five lifeboats, which were launched before the ship sank with a loss of twenty-nine lives.

Although she never sailed her intended Atlantic route as a passenger liner, *Britannic* had been afloat for three days short of 1,000. During this time, she had completed five voyages and repatriated more than 15,000 sick and wounded. She was the largest marine casualty in the First World War.

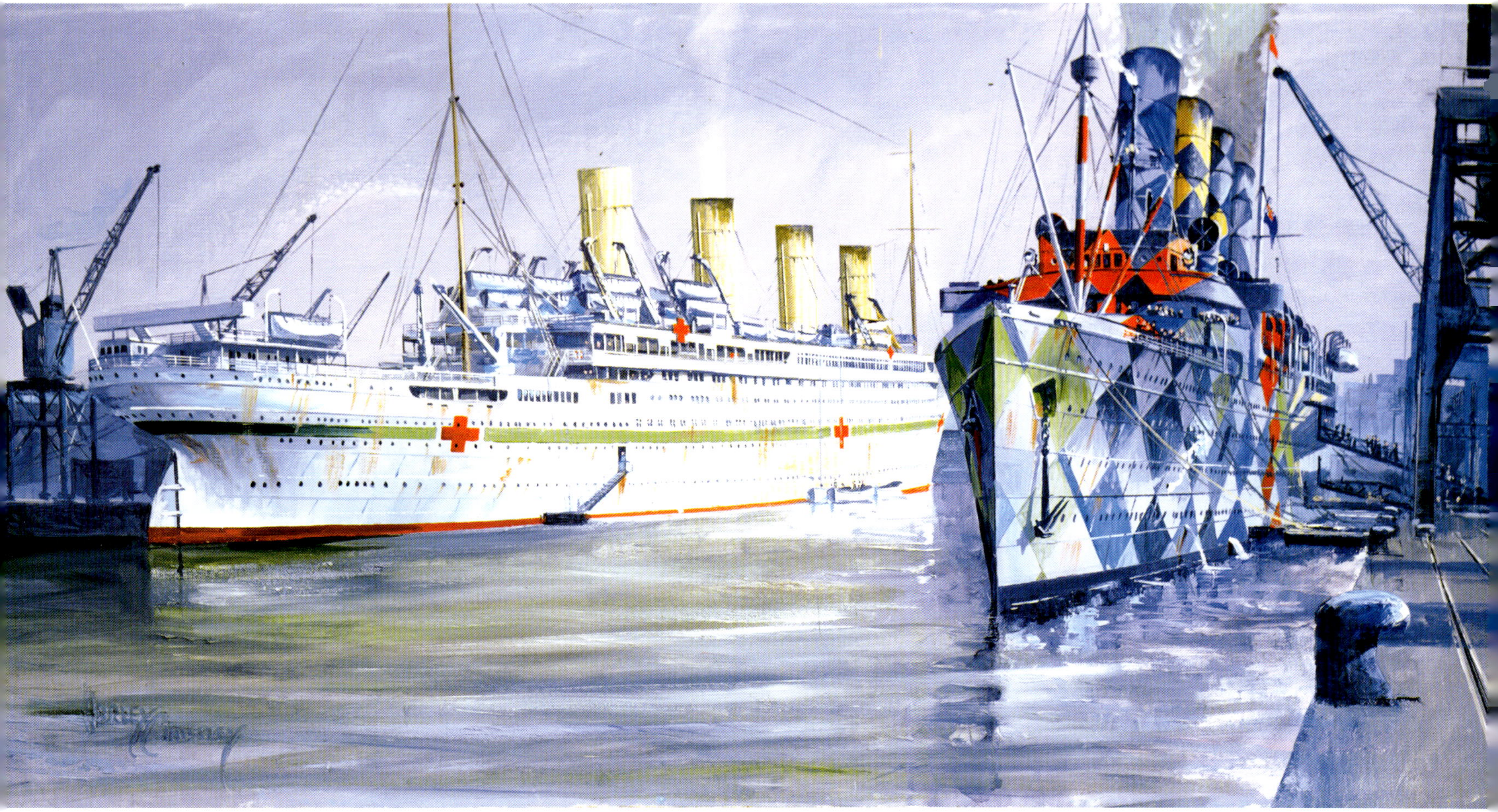

Britannic and *Mauretania* in Ocean Dock, Southampton

ARUNDEL CASTLE

630 feet x 72 feet 19,023 grt

Laid down in 1915 at Harland & Wolff, Belfast, as the *Amroth Castle*, work was suspended during the First World War, and she was finally launched as the *Arundel Castle* in 1919, after four years on the stocks. She was the largest vessel to be completed for Union Castle Line and the first new mailship for over eleven years.

The original design was for coal-burning boilers, and the company insisted on keeping to this even though most ships were now using oil, which was proving more efficient and cost effective. *Arundel Castle* consumed 4,000 tons of coal per voyage – an expensive commodity. With a speed of 17 knots, she and her sister ship *Windsor Castle* were the last four-funnelled ships to be built.

Her maiden voyage began in April 1921 from Southampton to Cape Town. With a crew of 440, her passenger capacity was a total of 1,170 in four classes.

Although considered by many to be rather outdated in appearance, she was the first on the Cape Service to have suites and cabins with private bathrooms, and some even had beds instead of bunks. She soon became a popular and well-loved ship on the Cape route.

In 1937, she was rebuilt by Harland & Wolff and fitted with new boilers, a new bow and two funnels in place of four. This work not only altered her appearance, increasing the length to 686 feet and grt to 19,118 but also increased her speed to 20 knots.

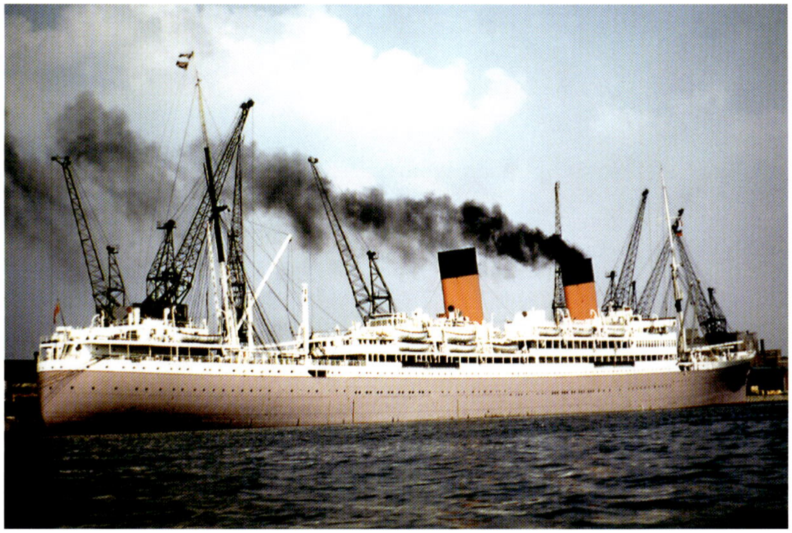

Arundel Castle at Southampton (Mike Lindsay)

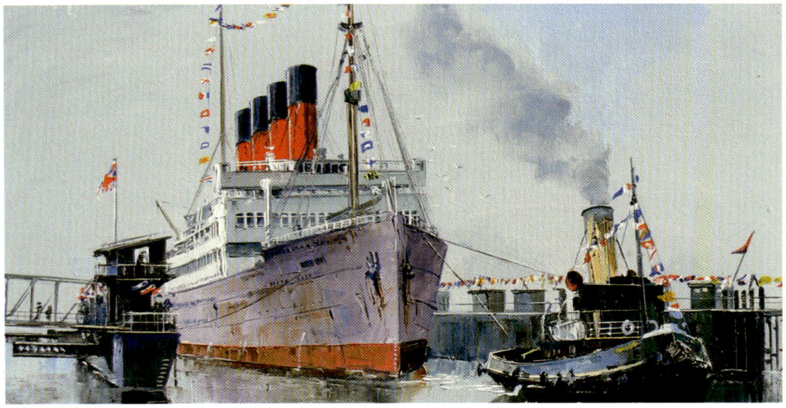

Arundel Castle opening Southampton Floating Dry Dock, 27 June 1924

During the Second World War, *Arundel Castle* was used as a troop transport and was one of the first through the Mediterranean. She also took part in the North African and Sicilian landings and was used twice as a protected vessel for repatriating badly injured personnel, first to Gothenburg, Sweden, and then to Marseille, France, in 1944.

At the end of the war, a repatriation voyage lasting 160 days took her to Gibraltar, Suez, India, Indonesia, Malaya, Japan, Ceylon and West Africa, during which time, she covered 45,225 miles. From 1947 to 1949, she was used to transport emigrants to South Africa with accommodation for 846 passengers. As there had not been time to convert the ship from a trooper, they travelled in rather austere conditions. She was the last Union Castle ship to be handed back to the company after the war, and during her war service, she had carried 200,000 troops and sailed 500,000 miles.

After a general overhaul and refit by Harland & Wolff lasting nearly a year, she was increased to 19,216 grt and returned to regular passenger service from Southampton to Cape Town on 21 September 1950. The accommodation was now redesigned for 164 First Class and 371 Tourist Class passengers. She remained in service on the South African run until 1958.

Withdrawn from service after thirty-seven years, *Arundel Castle* departed from Southampton for the scrapyard at Kowloon in 1959. During her life, she had steamed a total of nearly 3½ million miles.

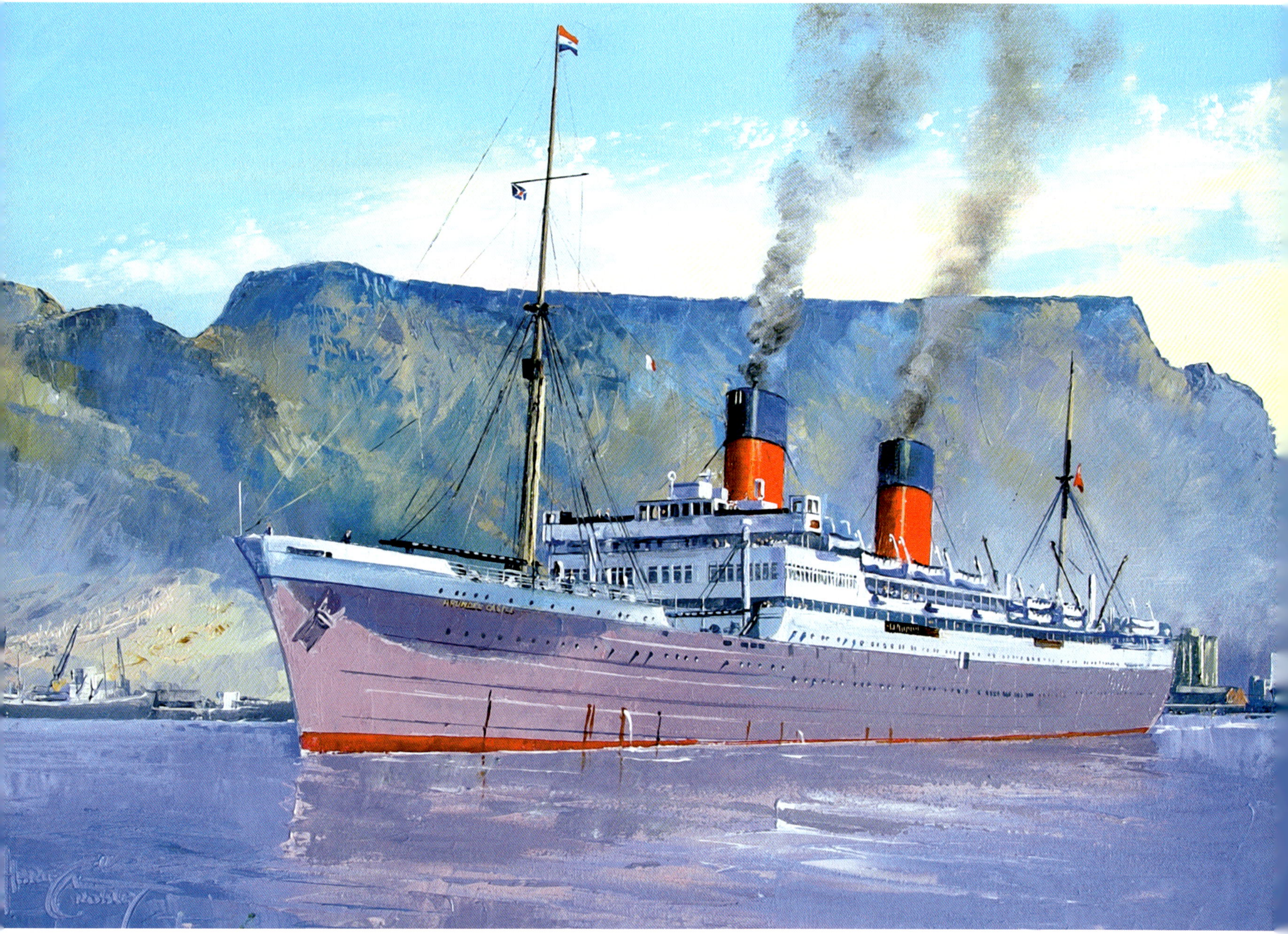

Arundel Castle leaving Cape Town

EMPRESS OF SCOTLAND

660 feet x 84 feet 26,032 grt

In June 1928, Canadian Pacific Steamship Company ordered the *Empress of Japan* from Fairfield shipyard on the River Clyde in Scotland for trans-Pacific voyages. Launched on 17 December 1929, she sailed on her maiden voyage from Liverpool to Quebec in June 1930.

Twin screws powered by Parsons turbines gave a speed of 21 knots. A special stowage area of 59,000 square feet was designated for silk cargoes, with an additional area of the steerage accommodation able to be converted quickly if required.

Her first trans-Pacific voyage was in August 1930. She was the fastest ship on the route, crossing from Vancouver to Yokohama in 8 days, 6 hours. She made fifty-eight round trips from Vancouver via Hong Kong until the outbreak of the Second World War.

In Shanghai, on the day that war was declared, *Empress of Japan* immediately sailed for Honolulu, where her funnels, masts and ventilators were painted grey, before going on to Victoria, Australia. Here, with the hull painted grey and two guns mounted, she was requisitioned by the Admiralty for use as a troop transport. The mainly Chinese crew demanded double pay for sailing into a war zone.

On 3 August 1940, the ship left Hong Kong for the Clyde via Sydney, Bombay, Suez and Durban, a voyage of 29,915 miles. When 400 miles west of Ireland, she was attacked by enemy aircraft, sustaining damage to her rudder and shaft bearings. Subsequent repairs were undertaken in Belfast.

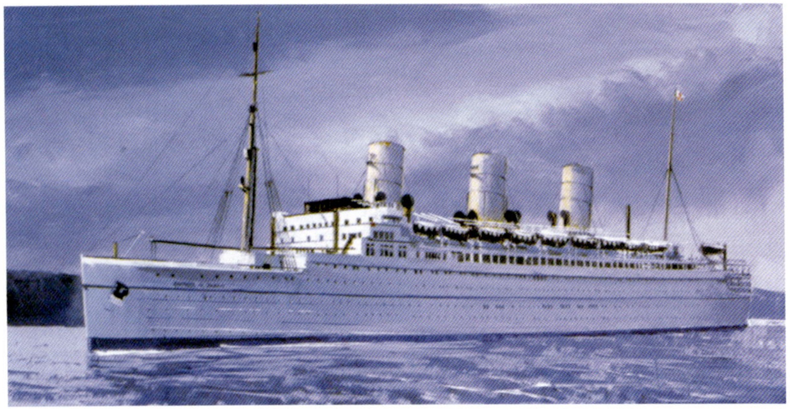

Empress of Japan

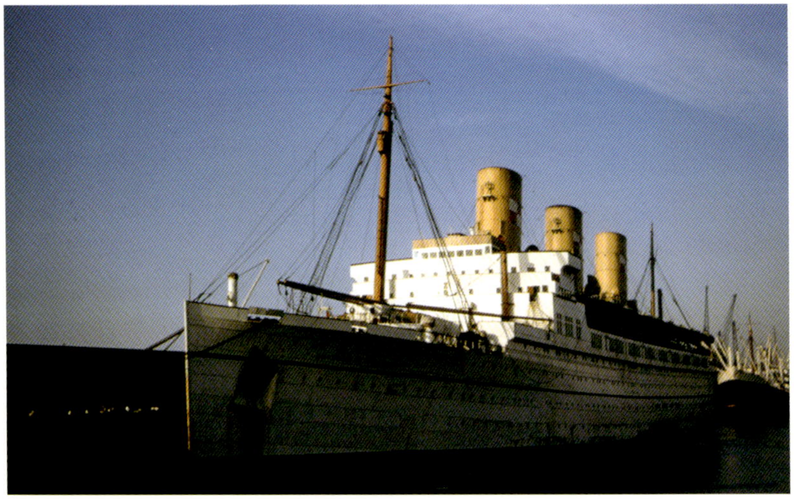

Empress of Scotland laid up in Liverpool, 1957

On one voyage in June 1941, she carried 2,993 troops to Singapore. Pearl Harbour was attacked by the Japanese on 7 December 1941, but it was not until October 1942 that the ship was renamed *Empress of Scotland*.

Most of 1943-44 was spent on the transatlantic shuttle, when she transported 72,000 troops in twelve months. Not decommissioned until 1948, she had carried 258,000 passengers and 30,000 tons of cargo, whilst steaming more than 720,000 miles during her eight and a half years of Admiralty service, all under just two captains.

Having spent a total of only 125 days in repair yards during this time, she returned to Fairfield's for a complete refit. After two years, she returned to service in May 1950 with the company flag painted on her three funnels.

In the winter of 1950/51, *Empress of Scotland* made the first of many cruises from New York to the West Indies, and between 1950 and 1957, she made ninety round trips from Liverpool across the North Atlantic.

Sold to Hamburg Atlantic Line in 1958, she sailed to Hamburg under the name of *Scotland*, where she underwent an extensive refit and modernisation, including replacing her three funnels with just two modern ones. For the next few years, she sailed from Cuxhaven to New York via Le Havre, Southampton and Cobh under the name of *Hanseatic*. This was to be her regular route, with some winter cruising, until a fire broke out in her engine room whilst she was in New York in 1966, causing extensive damage.

She was towed across the Atlantic to Hamburg in October 1966, where she was sold and scrapped.

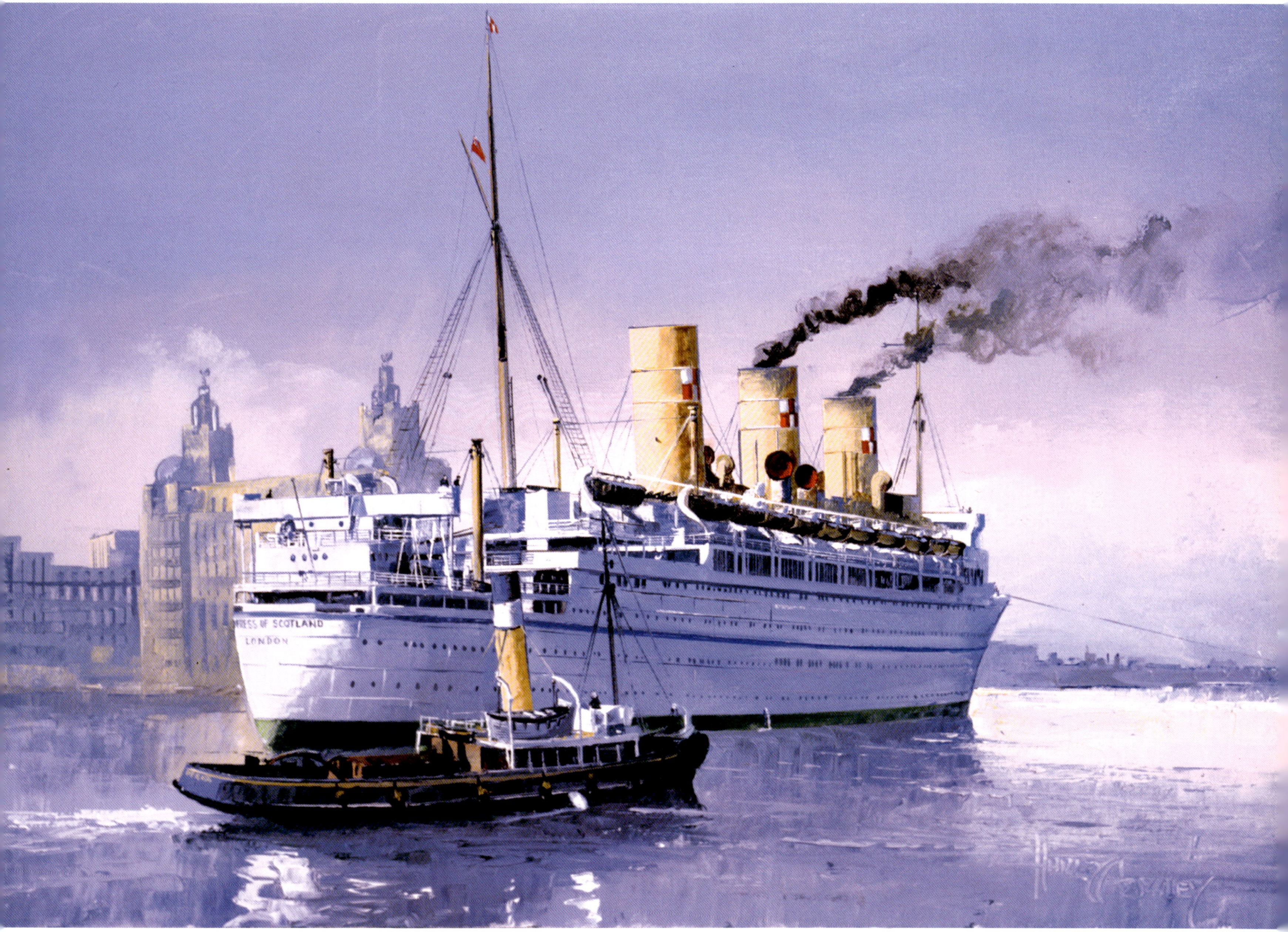

Empress of Scotland at Liverpool

EUROPA

941 feet x 102 feet 49,746 grt

Europa and her close sister ship *Bremen* were launched on consecutive days in August 1928 in a blaze of publicity for the German company Norddeutscher Lloyd. Both ships were designed as fast and luxurious record-breaking liners and were very similar in appearance. *Europa* was built at the Blohm & Voss yard in Hamburg, and Bremen was from AG Weser at Bremen.

The original plans were for the two ships to make simultaneous record-breaking maiden voyages in April 1929. However, *Europa* suffered a disastrous fire whilst fitting out, and she sank at her berth. Despite the original appraisal stating that she was only fit for scrap, after further discussions, it was decided that she could and should be repaired. Thus her completion was delayed by eleven months.

On her maiden voyage in March 1930, *Europa* gained the Blue Riband with a record speed of 27.91 knots on the westbound crossing of the Atlantic, wresting the trophy from her sister ship Bremen. From then on, Norddeutscher Lloyd used *Europa* together with *Bremen* and the smaller *Columbus* to operate a weekly transatlantic service in each direction.

It was after complaints from passengers about funnel gases and smuts over the rear decks that the two rather squat funnels were heightened to get rid of this problem.

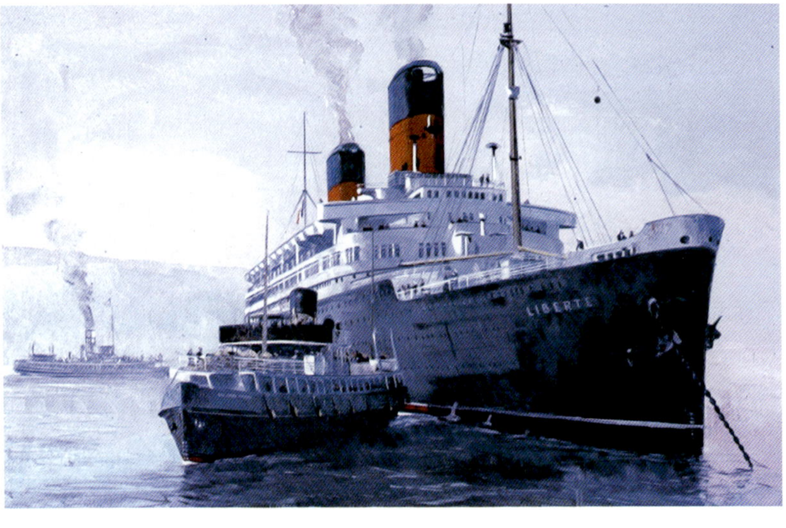

Liberté offloading mail at Plymouth

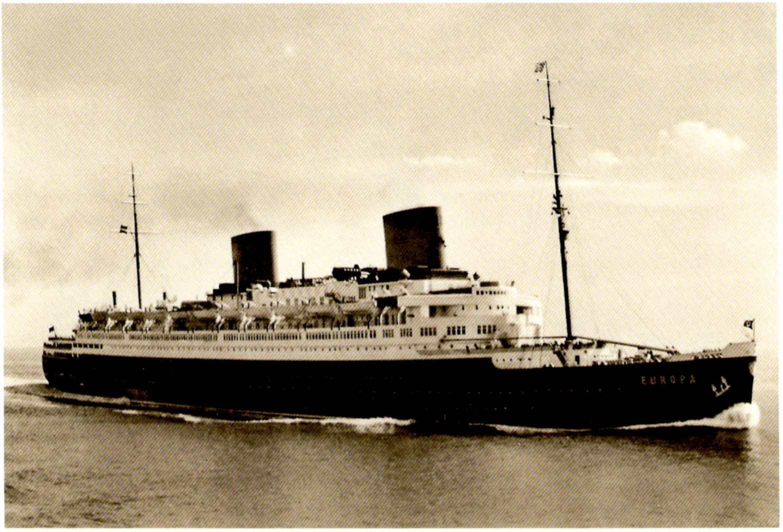

Europa

Like *Bremen*, *Europa* was fitted with a catapult and seaplane on the upper deck, between the funnels. This plane was launched before the ship reached New York to speed the arrival of the mails.

Late in 1939, she was used as a German naval accommodation vessel at Bremerhaven. In 1940, she was transferred to Hamburg, where plans were made to fit her out to carry tanks for the projected invasion of England, but these were abandoned when it was realised that they would adversely affect her stability. Further detailed plans were made in 1942 to convert the ship to an aircraft carrier but were not carried out.

At the end of the war, she was seized by the Americans, who renamed her AP-177 and used her as a troop ship. In 1946, she was awarded to the French as compensation for the loss of the *Normandie* and was renamed *Liberté* for French Line.

In December 1946, she sank in Le Havre, when, during a storm, she broke her moorings and hit the wreck of the capsized *Paris*. She was finally raised in April 1947 and towed to St Nazaire for reconstruction. Further delay occurred when a serious fire broke out during the refit.

Liberté re-entered service in August 1950 in the colours of French Line and crossed the Atlantic for the next eleven years.

In 1962, she was scrapped in La Spezia, Italy, having been replaced by the new liner *France*.

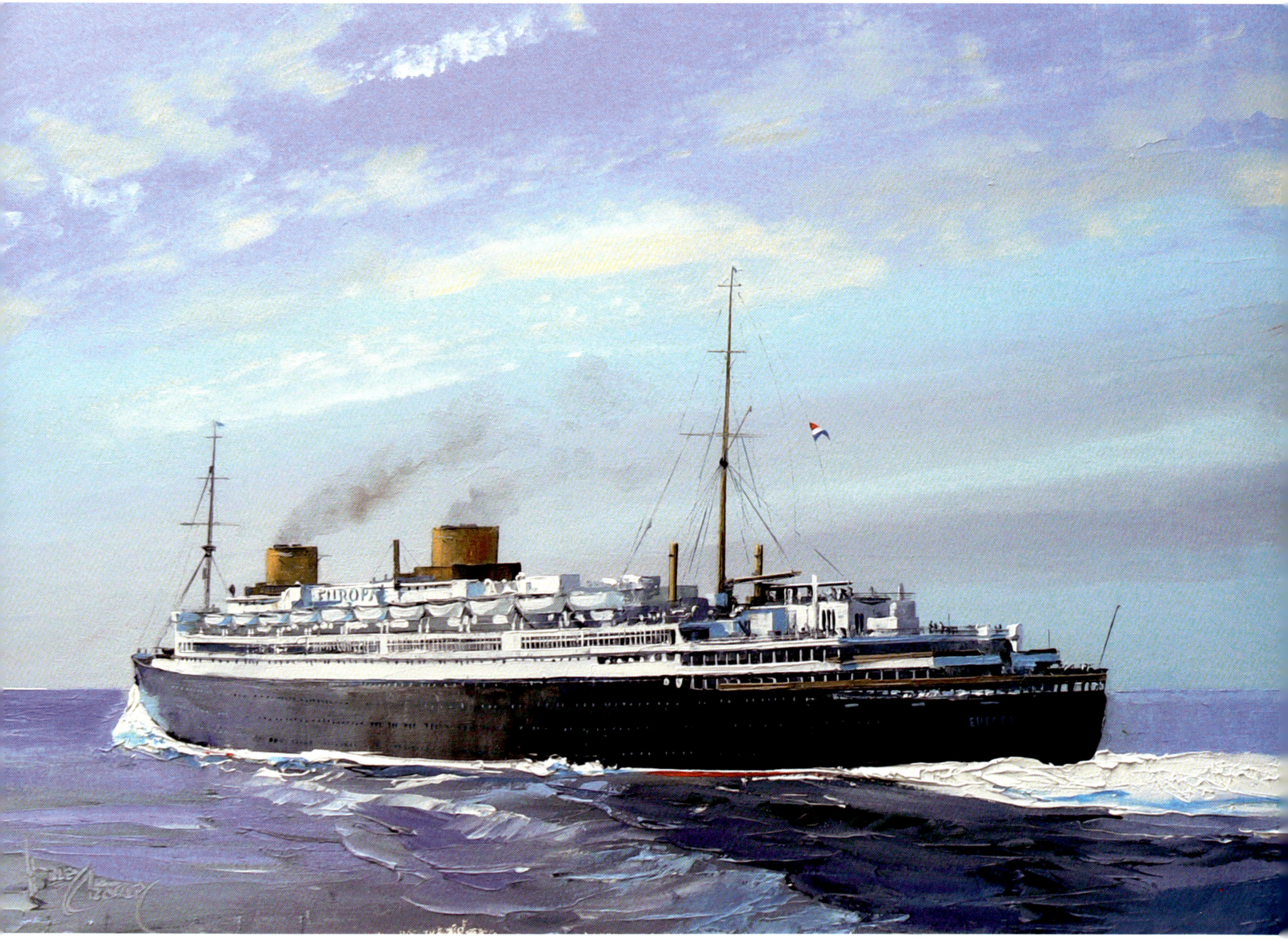

Europa at sea

NORMANDIE

1,030 ft x 117 ft 79,280 grt

Built for CGT (French Line), the first plates of this magnificent ship were laid in January 1931. She was designed by a Russian naval architect, Vladimir Yorkovitch, who had been trying to interest navies and shipping companies in his revolutionary designs for years.

The hull was completed by Penhoët at St Nazaire in October 1932. Watched by an estimated crowd of 200,000 people, she was launched by Madame LeBrun, the wife of the French President, with the world's largest bottle of champagne.

Normandie was the first ship to exceed 1,000 feet, the first over 60,000 grt, and the first large turbo-electric transatlantic liner. Equipped with an early form of radar to warn of anything ahead of the ship within a 45-degree arc, she was the largest ship in the world until 1940. The pride of France, she was financed by the Government, and her fabulous interiors, reflecting the exuberance and style of the French way of life, were built regardless of cost.

Although they accounted for only 848 of the 1,972 passengers, 75 per cent of the ship was devoted to First Class passengers. In the First Class, there were two attendants in each lift, one to ask your destination and the other to operate the lift.

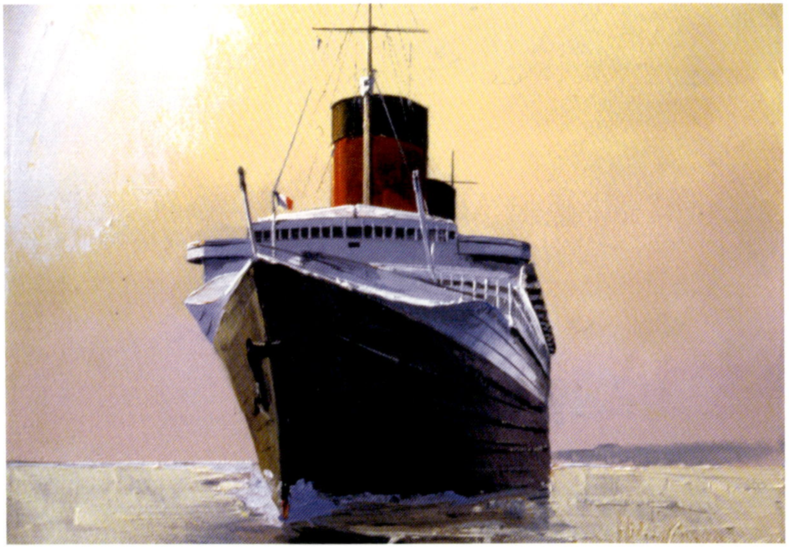

Normandie

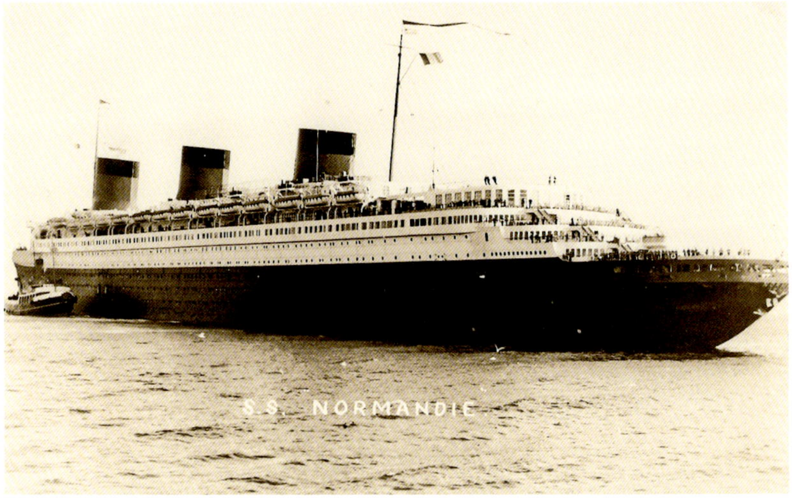

Normandie moored in Cowes Roads

Dining was a strictly formal occasion in the Great Dining Room, which was 282 feet long with 150 tables seating over 700 passengers. She had the largest interior swimming pool ever installed in a ship, 75 feet long and 19 feet wide. All portholes were hinged outwards to aid escape in an emergency.

On her maiden voyage from Le Havre to New York in May 1935, carrying 1,261 passengers and 1,341 crew, *Normandie* took the Blue Riband from the Italian liner *Rex* with a speed of 29.98 knots. On her return, she averaged 30.31 knots, the first ever crossing of the Atlantic at over 30 knots.

During her maiden season, she averaged only 993 passengers per voyage, just over half of her carrying capacity. Throughout her life, the ship never made a profit.

Before being laid up in New York at the start of the Second World War, *Normandie* had made 139 transatlantic crossings. In December 1941, she was seized by the American Navy for conversion into a troopship and renamed *Lafayette*.

During interior welding work on 9 February 1942, she caught fire, the flames rapidly spreading throughout the ship. As the New York fire brigade pumped tons of water into the ship, she listed heavily and eventually capsized at her berth at 2.45 a.m. on 10 February.

Eighteen months later, with most of her superstructure having been removed, she was finally raised and towed down the Hudson to Brooklyn. She was eventually scrapped in October 1946 after the end of the war by Lipsett Inc., an American scrap dealer.

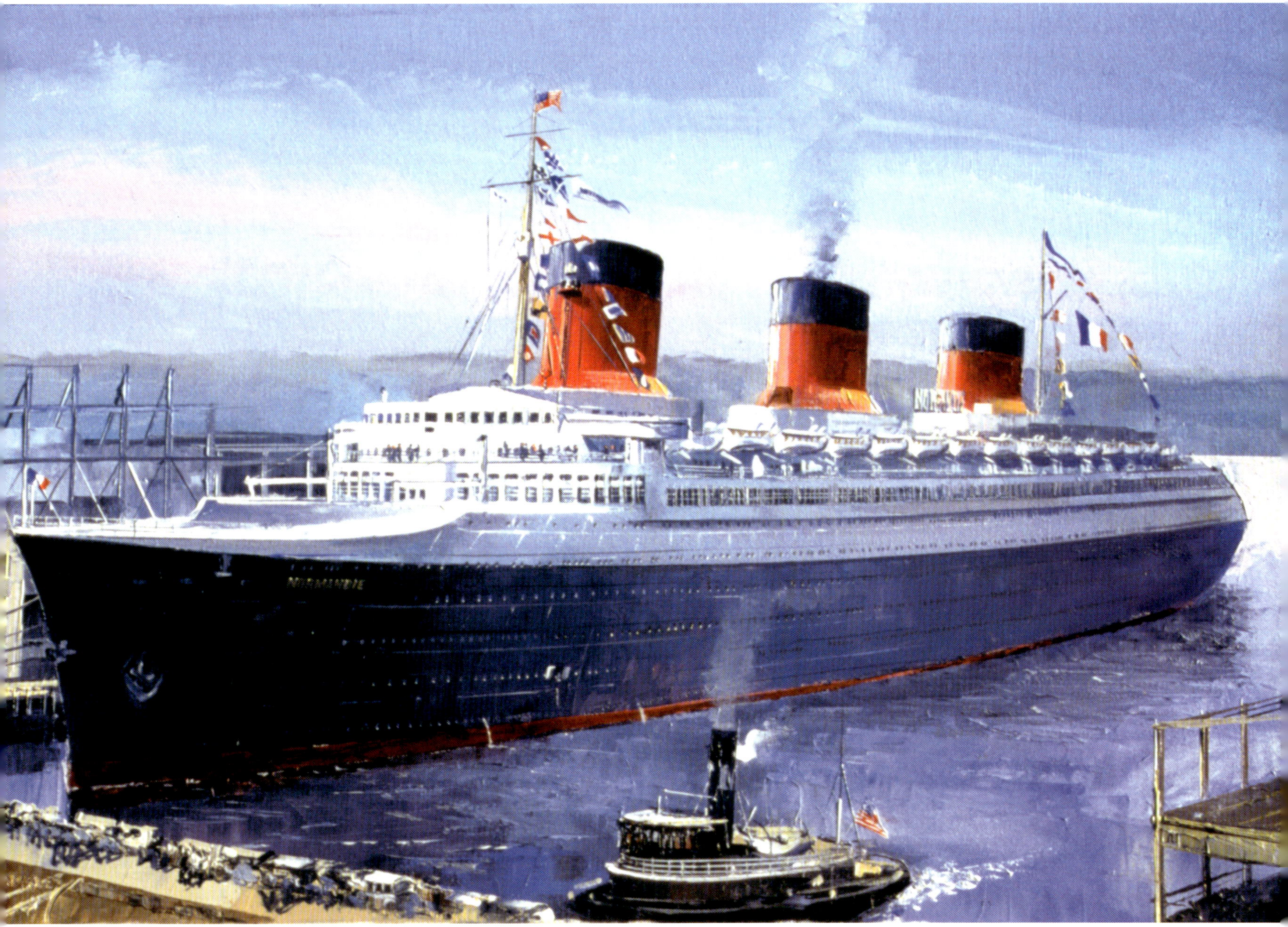

Normandie in New York

QUEEN MARY

1,019 feet x 118 feet 80,774 grt

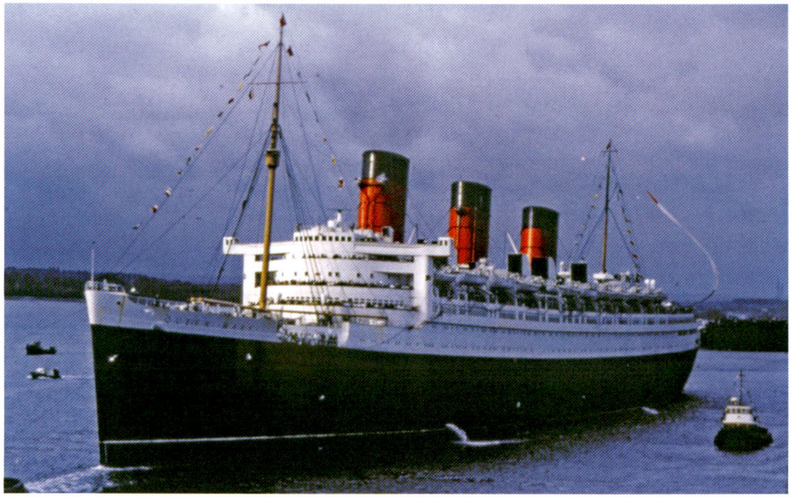

Queen Mary, Final Departure from Southampton

Work began on what was known as contract 534 in December 1930 – a new ship to be built by John Brown of Clydebank for Cunard. Twelve months later, in December 1931, the hull was painted with red lead and all work suspended, due to financial problems caused by the worldwide economic depression.

After complicated negotiations between Cunard, IMM, (owners of White Star Line), and the Government, Cunard White Star Steamship Company was formed with a £9.5 million low-interest loan from the Government, which ensured the completion of 534 and the building of a new, future sister ship, *Queen Elizabeth*. In April 1934, the shipyard reopened and work recommenced on the ship.

The name of the ship had been kept a closely guarded secret right up until the launch on 26 September 1934, when Her Majesty Queen Mary christened hull 534 as *Queen Mary*.

After successful trials in April 1936, during which she achieved 32.84 knots, Cunard White Star took possession of the ship. *Queen Mary* left Southampton on 27 May for her maiden voyage to New York. In August, she gained the Blue Riband from *Normandie* with a speed of 30.14 knots east to west, but severe vibration was a problem when the liner was driven at speed. The ship was dry-docked in December that year, and extensive work was undertaken to reduce the vibration.

At the beginning of the Second World War, she was laid up in New York, where she was eventually joined by the new but unfinished *Queen Elizabeth*, the new *Mauretania* and the French liner *Normandie*.

In March 1940, *Queen Mary* sailed to Australia, where she was converted to a troopship.

During her third transatlantic trooping voyage with over 10,000 troops on board, on 2 October 1942, she collided with an escorting cruiser, HMS *Curacoa*, which sank with the loss of 331 lives.

On an eastward Atlantic crossing in July 1943, she carried a total of 16,683 people (including the crew), a record that has never been broken. During her wartime service, *Queen Mary* had transported a total of 810,730 passengers to destinations worldwide and travelled over 600,000 miles.

Released by the Government in September 1946, she was returned to her builders John Brown to be renovated. Restored to her former glory, she resumed her role as a passenger liner, sailing on her first postwar crossing of the Atlantic from Southampton to New York on 31 July 1947.

For the next fifteen years, she operated an extremely profitable service alongside the *Queen Elizabeth* across the North Atlantic, and in 1963, she also began cruising.

She was sold out of service to the City of Long Beach, California, in 1967 for use as a museum, hotel and conference centre.

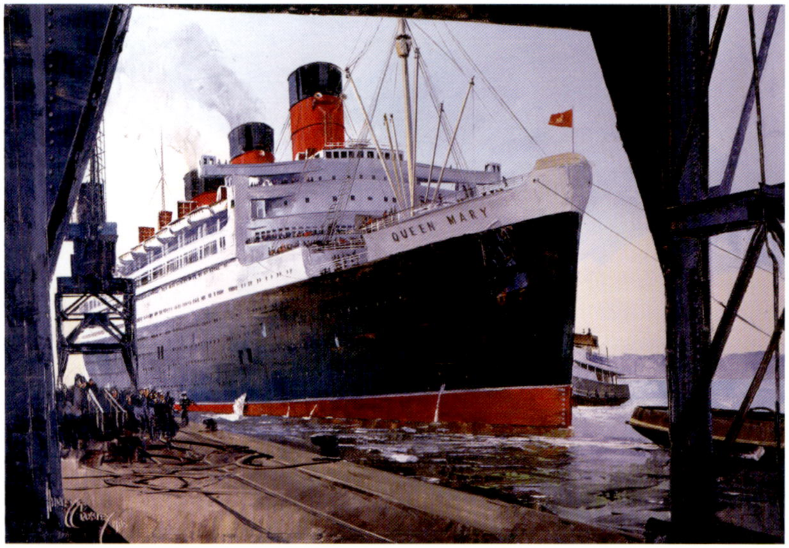

Queen Mary

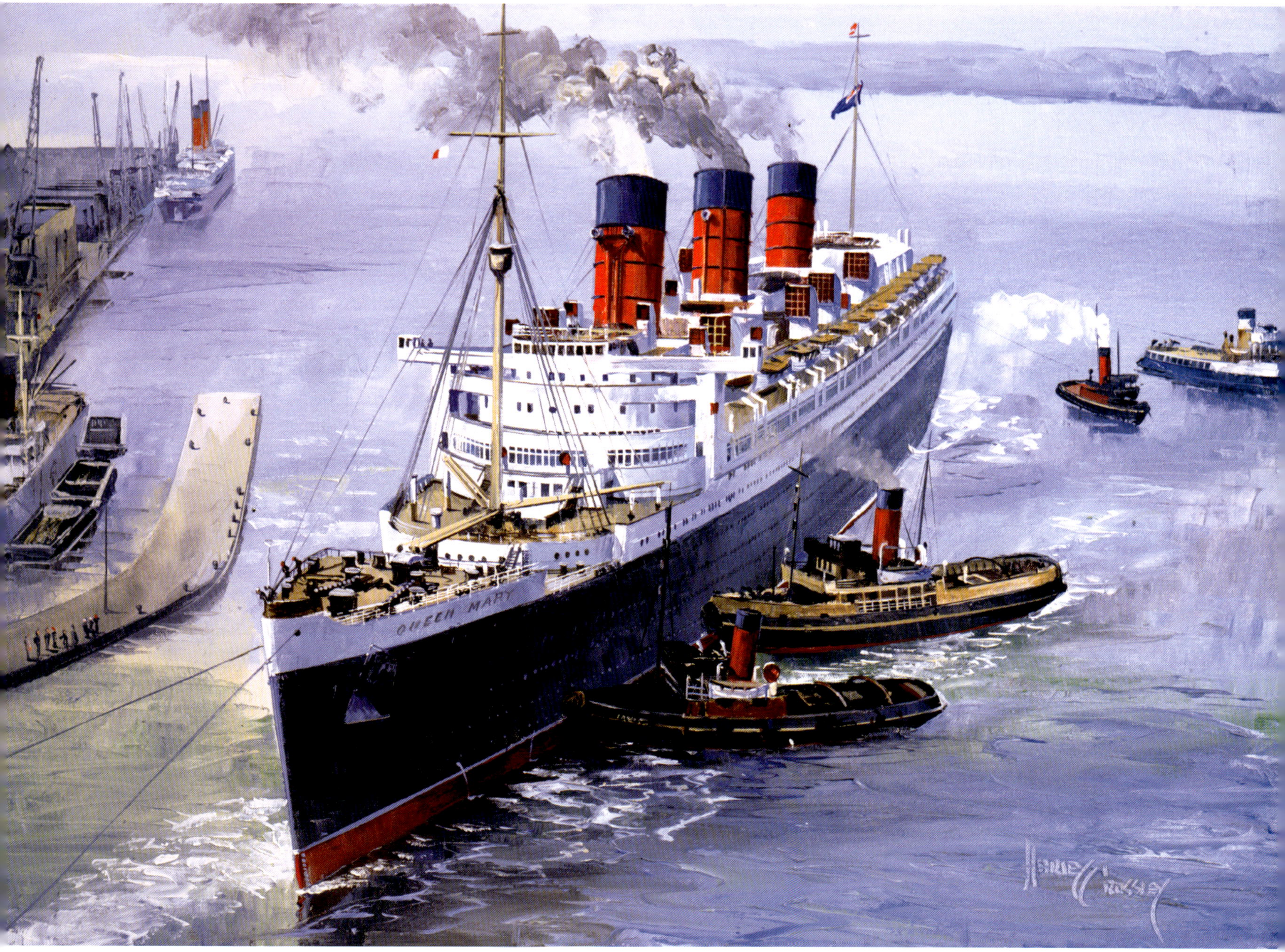

Queen Mary, first arrival in Southampton

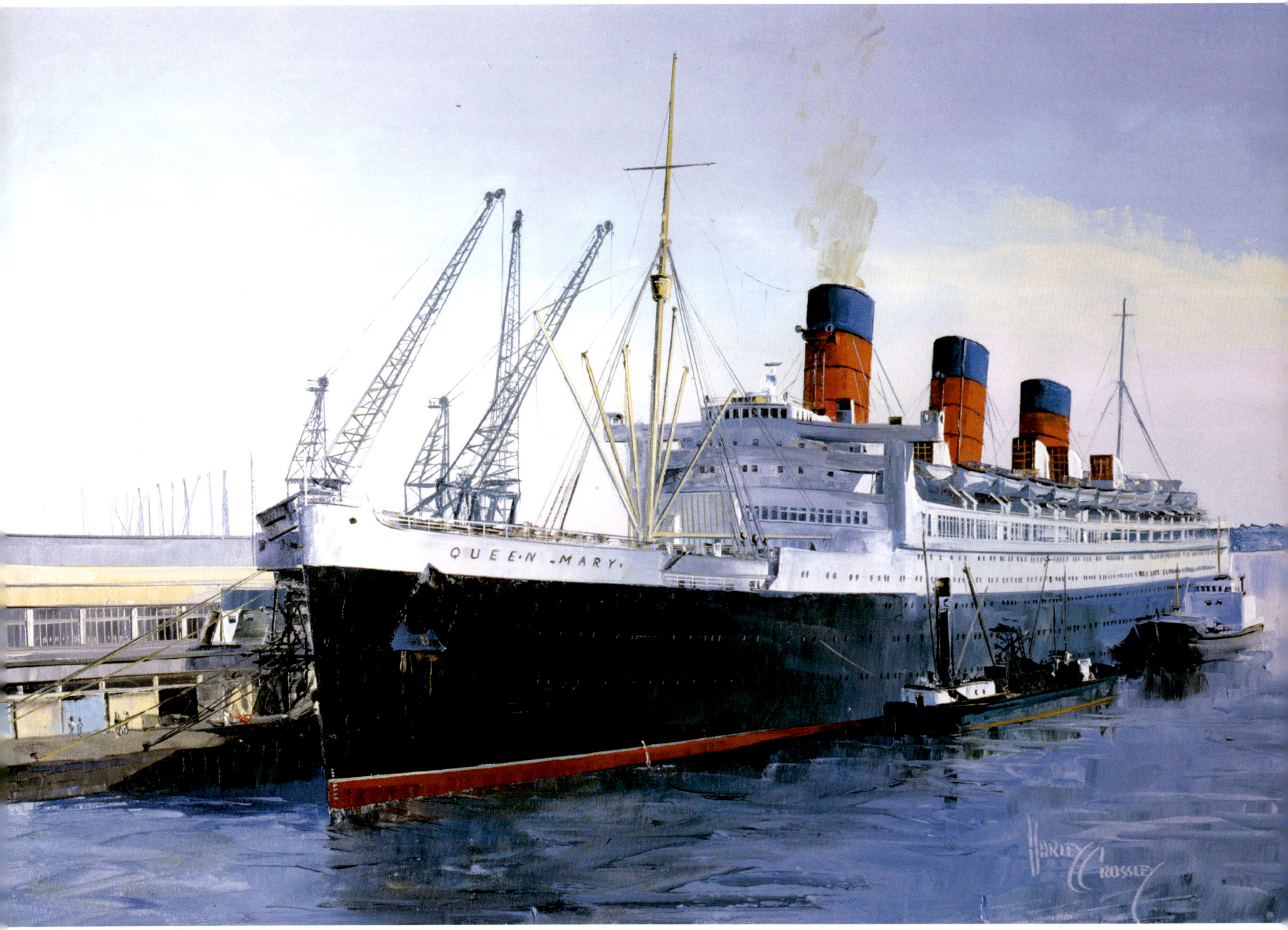

Queen Mary alongside Southampton Ocean Terminal

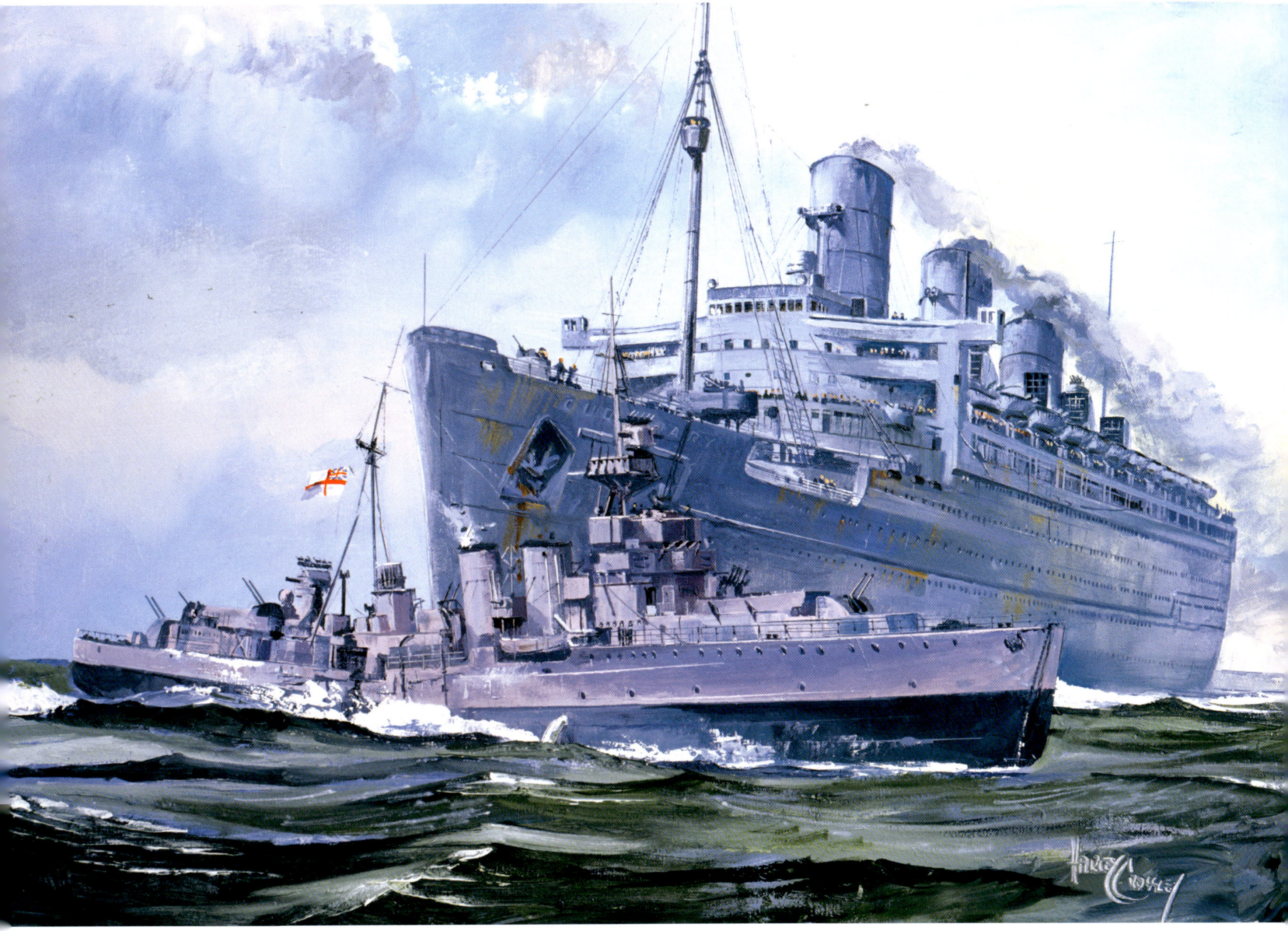

Curacoa incident

QUEEN ELIZABETH

1,029 feet x 118 feet 83,673 grt

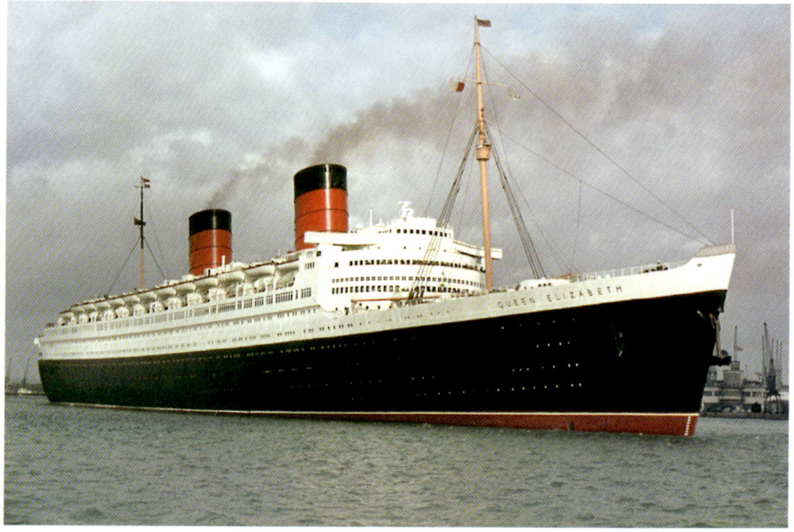

Queen Elizabeth (Mike Lindsay)

Built at Clydebank by John Brown & Co. Ltd for Cunard White Star Line in December 1936, the *Queen Elizabeth* was designed to provide a two-ship express weekly transatlantic service together with the *Queen Mary*. The world's largest liner when built, she was powered by Parsons geared turbines driving quadruple screws developing 200,000 shp.

Launched on 27 September 1938 by Her Majesty Queen Elizabeth, her maiden voyage was planned for April 1940, but the outbreak of war intervened.

At the start of the Second World War, she was painted grey and degaussing cables were fitted to protect against magnetic mines. Uncompleted, she left the Clyde on 2 March 1940 for an undisclosed destination, although the rumour was that she would go to Southampton for fitting out to be completed. In command was Captain Townley, who had signed for the ship 'untried and untested'.

Instead, she arrived safely in New York on 7 March and berthed next to the *Queen Mary*, *Normandie*, and the new *Mauretania*. She remained for eight months, whilst basic fitting out was completed, and eventually sailed for Australia via Singapore to be completed as a troop ship.

Throughout the war, the *Queen Elizabeth* and the *Queen Mary* operated independent of convoys, their high speed being considered to be the best protection against attack from German U-boats. Prime Minister Winston Churchill estimated that the troop-carrying capacity of the two Queens shortened the war by one year.

Queen Elizabeth arrived at Southampton for the first time on 20 August 1945, but her war service did not end until March 1946.

After extensive renovation, she sailed on her maiden voyage as a passenger liner from Southampton to New York on 16 October 1946, the first British vessel to start a scheduled transatlantic service after the war.

She was very profitable until the mid-1950s but was losing money by the early 1960s, when she was fitted with stabilisers and went cruising for the first time. The 1966 British seamen's strike hastened the sale of the vessel, and her final scheduled service was in November 1968.

She sailed from Southampton for the last time, arriving in Port Everglades on 8 December 1968.

After languishing in the USA for two years, during which time she was renamed *Elizabeth*, she was sold at auction for $3.2 million to the Chinese ship owner C. Y. Tung and renamed *Seawise University*. She sailed to Hong Kong arriving on 16 July 1971 to be renovated for passenger service in the Pacific.

On 9 January 1972, a series of fires were discovered on board. She burned for a day, heeled over and sank.

Most of the wreck was removed in 1974, but some of it remained under the newly built Hong Kong International Airport.

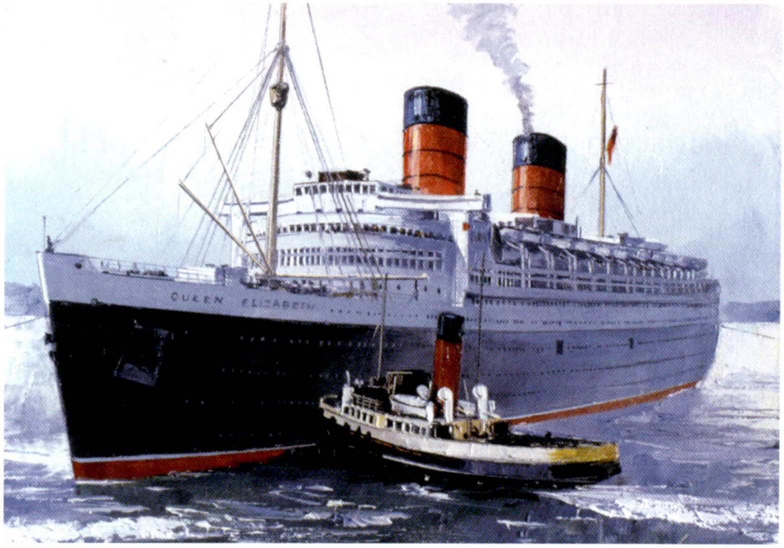

Queen Elizabeth with *Calshot*

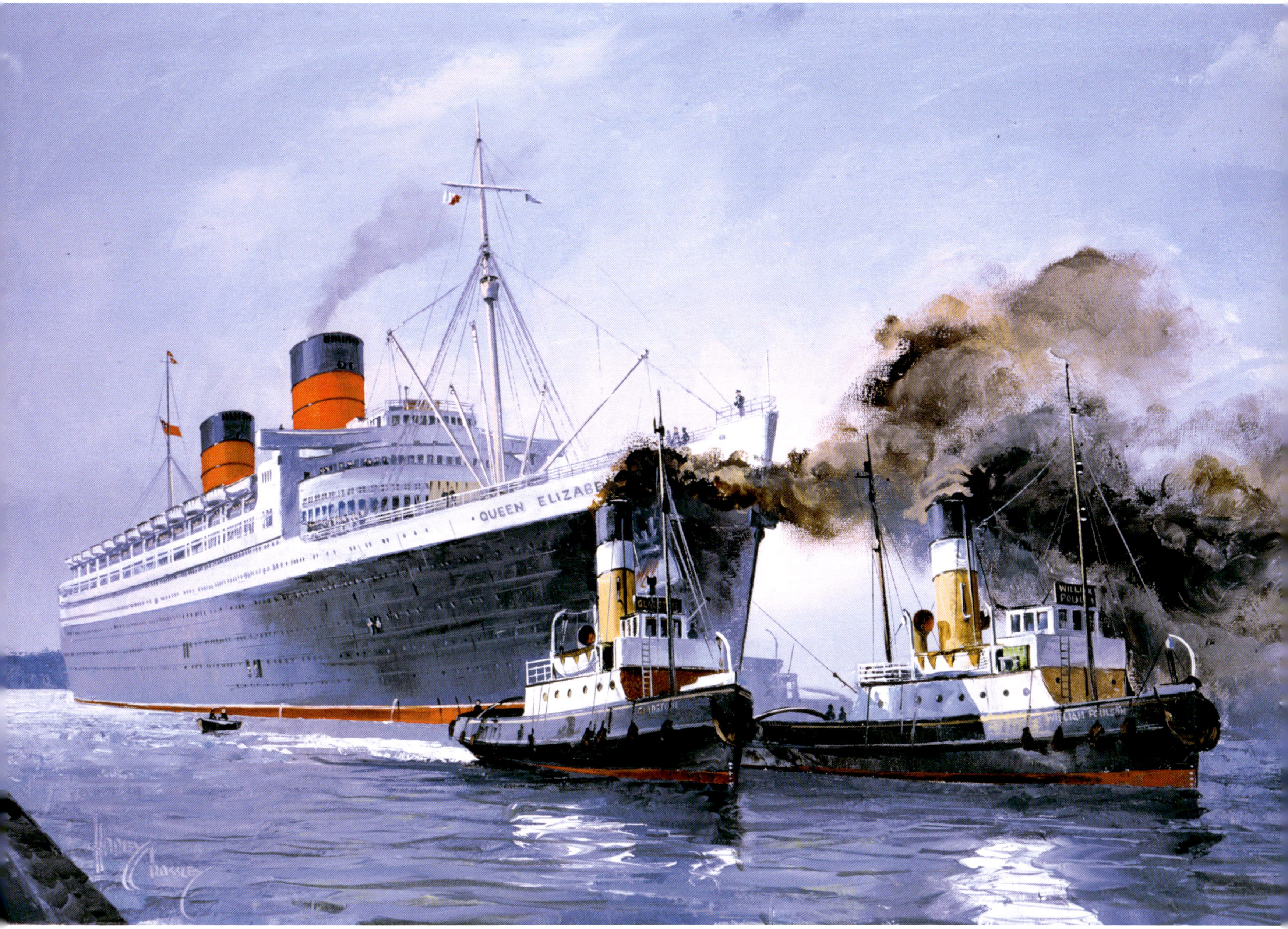

Queen Elizabeth, arrival at Southampton

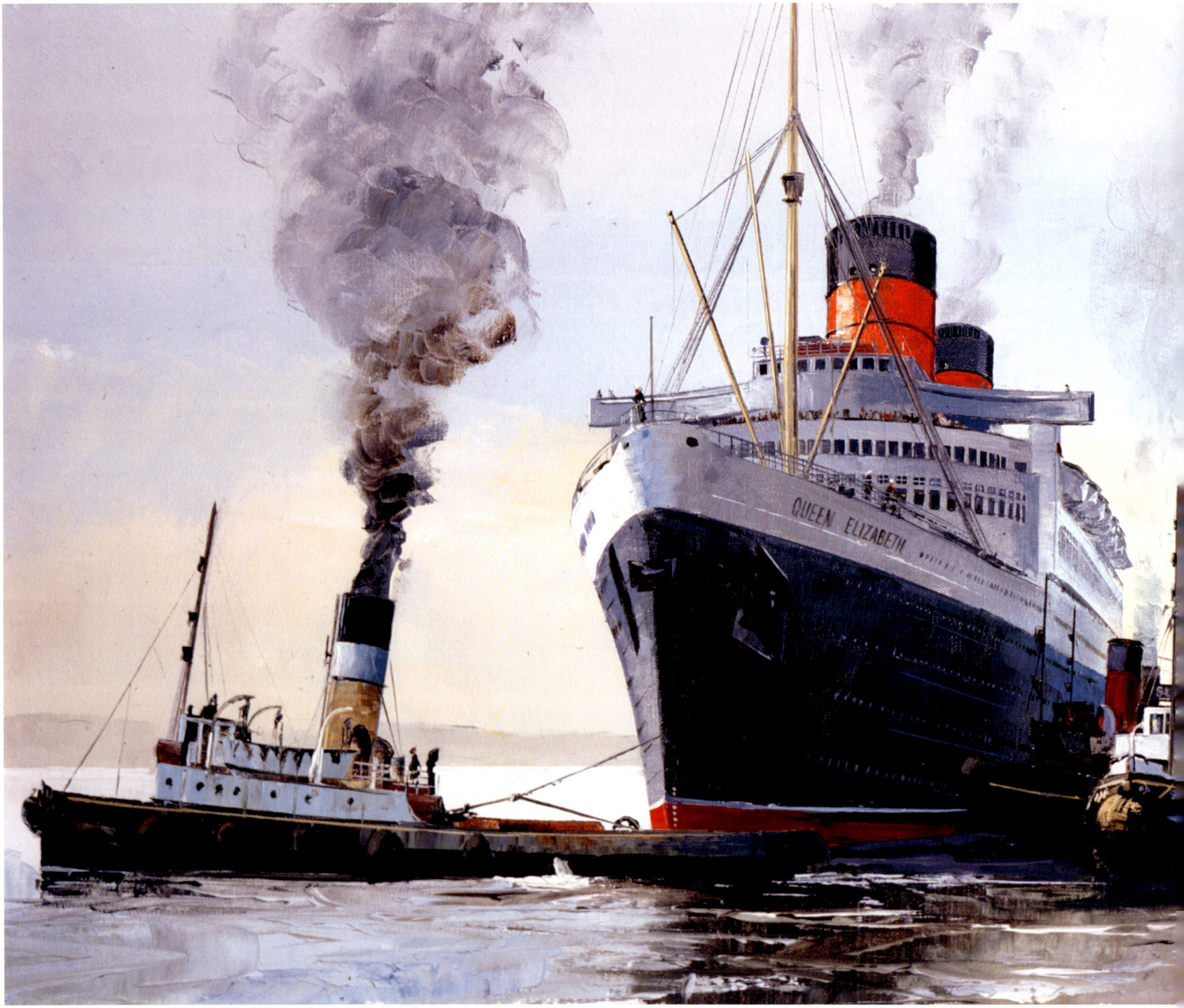
QUEEN ELIZABETH

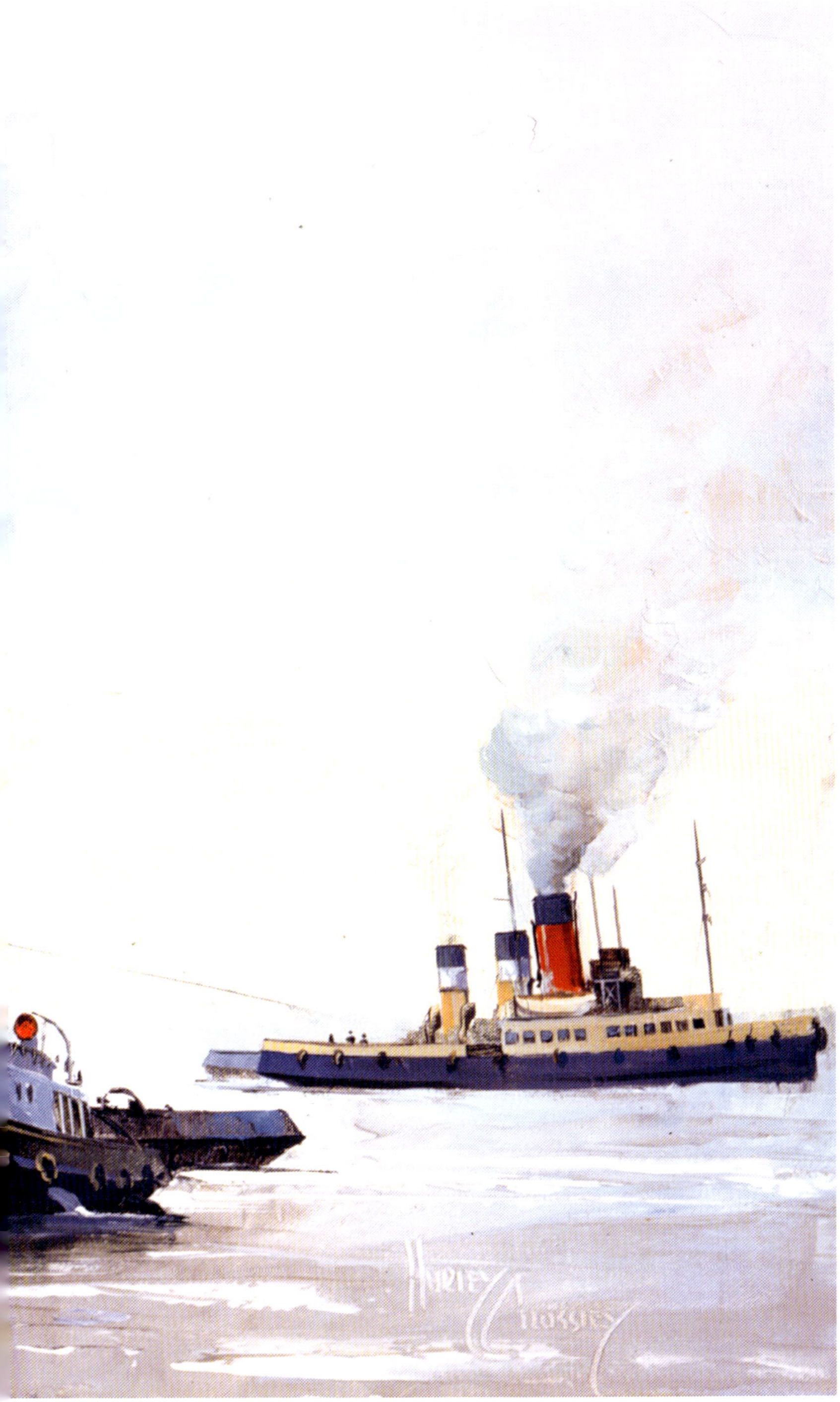

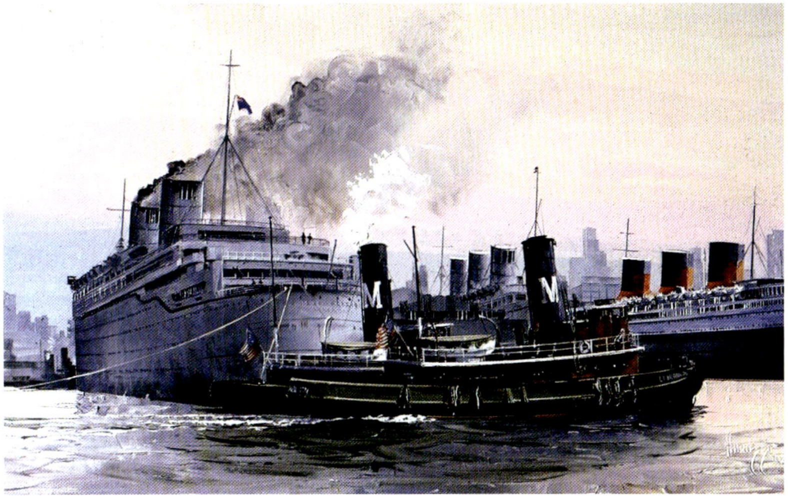

Left: Queen Elizabeth, departure from Southampton

Above: Queen Elizabeth, first arrival in New York

ANDES

669 feet x 83 feet 25,689 grt

Andes was launched from the Belfast yard of Harland & Wolff in March 1939 for Royal Mail Lines. She was scheduled to make her maiden voyage to Buenos Aires on 26 September that year to mark the centenary of the royal charter that established the company.

Originally designed to accommodate 600 passengers in two classes, she was rapidly converted instead to carry 4,000 as a troopship. Her maiden voyage was from Liverpool in December 1939, when she sailed to Canada to embark Canadian troops for Britain.

In 1942, *Andes* steamed over 38,000 miles on a trip around the world, during which time, she carried over 14,000 troops. She covered the world during the war, and on her transatlantic trips, she carried 4,500 troops per voyage.

At the end of the war in 1945, she carried the Norwegian government-in-exile back to Oslo. In June, she left Britain for New Zealand and Australia via the Panama Canal with returning troops, and during this voyage, she created a record by circumnavigating the world at an average speed of 15 knots. *Andes* later made another record-breaking voyage from the UK to Melbourne in twenty-three days.

Released from Government service in 1947, she returned to her builders in Belfast for a refit. In January 1948, *Andes* at last made her maiden voyage as a luxury passenger liner, sailing from Southampton to La Plata in Argentina.

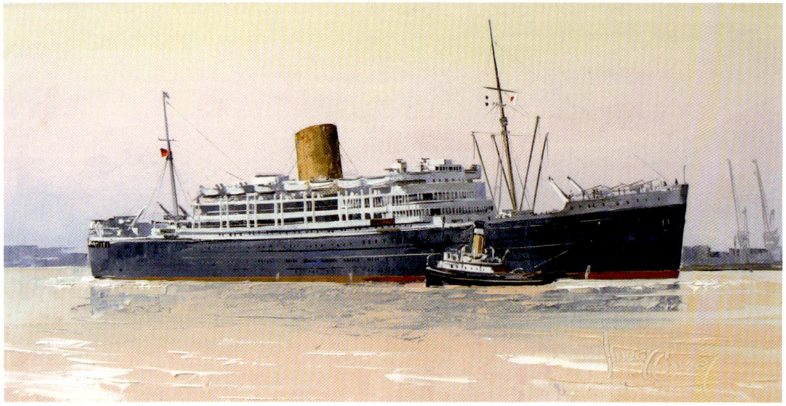

Andes

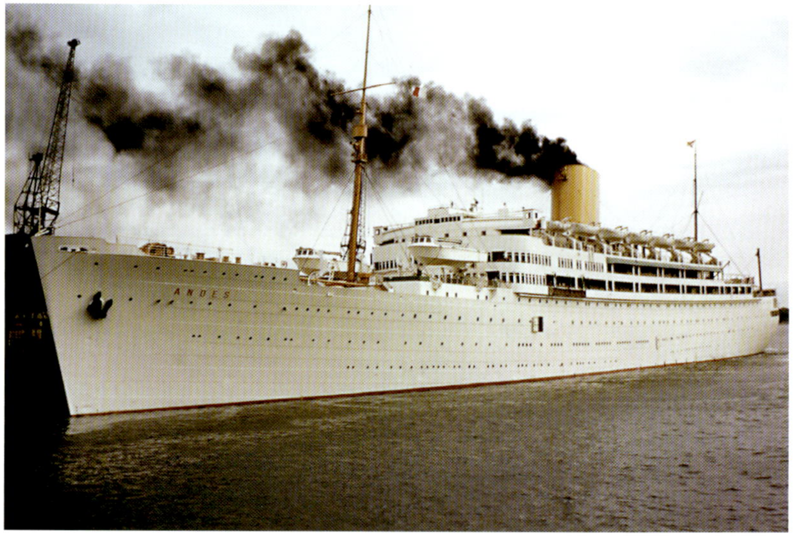

Andes (Mike Lindsay)

Andes was one of the first transatlantic liners to be fitted with Denny-Brown stabilisers. With her handsome profile, she became known as the Queen of the South Atlantic.

The increase in the popularity of air travel resulted in a decline in passenger numbers, and she was withdrawn from the South American route in 1959. Companies realised that, in order to stay viable, cruising was to be the way forward, and *Andes* led the way as a ship converted solely for cruising to meet this need. In November of that year, she sailed to Vlissingen and was converted to a cruise ship at the De Schelde shipyard with an increased grt of 25,895. This marked the end of a passenger service that Royal Mail Line had run from Southampton for 108 years.

With her new, all-white hull and large motor tenders mounted on her fore-deck, *Andes* proved to be a popular cruise ship, carrying 480 passengers in one class. Her first cruise after the refit was in June 1960. A luxury cruise ship, she attracted many wealthy passengers with around 60 per cent repeat bookings. She carried nearly as many crew as she did passengers and cruised for the next ten years until she was sold in 1971.

Andes sailed for Ghent in May the same year to be scrapped by van Heyghen Frères.

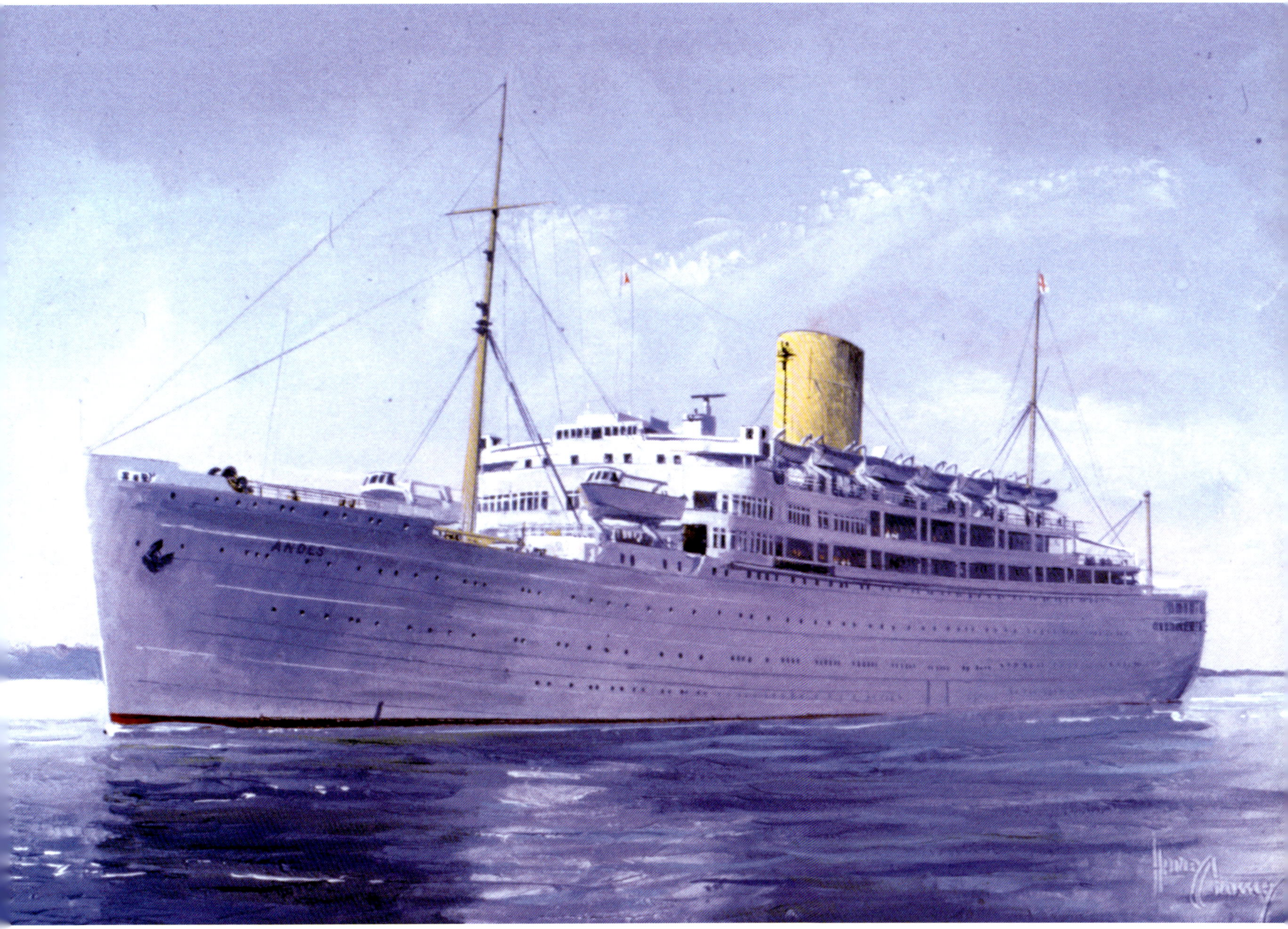

Andes as a cruise ship

CARONIA

715 feet x 91 feet 34,183 grt

Caronia was the first new large ship to be ordered by the Cunard White Star Company after the Second World War.

She was built by John Brown & Co. on Clydebank in Scotland where the *Queen Mary* and *Queen Elizabeth* had been built before the war. Launched in October 1947 by the then Princess Elizabeth, now Her Majesty the Queen, her maiden voyage was from Southampton to New York in January 1949.

Designed from the outset mainly for cruising, Cunard introduced many new features on her, including the largest funnel ever fitted to a ship. Six 45-foot covered launches carried passengers ashore when cruising, and she was Cunard's first ship to have en-suite bathrooms in each cabin and a permanent outdoor swimming pool. *Caronia* was also the first two-class Cunarder, although she was always a one-class ship when cruising.

Her crew-to-passenger ratio was the highest ever, ensuring superb service, and her unusual colour scheme of four shades of green soon earned her the nickname of Green Goddess.

In January 1951, she left New York on her first 100-day around-the-world cruise, and every year from then on, she would begin her world cruise in January. Several passengers lived on board the year round and a Mrs Clara MacBeth lived on the ship for fifteen years, spending an estimated $20 million in fares! *Caronia* was one of the biggest earners of dollars for Britain in the 1950s and 1960s.

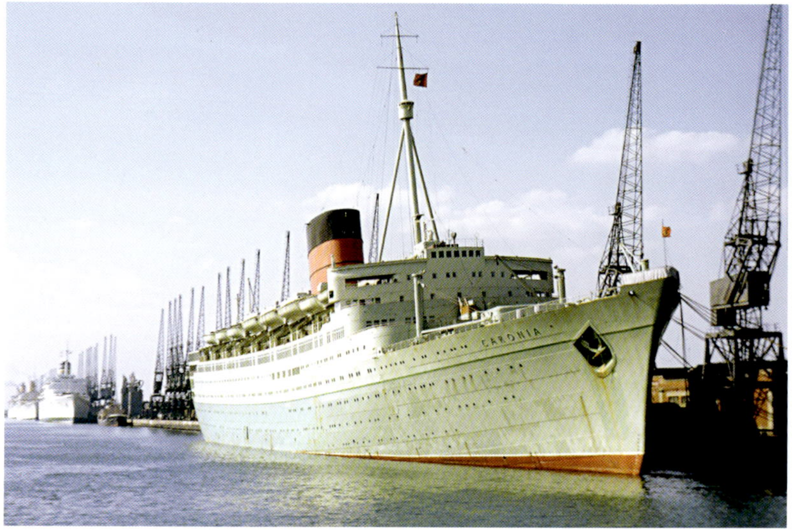

Caronia (Mike Lindsay)

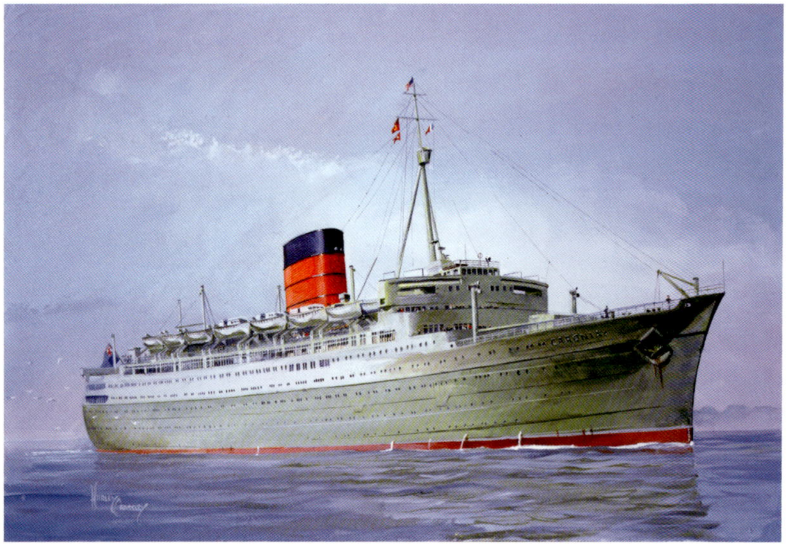

Caronia

The ship was occasionally used for line voyages during the European summer.

In 1965, *Caronia* had an extensive refit when her passenger accommodation was upgraded, but with increasing competition from other, more modern ships, she was put up for sale in 1967. She was eventually sold to Greek shipping magnate Andrew Kostantinides and renamed *Columbia*.

After a refit in Piraeus she was renamed *Caribia* and sent to New York for cruising to the West Indies. On her second cruise in March 1969, a man was killed by an explosion in the engine room. After drifting without power for twenty hours, the ship limped into St Thomas, where she disembarked her passengers, then went on to Curacao for repairs. She then returned to New York, where she was laid up for five years.

Eventually sold for scrapping in Taiwan, she left New York in April 1975, being towed by the German tug *Hamburg*. During a storm, the ship struck a breakwater at Guam and broke into three sections. The harbour entrance was blocked by the bow section for some time before the remains were scrapped on the spot.

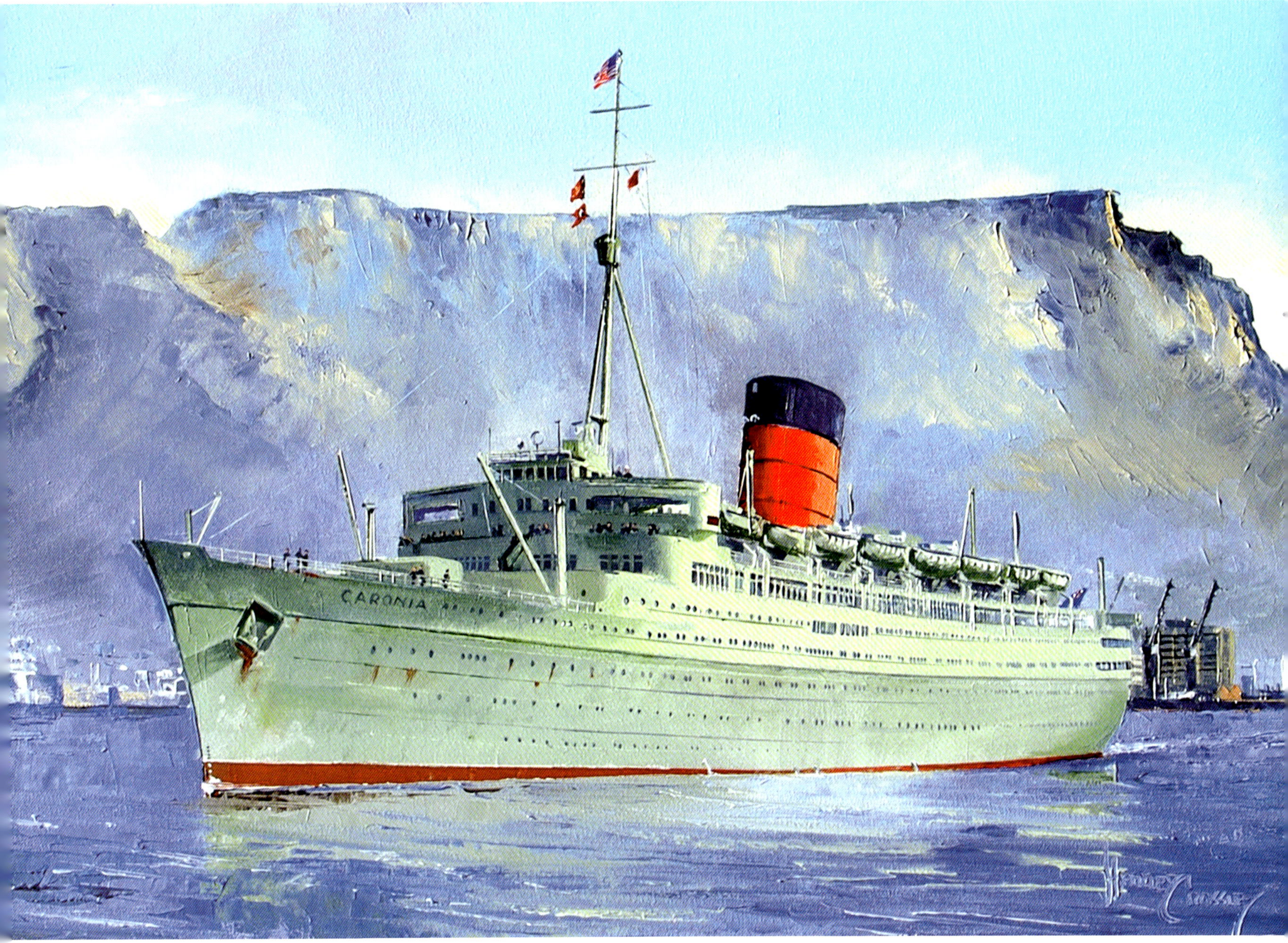

Caronia at Cape Town

HIMALAYA

709 feet x 90 feet 27,955 grt

Built by Vickers Armstrong in Barrow, *Himalaya* was the first passenger liner to be ordered by P&O after the end of the Second World War and was intended for the Australian market. Launched on 5 October 1948 by Lady Currie, the wife of the chairman of P&O, she was, at the time, the largest and fastest liner ever built for the company.

Geared turbines drove twin screws, giving a regular service speed of 22½ knots, although on her trials she achieved a speed of 25.13 knots. An important feature of her design was the installation of a Weir evaporating plant for converting seawater into fresh water at the rate of 350 tons a day, estimated to save the company £1,500 on a ten-week round voyage. She was the first passenger/cargo liner to be fitted with such a plant.

Delivered to P&O in Southampton on 1 September 1949, *Himalaya* sailed on her maiden voyage from Tilbury to Sydney on 6 October. She immediately reduced the passage time to Bombay by five days and the time to Australia by ten days, making her an instant success with passengers.

After complaints from passengers about soot, the funnel was fitted with a 'Thornycroft' top, which raised the top of the funnel by about twelve feet. During the 1950s, she also began cruising, continuing to build on her popular success.

In August 1956, whilst in the Mediterranean, there was an explosion in a refrigeration chamber, which tragically killed five members of the crew and injured twelve others. After landing the injured at Malta, she continued on her way to Australia.

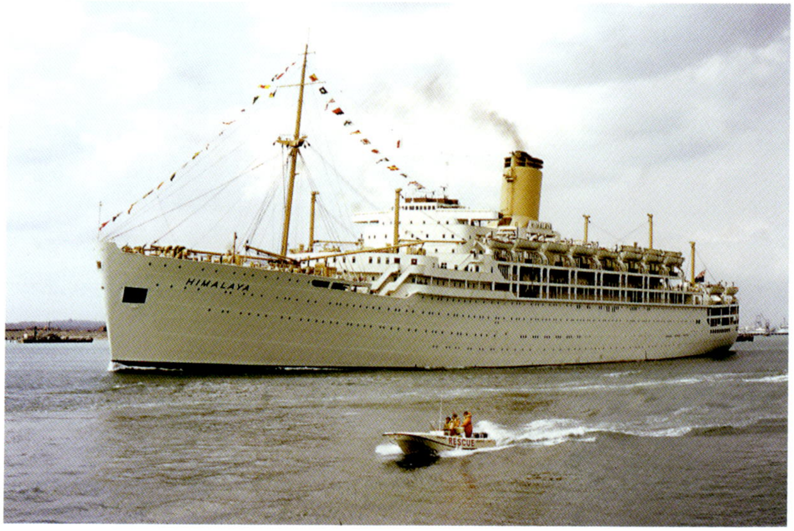

Himalaya (Mike Lindsay)

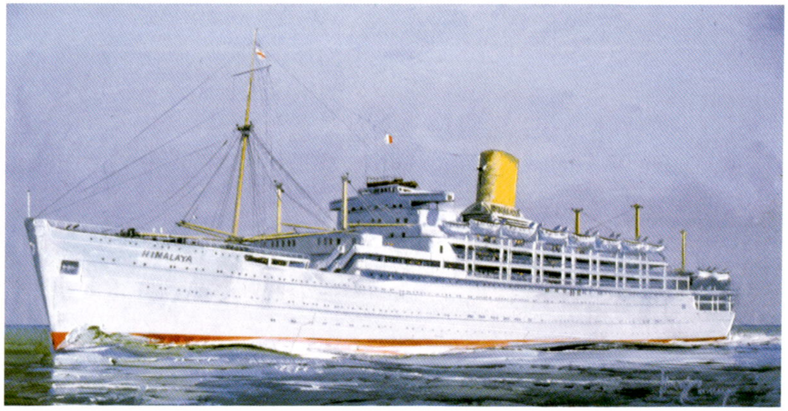

Himalaya

Fitted with stabilisers in 1958, *Himalaya* made her first crossing of the Pacific from Sydney to San Francisco. In February 1959, she left London for Australia, New Zealand, America, Japan and Singapore, a round trip of 49,391 miles. Air-conditioning was installed during her refit in Rotterdam in 1959-60. In March 1961, she carried the Australian cricket team, captained by Richie Benaud, to England in their quest for the Ashes.

In late 1963, she was converted to a one-class ship, and by the end of the decade, she was primarily being used for cruising. In October 1969, P&O transferred their passenger operations from Tilbury to Southampton, and *Himalaya* soon became a familiar sight in the Western Docks.

The next few years were spent mostly cruising from both Southampton and Sydney with positioning voyages linking the two operations each year.

On 16 May 1974, *Himalaya* departed from Southampton for the last time and sailed to Sydney for her final season of cruising. She was sold to Mitsui Co., who then sold her on to Tong Chen Steel for scrapping. She left for the breaker's yard in Kaohsiung, Taiwan, arriving there on 28 November 1974 after a successful career spanning twenty-five years.

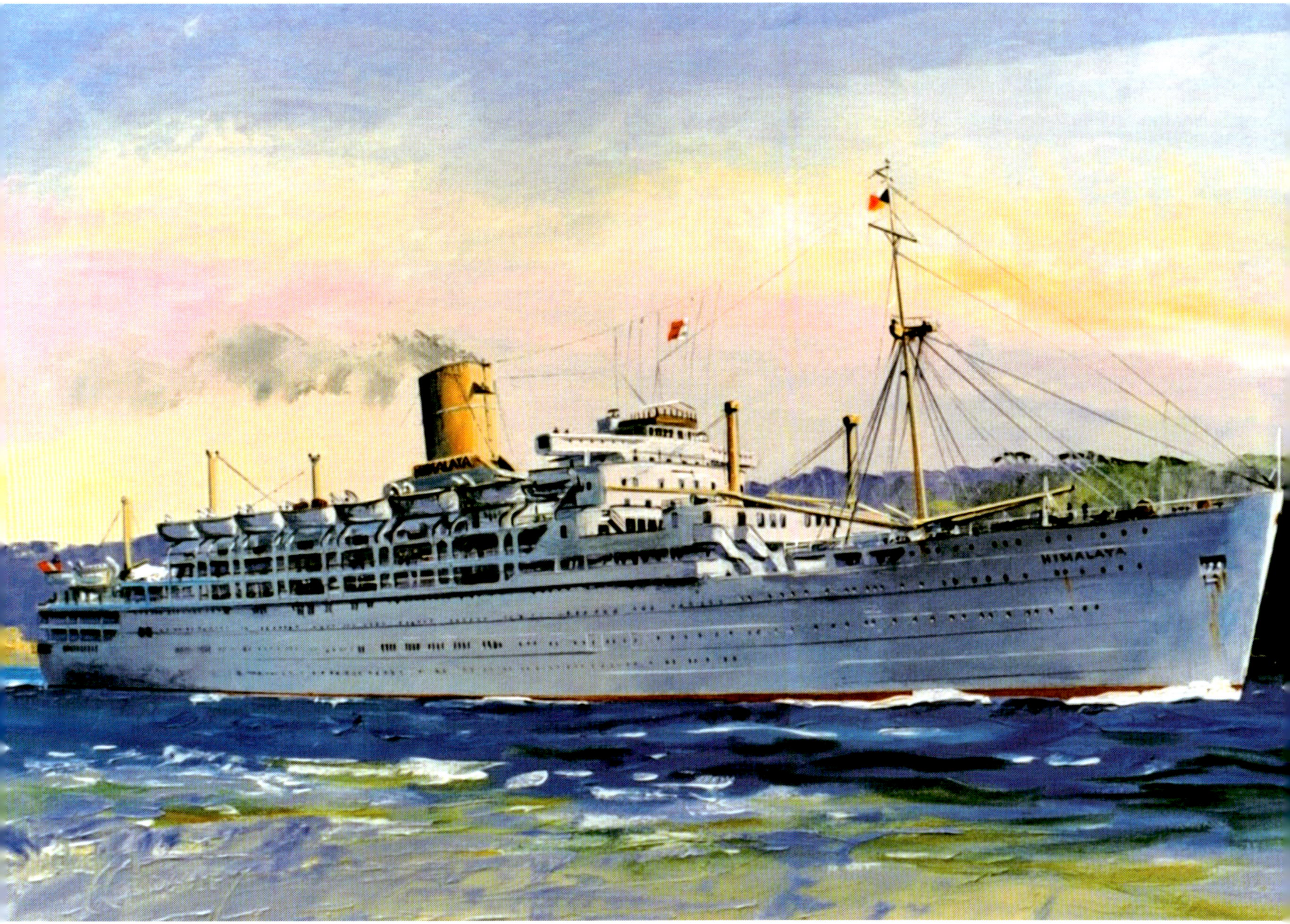

Himalaya passing the Isle of Wight

UNITED STATES

990 feet x 101 feet 53,329 grt

Built by the Newport News Shipbuilding & Drydock Company, the *United States* was the first large liner to be built in a dry dock as opposed to a slipway. Although built for United States Lines, over half of her estimated $78 million building costs were met by the Government, making her the most expensive and largest merchant ship ever built in America.

Designed as a liner, the Government nonetheless dictated that she should be capable of being quickly converted to a troop carrier for transporting 14,000 troops at high speed to any destination in the event of war. Consequently, the US Navy oversaw the planning of the ship.

To save weight, there was extensive use of aluminium in the superstructure, funnels, mast and lifeboats. Extraordinary efforts were made to ensure that the ship was fire proof, the only wood on board being a butchers' block and the Steinway grand piano. On 23 June 1951, the ship, 70 per cent completed, was floated out of her building dock and named *United States* by Mrs Tom Connolly, wife of a senator.

During her trials in the spring of 1952, she reached an incredible speed of 43 knots for a short while, and amazingly managed 20 knots in reverse. To attain these high speeds, her engines developed 241,785 shp, nearly 100,000 more than the *Queen Mary*. These details and speeds during the trials remained a state secret for many years.

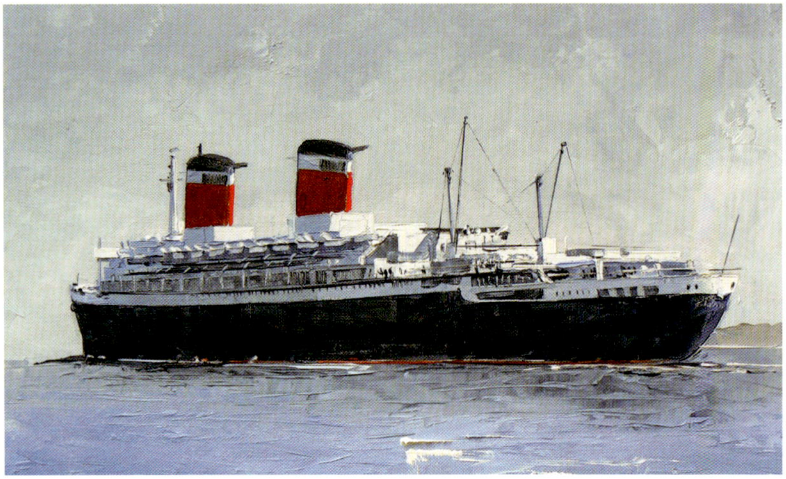

United States

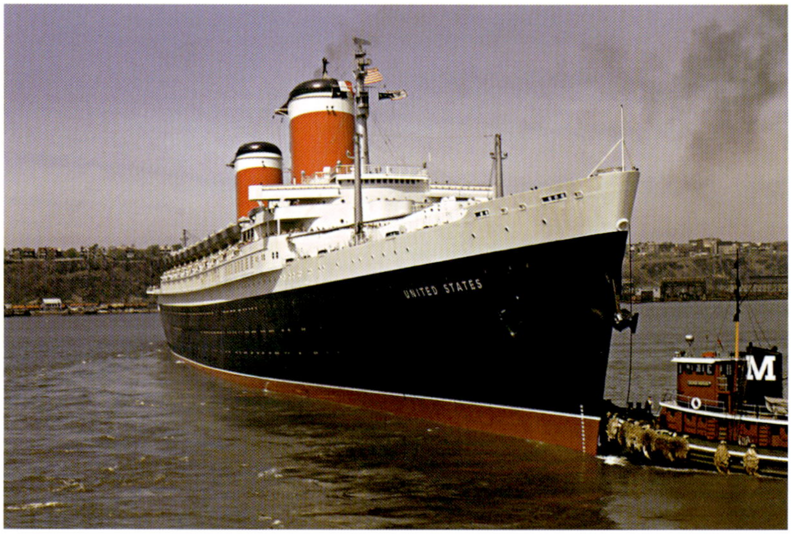

United States departing from New York

On 3 July 1952, *United States* sailed on her maiden voyage from New York to Southampton. At an average speed of 35.39 knots, the crossing between Ambrose lightship and Bishop Rock took 3 days, 10 hours, 40 minutes. On her return homeward, she covered the same stretch in 3 days, 12 hours, 12 minutes at an average speed of 34.51 knots, winning her the coveted Blue Riband. This record still stands today for a passenger liner.

During the 1950s and early 1960s, the ship was immensely successful, often crossing with 90 per cent occupancy. The Duke and Duchess of Windsor regularly travelled on her, as did many famous film stars and celebrities. By the late 1960s, the number of passengers crossing the Atlantic declined, and the *United States* began cruising. She visited some unusual ports, including Gibraltar and Cape Town. The annual government subsidy was $12 million, but by 1969, she was losing $4 million per year, meaning an average subsidy per ticket of $400.

The subsidy was withdrawn, and on 8 November 1969, the ship was decommissioned and laid up in Newport News. She was later moved to Norfolk, Virginia, where she remained for the next twenty-three years.

United States had been in service for seventeen years, travelled 2,772,840 miles and carried 1,002,936 passengers.

In 1992, she was towed to Turkey and the Ukraine for removal of the asbestos on board. In 1996, she was towed to pier 84 in South Philadelphia, where, although still afloat, she has been completely stripped and is in poor condition.

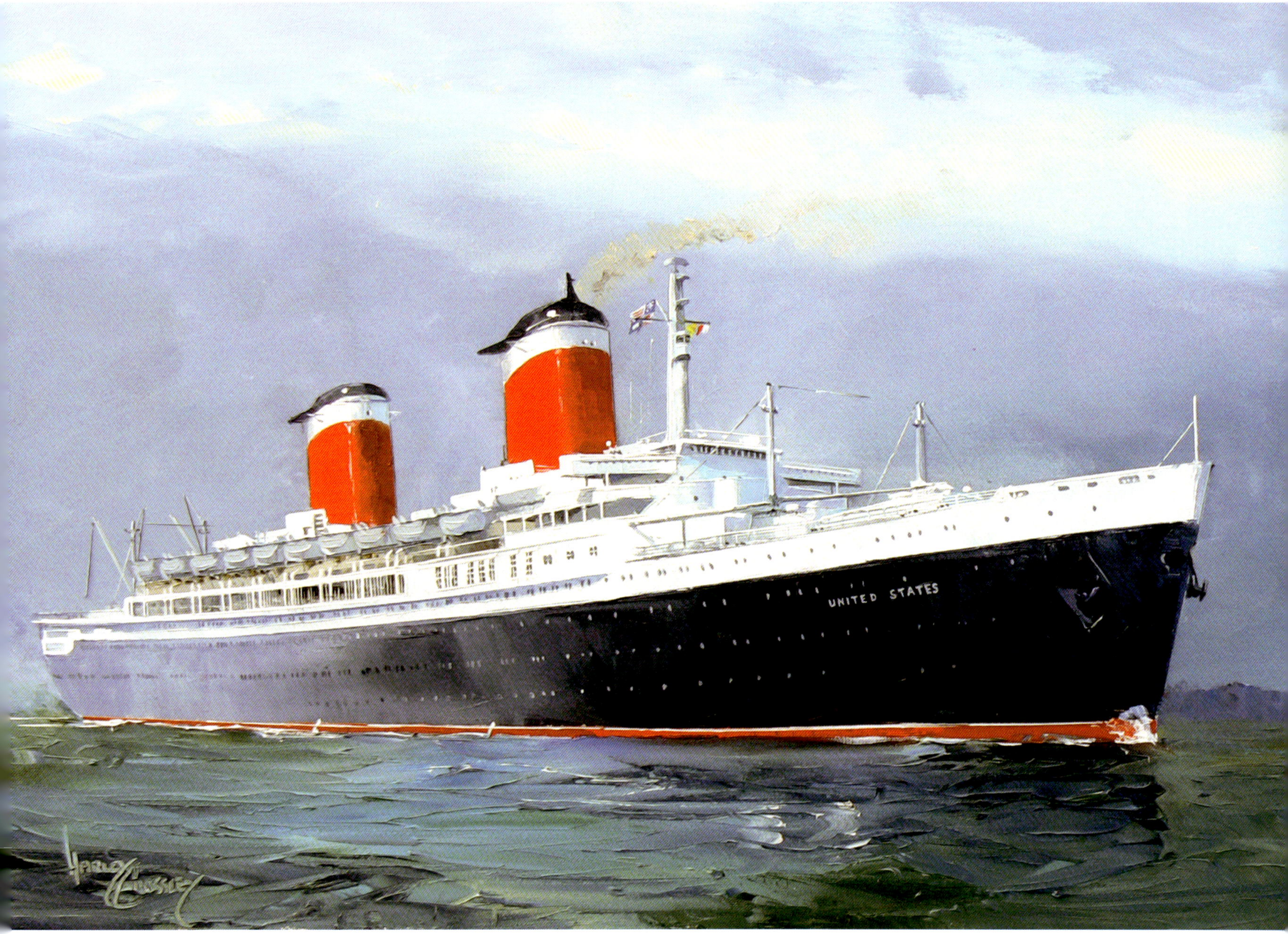

United States

OXFORDSHIRE

613 ft x 78 ft 20,586 grt

Built by Fairfield of Glasgow for Bibby Line, *Oxfordshire* was the last ship specifically built for transporting troops. The British Government agreed to charter the ship for twenty years, together with the *Nevasa*, being built for British India Steam Navigation.

Launched on 15 December 1955 by Lady Dorothy Head, wife of the Minister for War, *Oxfordshire* was delivered to her owners in February 1957. Four steam turbines gave a speed of 17 knots, although on trials she achieved 21 knots. The first Bibby ship to be fitted with Denny stabilisers, her capacity was for 1,000 troops plus 500 passengers, mostly the families of the men.

Her maiden voyage was from Liverpool on 28 February to Hong Kong via Cape Town. For the next five years, *Oxfordshire* averaged four round voyages annually transporting troops between Britain and Ceylon, Aden, Port Said and Suez. However, due to the decline in British garrisons abroad and the advent of air travel, the Government terminated the contract early. At the end of 1962, *Oxfordshire* carried troops of the Royal Highland Fusiliers from Malta to the UK on her final trooping voyage. Withdrawn from service, she was laid up in the River Fal, Cornwall.

The following February, Bibby Line signed a six-year charter agreement, with an option for purchase, with Fairstar Shipping, a division of Sitmar Line, for carrying migrants to Australia. This was the era of the 'ten pound pom', a Government scheme of assisted passage for people wishing to leave Britain and start a new life in Australia.

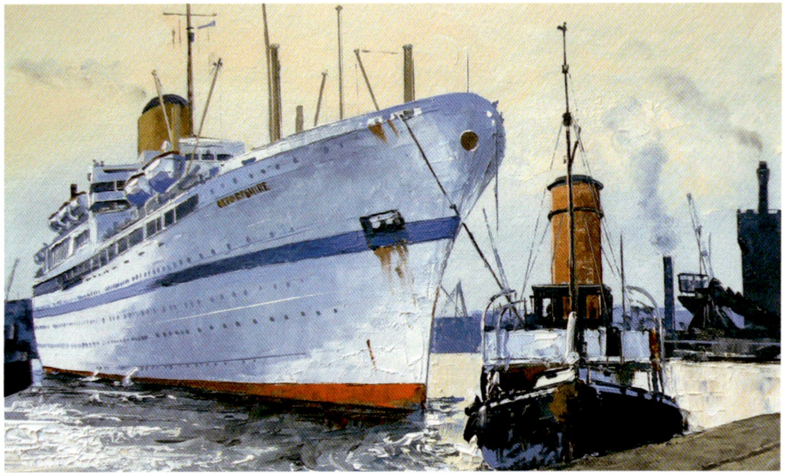

Oxfordshire in Liverpool Docks

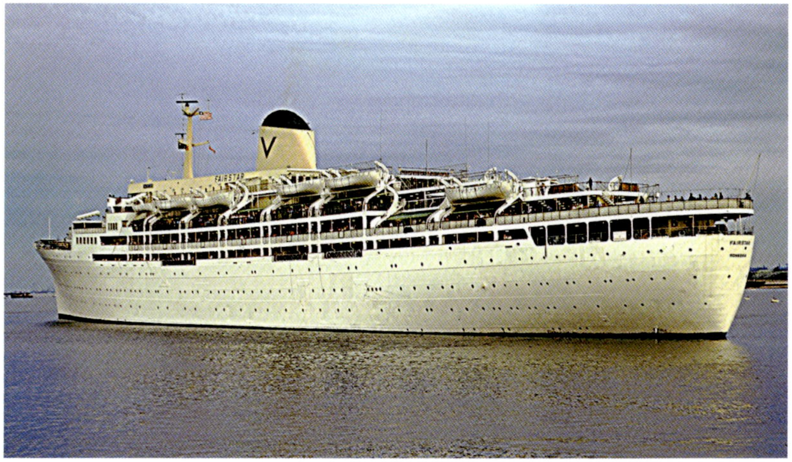

Fairstar (Mike Lindsay)

In May 1963, work began at the Wilton-Fijenoord Shipyard, Schiedam, in the Netherlands to convert *Oxfordshire* into a passenger-carrying liner. Lengthened fore and aft and with the funnel housing redesigned, her outward appearance was drastically changed. The interior was altered to provide accommodation for 1,868 passengers in one class, with most of the cabins having private facilities. Shipyard problems delayed the work and costs escalated, resulting in the ship being sent to Harland & Wolff in Southampton for completion.

Renamed *Fairstar* and now 21,618 grt, the ship left Southampton on 19 May 1964 for her maiden voyage, carrying emigrants to Sydney. Out of season, she cruised from Sydney to the Pacific. During the next ten years, she cruised more often, proving popular with her Australian passengers, earning the nickname of 'The Fun Ship'.

Her final line voyage left Southampton in November 1974. Sailing mainly to the South Pacific from Sydney, now her home port, *Fairstar* cruised to Asia once a year for an annual overhaul and dry docking in Singapore.

In 1989, shortly after Sitmar was sold to P&O Cruises, the cabins were upgraded and her capacity was reduced to 1,280 passengers. During the 1990s, the ship suffered numerous problems, including a boiler breakdown, which left her adrift in the South China seas for two days, before being towed to Singapore for repair.

To comply with the 1997 SOLAS regulations would have involved considerable expense, and the company decided to withdraw the ship from service. *Fairstar* sailed from Sydney on her final cruise on 21 January 1997. Three weeks later, renamed *Ripa*, she left Sydney for the last time on her journey to the breaker's yard in Alang, India.

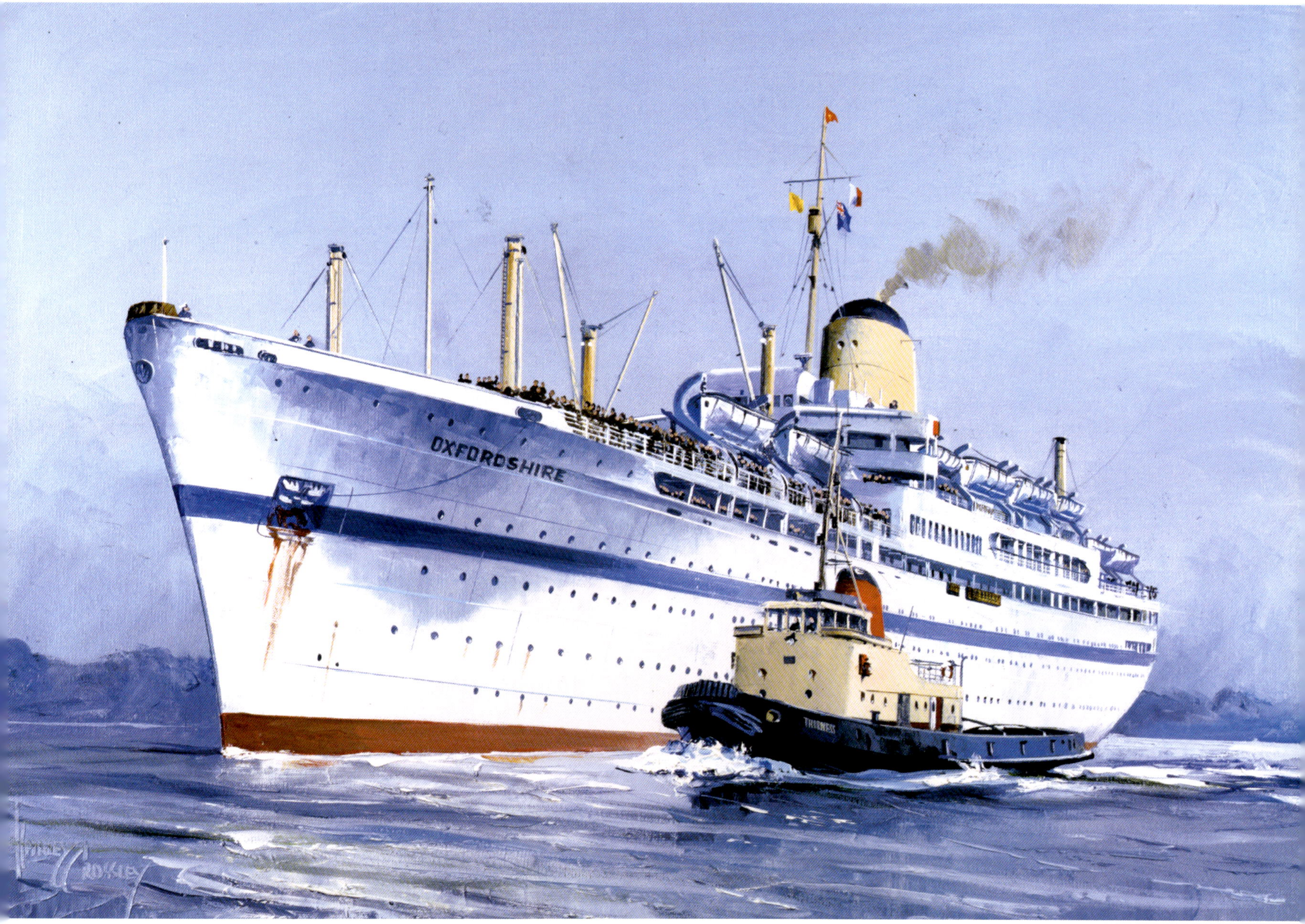

Oxfordshire in Southampton Water with tug *Thorness*

WINDSOR CASTLE

783 feet x 93 feet 37,640 grt

The only Union Castle Line ship ever ordered from the Cammell Laird yard at Birkenhead, *Windsor Castle* was the largest liner to sail on the mail service between Southampton and South Africa. Laid down in late 1957, she was launched on 23 June 1959 by Her Majesty Queen Elizabeth, the Queen Mother. For the first time, live television coverage of the launch of a ship was carried out by BBC Television.

Just over a year later, there was an unofficial strike by seamen, which threatened to disrupt the ship's entry into service. The original plan for a shake-down cruise from Liverpool to Southampton via the Scottish Islands and Rotterdam had to be cancelled due to the seamen's strike. Fortunately, the company secretly managed to assemble a loyal crew, and the ship sailed direct to Southampton, carrying out trials on her way.

Windsor Castle left Southampton on 18 August 1960 on her maiden voyage to Cape Town and Durban, the flagship of the great Union Castle Line. On her second voyage, off Las Palmas, she went to the assistance of *Capetown Castle*, which had suffered an explosion in her engine room.

In July 1965, the Union Castle ships inaugurated a mail service of 11½ days between Cape Town and Southampton. It was then that the time of

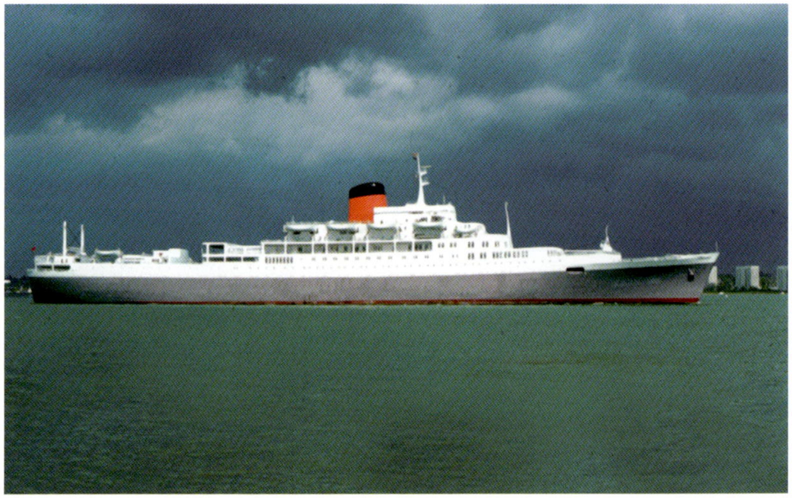

Windsor Castle

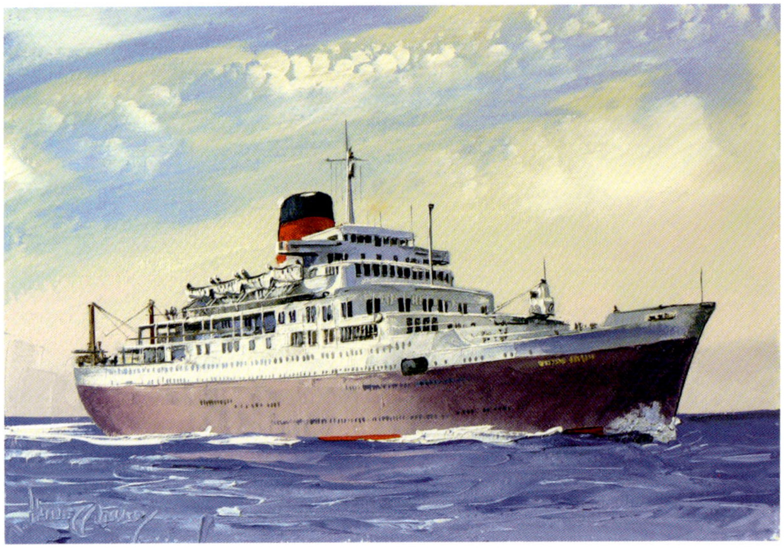

Windsor Castle

sailing from Southampton was altered from 4 p.m. on Thursday to 1 p.m. on Friday.

Fitted with air-conditioning and stabilisers, *Windsor Castle* was a popular ship with passengers, and her lavender-coloured hull became a familiar and well-loved sight in Southampton.

The advent of air travel and also the introduction of containers brought about the withdrawal of mail ships, and her final arrival in Southampton on 19 September 1977 marked the end of an era. For seventeen years, RMS *Windsor Castle* had travelled the seas between England and South Africa, carrying passengers, cargo and mail, completing 124 round voyages and covering 1,662,000 miles.

Sold in 1977 to Margarita Shipping & Trading (Latsis Group), she was converted in Piraeus to a luxury accommodation vessel and renamed *Margarita L.* After being laid up for a year, she was then used in Jeddah to accommodate workers on various projects for the company during the next two years, before returning to Eleusis, Greece, where she was laid up again. The ship was put up for sale in 1998, but there was no interest in buying her, and she remained where she was until finally being sold for scrap in 2005.

Restored to steaming condition, she was renamed *Rita* and set off in April 2005 on her final voyage to be scrapped in Alang. She broke down off India and was finally taken under tow for the last stage of her journey. It is ironic that the scrapping of the *Windsor Castle* began on 18 August 2005, exactly forty-five years after the start of her maiden voyage from Southampton.

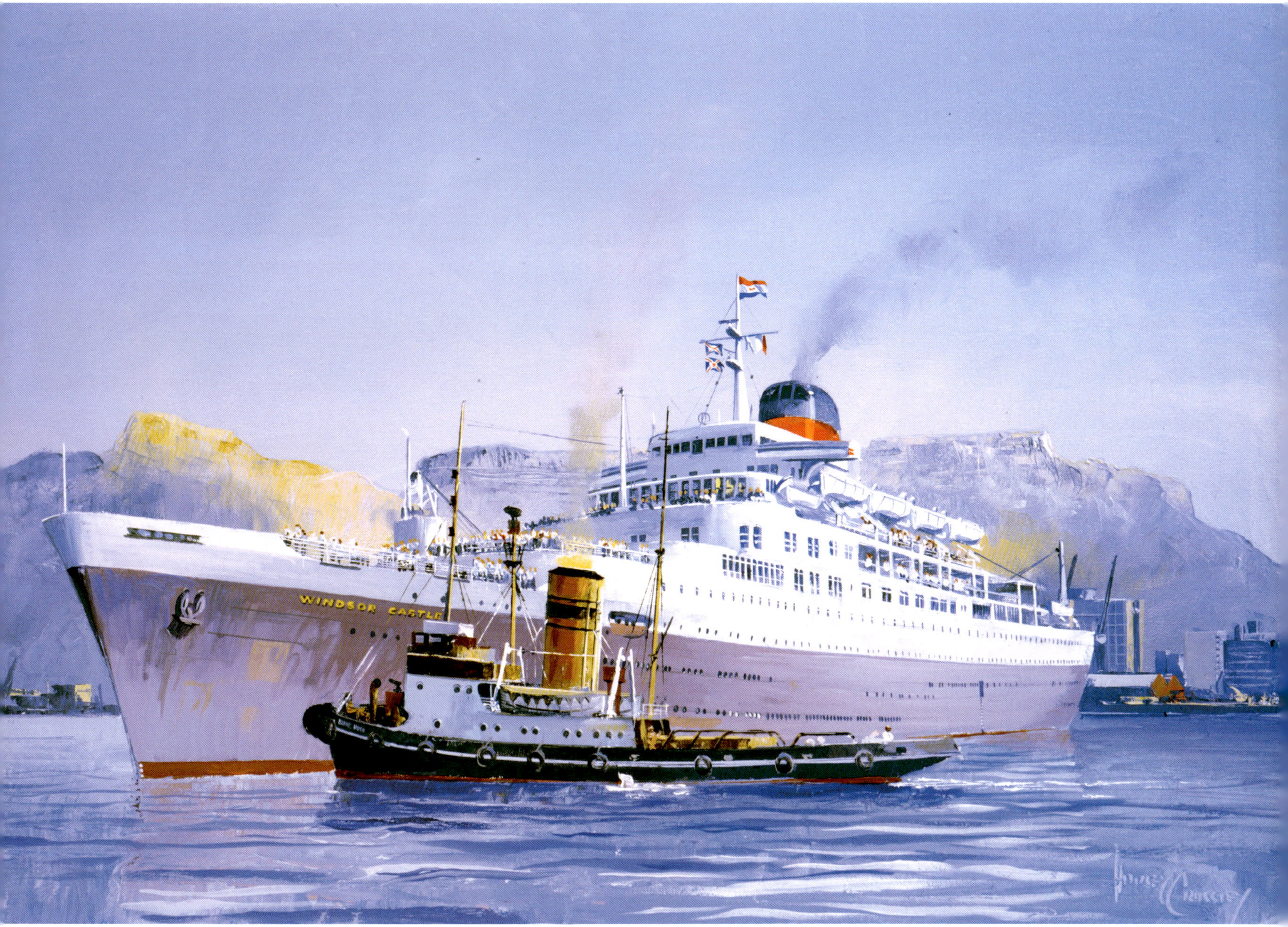

Windsor Castle Cape Town departure

CANBERRA

820 feet x 102 feet 45,270 grt

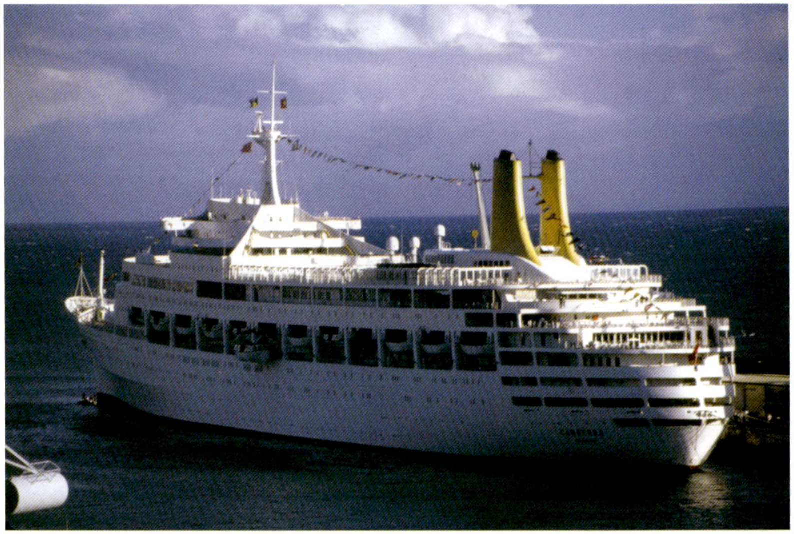

Canberra at Funchal

Canberra was launched from the Harland & Wolff yard in Belfast by Dame Pattie Menzies, wife of the Australian Prime Minister on 16 March 1960. Instead of the customary champagne, a bottle of Australian wine was used at the ceremony.

Fitted with two sets of stabilisers, bow thrusters, turbo-electric propulsion, and with the extensive use of aluminium, she was dubbed 'the ship that shapes the future'. Her engines developed 88,200 shp, and during trials off the Isle of Arran, she reached a speed of over 29 knots. She was air-conditioned and had three outdoor swimming pools on board. Harland & Wolff lost money on the contract.

Canberra sailed on 3 December 1960 on her maiden voyage, which was a ninety-day cruise around the world via Suez, carrying 2,238 passengers. However, she suffered from condenser and buoyancy problems, causing late arrivals at some of the ports. Stability was later adjusted by pouring tons of cement into the bow, but this increased the draught of the ship to over 35 feet, which prevented her from mooring in many ports around the world.

In 1963, the ship suffered a major mechanical breakdown whilst in the Mediterranean, resulting in most of the passengers being disembarked in Malta to fly home whilst the ship underwent emergency repairs. Nine days later, she left Valetta and returned to Harland & Wolff in Belfast for repairs.

During the 1960s, *Canberra* became less profitable, and after some modifications, she cruised out of New York as a one-class ship. This was a failure, and in 1973, she was laid up in America and offered for sale. There was no buyer, so she returned to the UK, and after more work had been carried out, she returned to cruising from Southampton and became very popular, despite 206 of her cabins not having private facilities.

Whilst homeward bound at the end of a world cruise in 1982, she was requisitioned by the British Ministry of Defence for use as a troop ship for the Falklands conflict.

She arrived at Southampton on 7 April, and sixty hours later departed for the South Atlantic. At the end of the conflict, she transported 4,167 prisoners of war from the Falklands back to Argentina. *Canberra* returned to the UK carrying 40 and 42 Commando having steamed 25,245 nautical miles during a ninety-four-day voyage, during which time she earned the nickname 'The Great White Whale'.

After an extensive refit, *Canberra* returned to cruising until her final voyage in September 1997, when she was sold for scrap. Her life ended when she was broken up at Gadani beach in Pakistan.

During her life, she had steamed more than 3 million miles and carried over 1 million passengers.

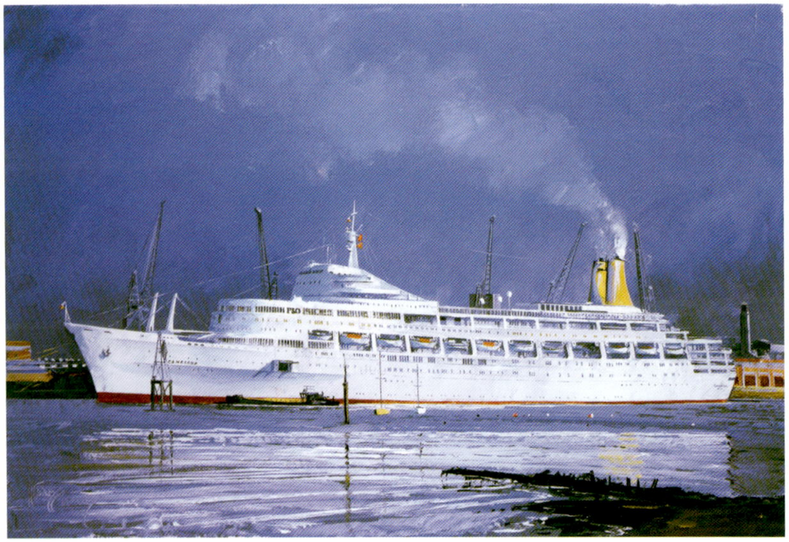

Canberra at 107 berth, Southampton

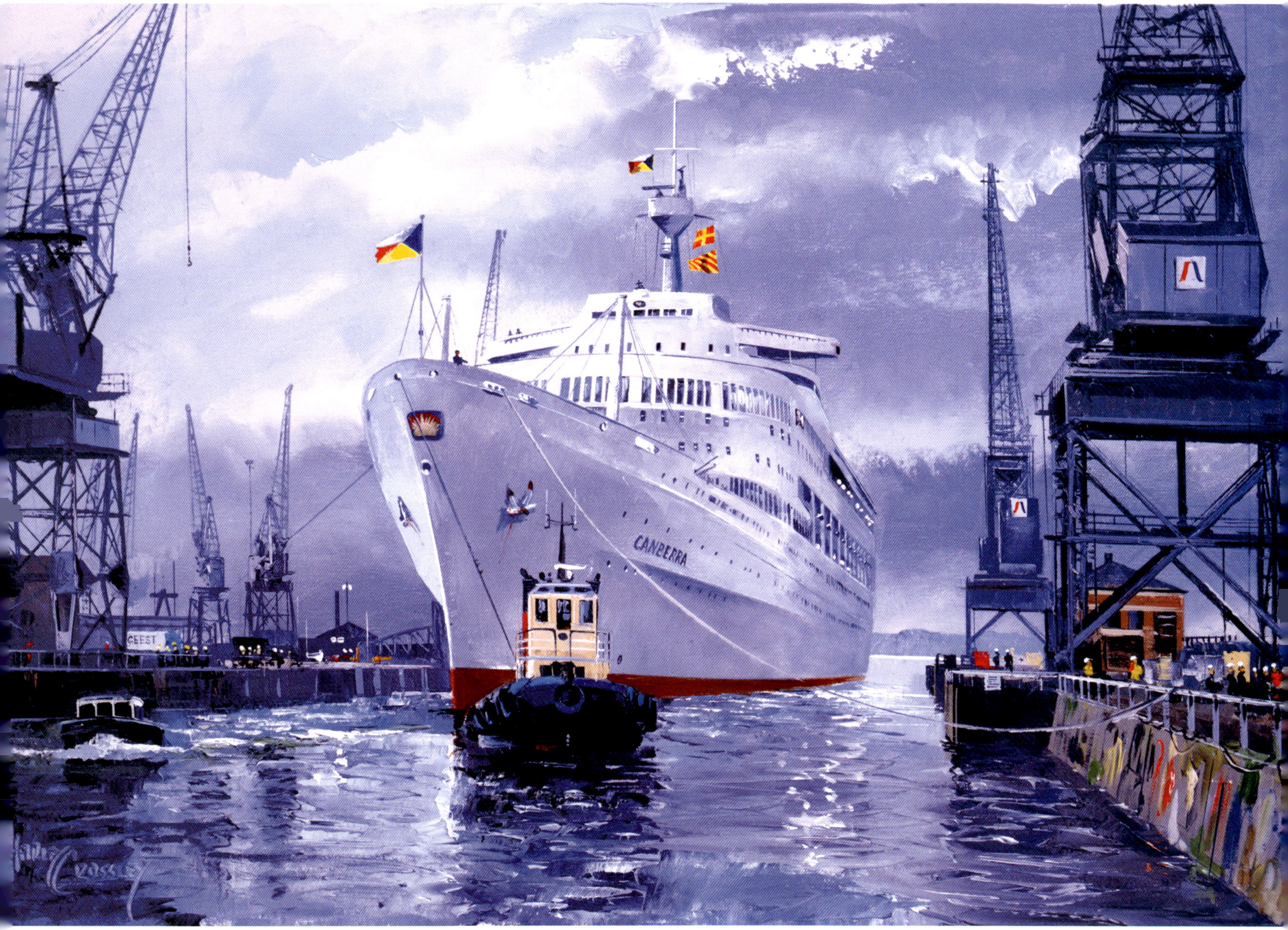

Canberra entering King George V Dry Dock in Southampton

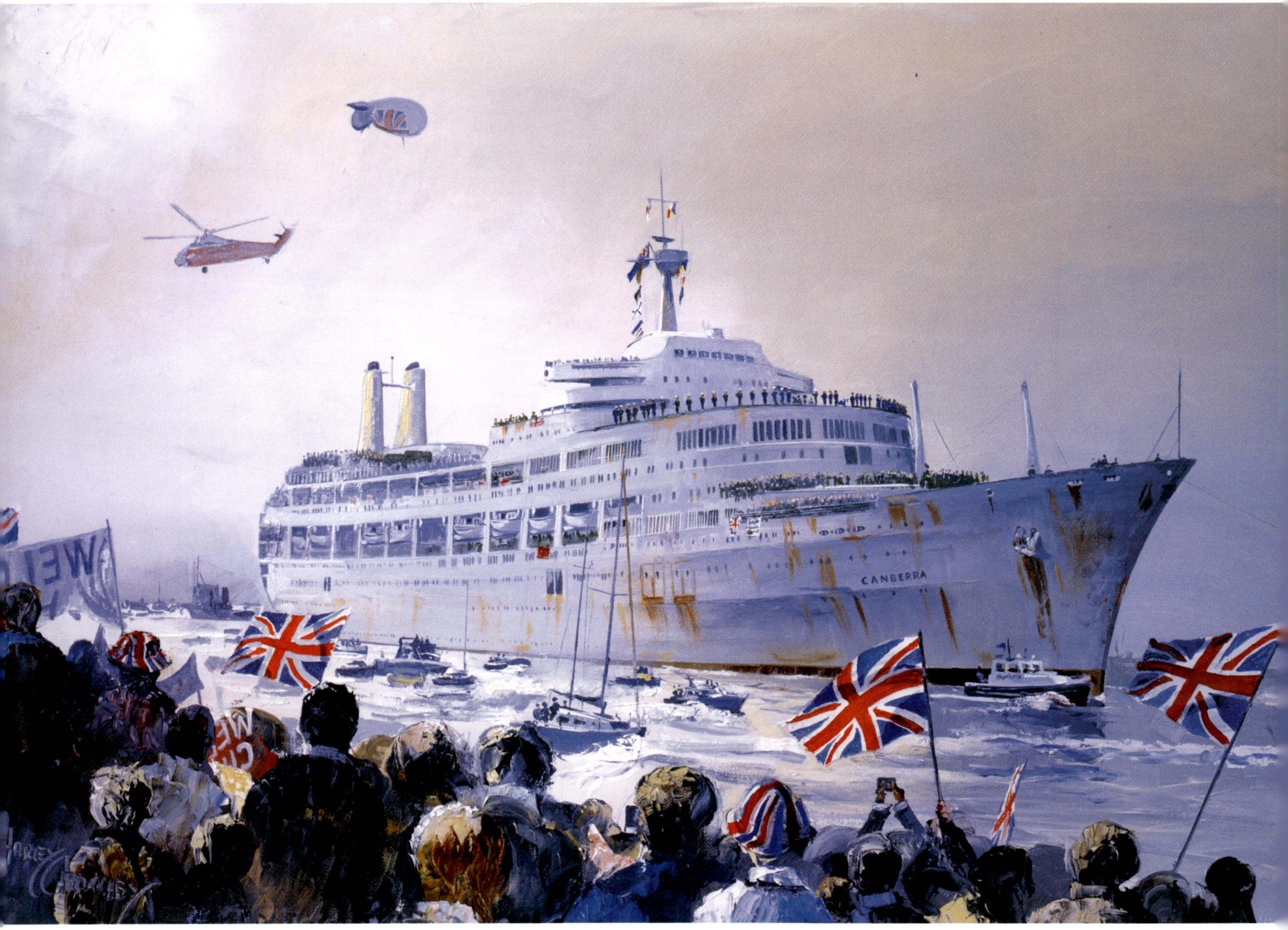

Canberra, return from the Falklands

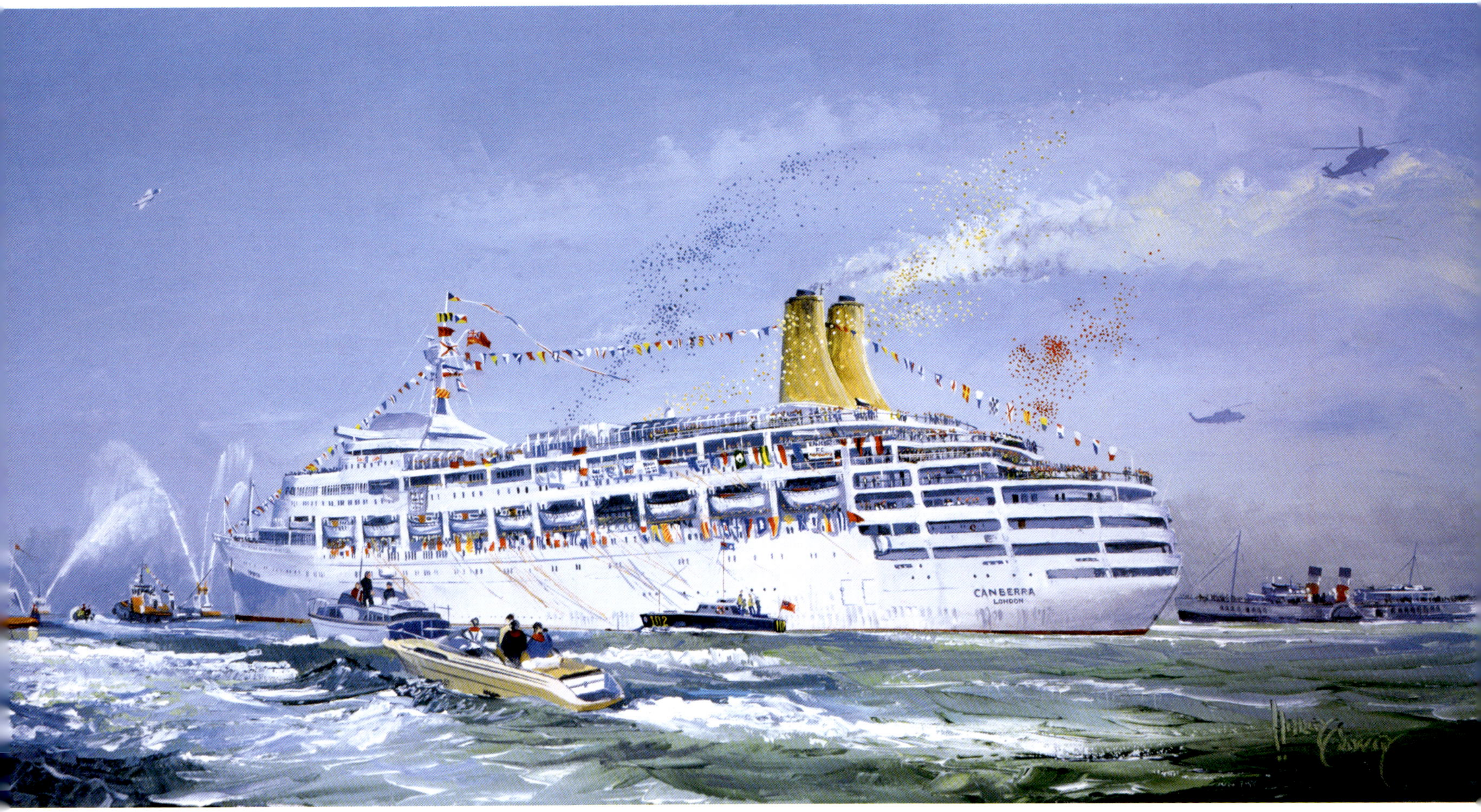

Canberra, final Southampton arrival

NORWAY

1,035 feet x 110.5 feet 66,348 grt

Work began in 1957 at Chantiers de l'Atlantique in St Nazaire on a new ship for CGT Lines, designed to be a showpiece for France: the longest and one of the fastest afloat. Launched on 11 May 1960, the new ship was christened *France* by Madame de Gaulle, wife of the French President.

Her twin funnels were fitted with unique side fins, which dispersed the smoke and fumes sideways, and she was equipped with four enormous propellers.

Although never as fast as the *United States*, holder of the Blue Riband, the *France* managed a speed of 35.21 knots during her trials in November 1961.

Following a 'shake-down' cruise to the Canaries, she finally departed on her maiden voyage from Le Havre to New York on 3 February 1962. Upon her arrival on 8 February, she was greeted with a gala reception, as New Yorkers welcomed this magnificent new ship. Her interiors were filled with the best in French art and décor, but it was her cuisine that drew many of her passengers.

An immediate success with line passengers, she began cruising in the 1970s.

Due to the advent of air travel and the vastly increased fuel costs, the French Government decided to withdraw their subsidy for the ship, and in October 1974, she was taken out of service and laid up in Le Havre.

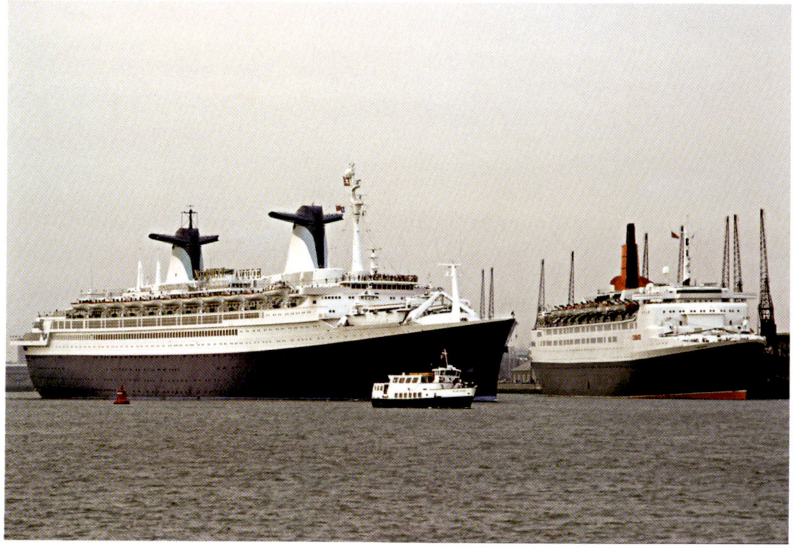

Norway passing *QE2* (Mike Lindsay)

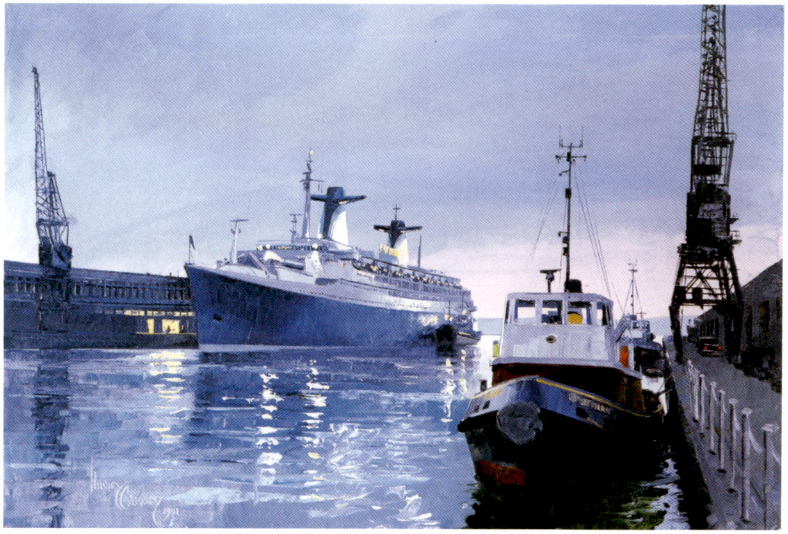

Norway at Southampton

Three years later, although bought by Akram Ojjeh, a Saudi Arabian billionaire, she still remained in Le Havre. Sold to Lauritz Kloster in June 1979, she was towed to Bremerhaven, where she underwent a major refit to drastically reduce her fuel consumption. This resulted in reducing her operating speed to around 18 knots for cruising.

Renamed *Norway* on 14 April 1980, she called at Oslo and Southampton before beginning her new career as a cruise ship for NCL sailing out of Miami. Immensely popular with passengers, she operated at around 90 per cent capacity on cruises in the Caribbean, returning to Bremerhaven in 1982 for further work to be carried out.

During 1984, *Norway* cruised from Southampton before a refit at Blohm & Voss in Hamburg and her subsequent return to Miami. When two rather unsightly new decks were added to the ship in 1990, her size was increased to 76,049 grt.

A major boiler explosion in May 2003 resulted in the death of eight crew members, and the ship departed from Miami under tow. Transferred to Star Cruises, NCL's parent company, a year later, it was announced that *Norway* would not sail again. In April 2006, she was sold for scrapping, renamed *Blue Lady* and set off to the breakers in Alang. The presence of asbestos on board proved a problem, and it was not until late 2008 that scrapping was finally completed.

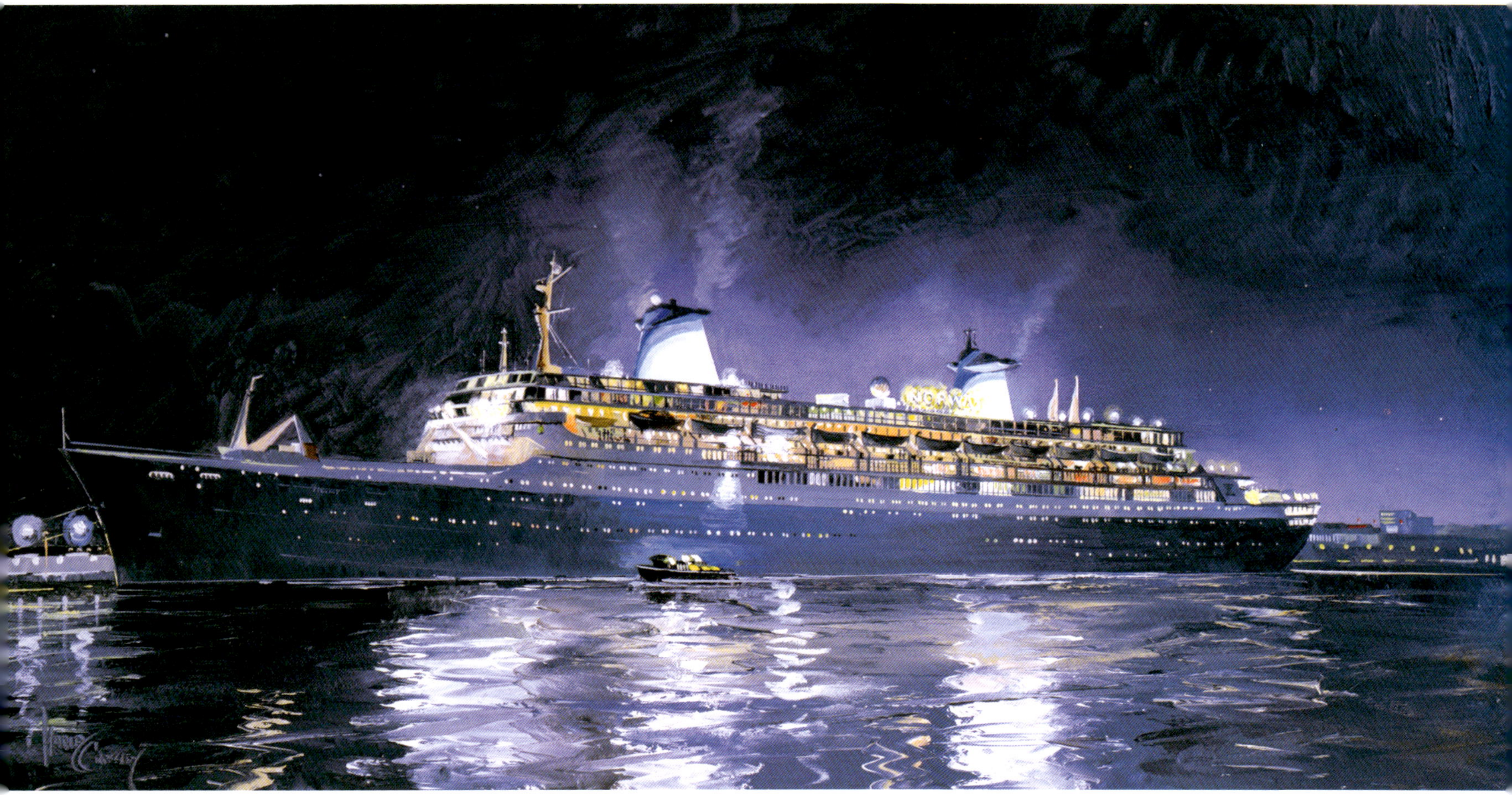

Norway at Puerto Rico

HEBRIDEAN PRINCESS

235 feet x 46 feet 2,112 grt

Built by Hall, Russell & Company of Aberdeen for the Secretary of State for Scotland in 1964, MV *Columba* was operated as an inter-island vehicle ferry by David MacBrayne Ltd. She was equipped with two Crossley diesel engines to give an operating speed of 12 knots in the rugged waters off Scotland.

Launched on 12 March 1964 by Lady Craigton, she began her service on 30 July that year, sailing from Oban to Lochaline via Mull. The ship had a capacity for 600 passengers and fifty cars. As West Highland piers had no linkspans at this time, vehicles were loaded using a hydraulic hoist. From 1972, *Columba* covered a variety of inter-island routes.

Caledonian Steam Packet Company acquired most of the MacBrayne ferries in 1973, and *Columba* continued her service under the CalMac name until she was sold in 1988 to Hebridean Island Cruises, a new cruise company. After undergoing a complete internal refit at George Prior Engineering Company in Great Yarmouth, she emerged as a luxury small cruise ship with a total passenger capacity of forty-six. She still retained a capacity to carry cars, allowing passengers to terminate their cruise at ports on the way if they wanted.

Renamed *Hebridean Princess* by the Duchess of York, she sailed on her maiden cruise on 26 May 1989 round the Western Islands of Scotland. Registered in Glasgow, her home port was Oban.

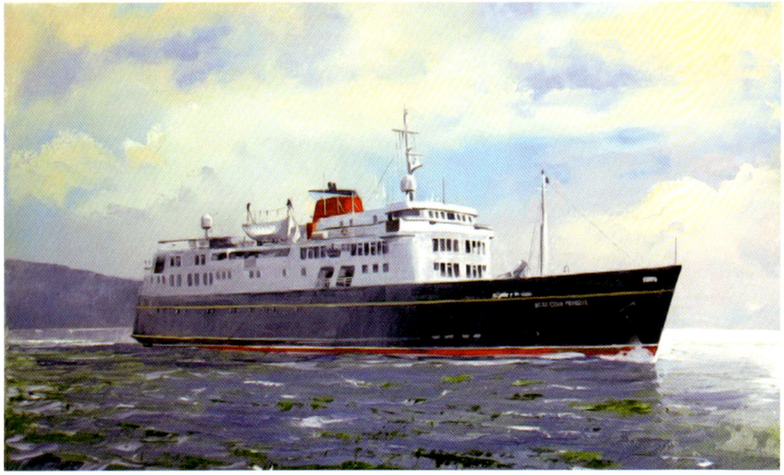

Hebridean Princess

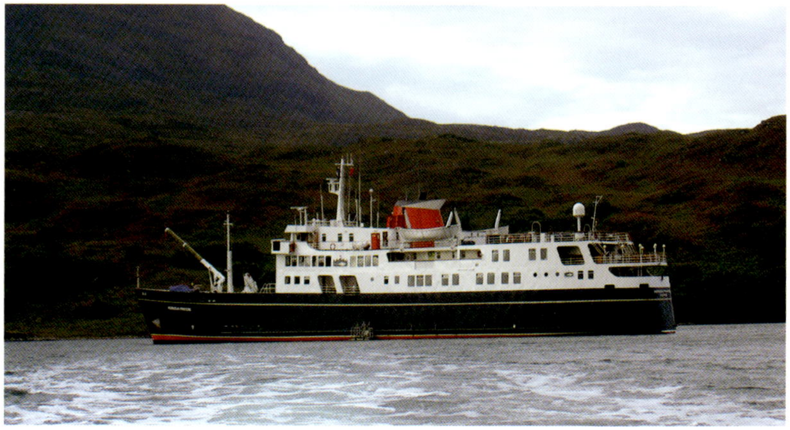

Hebridean Princess

Within two years, the car facility was removed, and her passenger capacity increased to forty-nine, with eleven of her cabins available for single occupancy with no surcharge levied.

The smallest luxury cruise ship in the world, her decoration is reminiscent of a Scottish country house, including a brick inglenook fireplace in the Tiree Lounge. Unlike larger cruise ships, *Hebridean Princess* is not fitted with entertainment facilities. She has no cinema, show lounge, casino, spa or swimming pool. Passengers liken a cruise on her to taking part in an intimate house party. With a crew of thirty-eight to a maximum of forty-nine passengers, the service is impeccable, the food freshly sourced and prepared, and the atmosphere one of total relaxation. She rarely sails at night, allowing her passengers to enjoy their sleep without any noise from the engines.

With the purchase of a second ship in 2001, the company changed its name to Hebridean International Cruises. *Hebridean Princess* continued cruising in Scotland and the Norwegian Fjords, whilst the larger *Hebridean Spirit* sailed to more exotic destinations.

In July 2006, to celebrate her eightieth birthday, Her Majesty Queen Elizabeth II chartered *Hebridean Princess* for a cruise in the Scottish Islands with her family.

The company was bought in June 2009 by All Leisure Group, who immediately sold *Hebridean Spirit*.

Operating once again under the company name of Hebridean Island Cruises, *Hebridean Princess* continues her luxury cruising around the Scottish Islands, retaining her exclusive niche in the market. In 2010, Her Majesty Queen Elizabeth II again chartered this delightful ship for a family holiday.

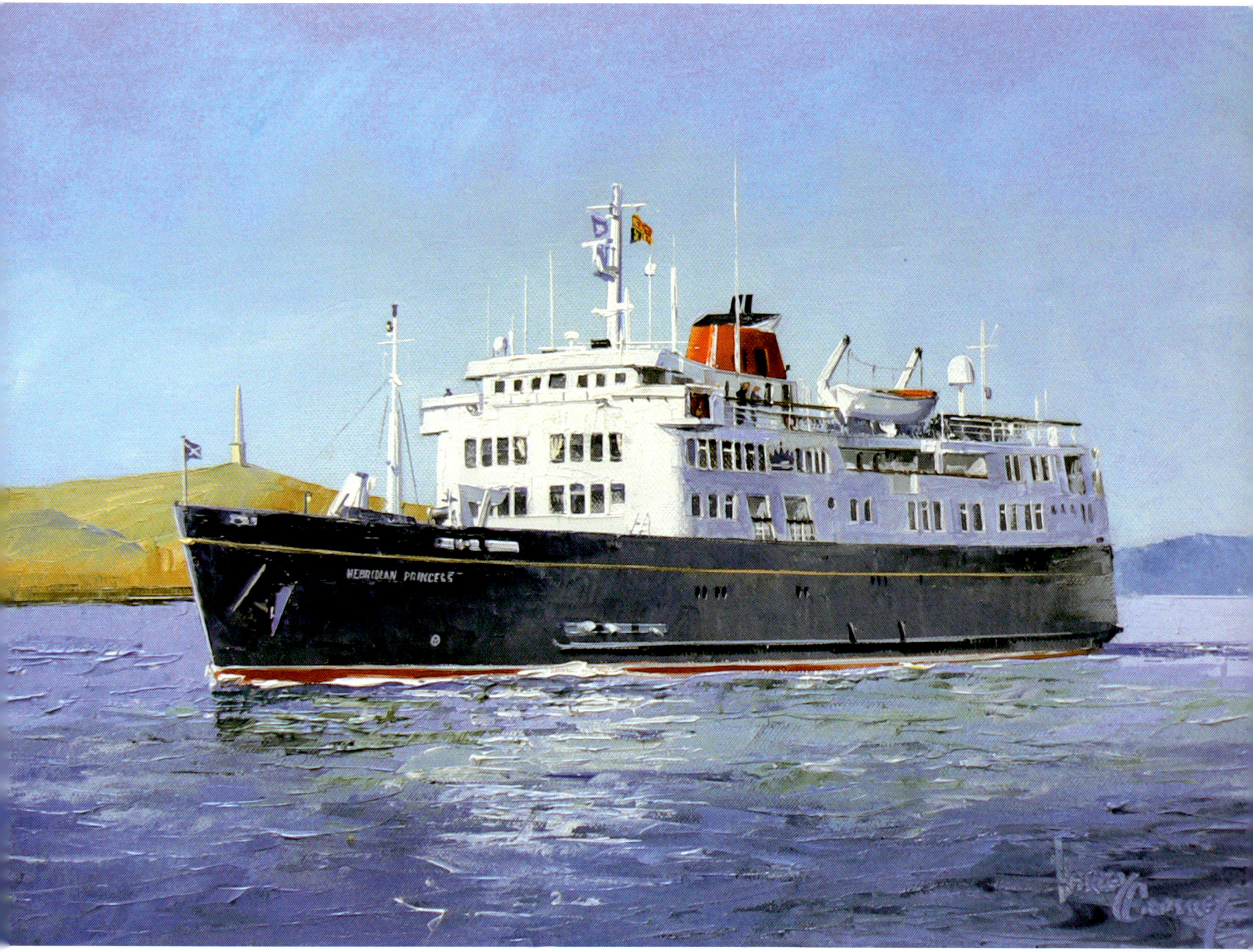

Hebridean Princess approaching Oban. This painting was specially commissioned for presentation to Her Majesty Queen Elizabeth II on the occasion of her chartering the vessel in July 2010.

SAGA ROSE

620 feet x 81 feet 24,002 grt

Built as the *Sagafjord* at the yard of Forges et Chantiers de la Méditerranée for Norwegian America Line, the keel was laid in June 1963. Built on classic lines with one funnel amidships, she had an operating speed of 20 knots. Nearly ten years later, these same classic lines were to be repeated in the building of her near sister ship *Vistafjord* on Tyneside.

Launched in June 1964, her sea trials took place in May the following year. Although strongly rumoured to be named *Norway*, she was christened *Sagafjord* on 18 September 1965 and sailed on her maiden voyage from Oslo to New York on 2 October.

Built to an extremely high standard, the builders lost so much money that they went out of business after her construction.

The ship was designed as a two-class liner for transatlantic passages, converting to one class for luxury cruises operating out of New York during the winter. Expensive luxury cruises soon became her mainstay, and she gained immense popularity. *Sagafjord* underwent a major refit at Blohm & Voss in Hamburg during 1980-81, including new engines and air-conditioning system. A new top deck was also added at this time.

When Norwegian America Line was taken over by Cunard in 1983, they continued to operate her under the same name, capitalising on her excellent

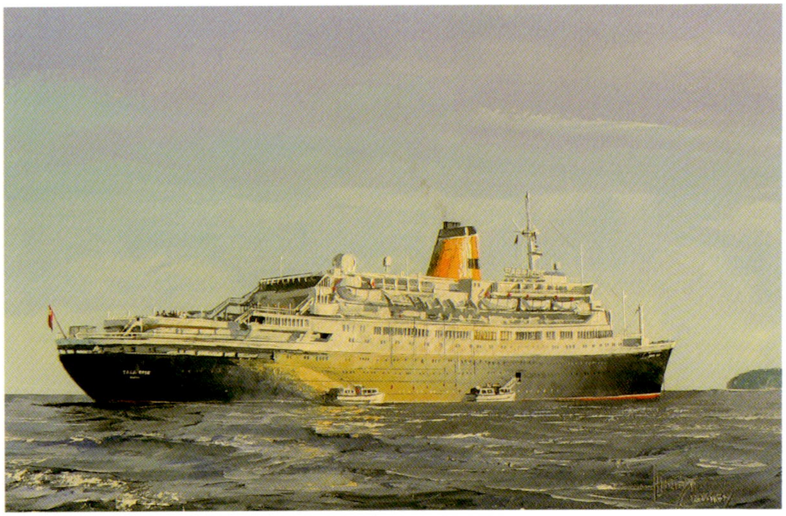

Saga Rose

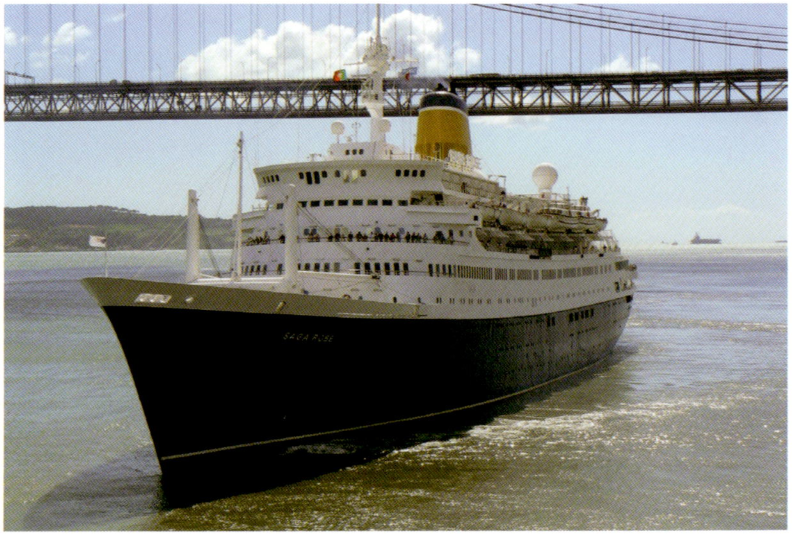

Saga Rose at Lisbon

reputation. Chartered to Transocean Tours in 1996, she sailed under the name of *Gripsholm*.

Sold to Saga Shipping in 1997, she was refurbished and renamed *Saga Rose*, the first ship for the company, which specialised in the market for people over the age of fifty. Sailing from the UK under her new owners, the ship continued her successful career, with her annual world cruise seeing many repeat bookings from her faithful followers.

On a cruise in November 2006, *Saga Rose* was caught in a storm on her way to Madeira and suffered damage to some of her cabins. During her world cruise in 2008, she suffered an electrical fault, leaving her without electricity for several hours, necessitating an unplanned stop in Cebu in the Phillipines. Later in the same cruise, she stayed in Singapore for five days for more repairs. On both occasions, the company accommodated passengers in hotels ashore whilst repairs were carried out.

In 2009, *Saga Rose* left on her forty-fourth world cruise, one for every year of her life, more than any other cruise ship had undertaken.

Unable to comply with the 2010 SOLAS regulations, *Saga Rose* sailed from Southampton on her final cruise on 30 October 2009. Saga announced that she was to be sold to become an accommodation ship in Walvis Bay, but in April 2010, it was reported that she never reached the port and was now 'on sea trials' south of Cape Town with a new destination of Port Elizabeth. *Saga Rose* was finally sold in June 2010 to Eckhardt Marine for breaking up in Jiangying, China.

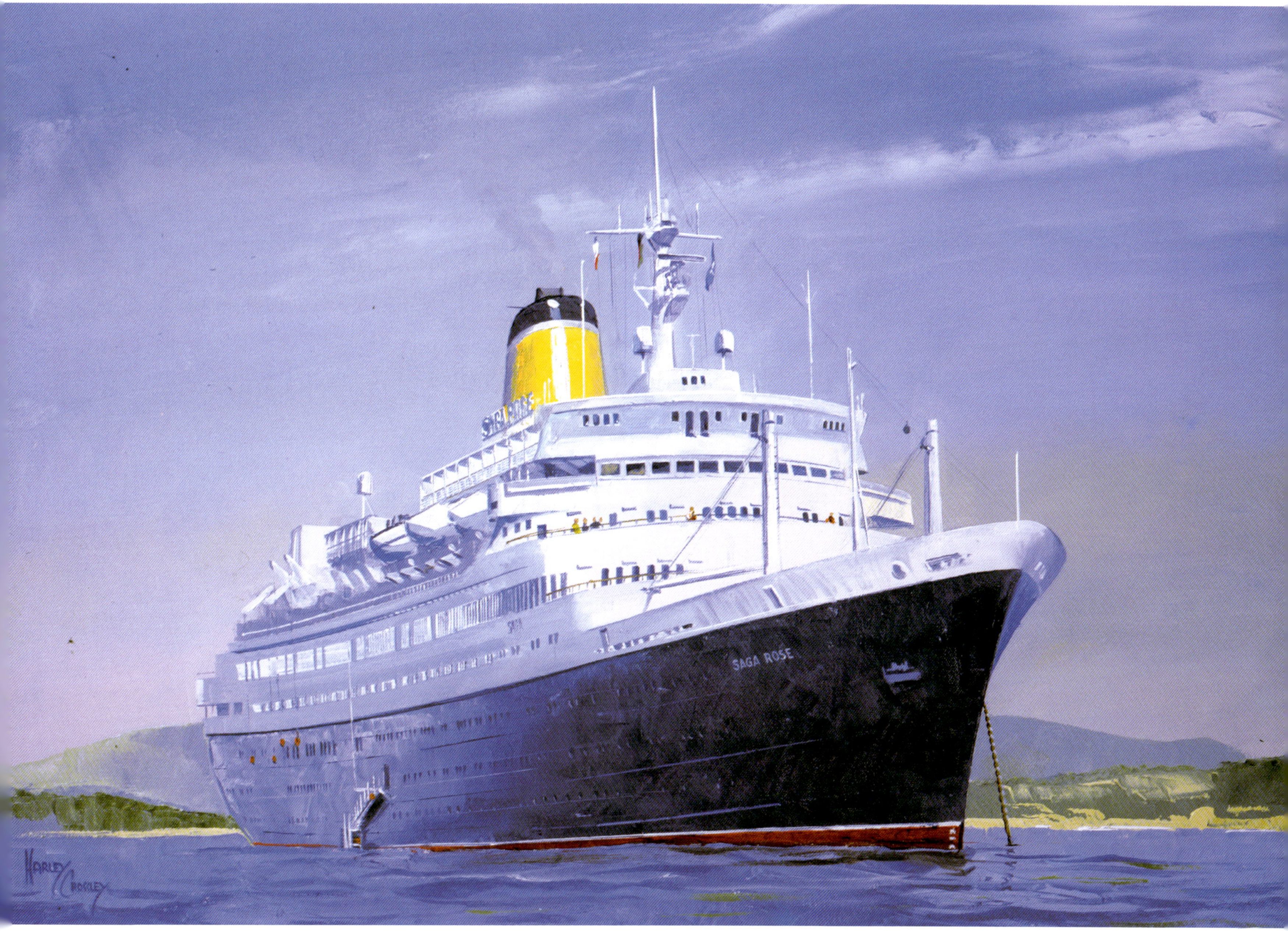

Saga Rose moored at Bora Bora

BLACK PRINCE

470 feet x 66 feet 9,499 grt

Black Prince was the second of two identical dual-purpose vessels built by Flender Werke AG of Lübeck, the first one being called *Jupiter*. Both ships had dual ownership and names, and when ordered, they were the world's largest car ferries.

She sailed on her maiden voyage in 1967 for Fred Olsen as *Black Prince* between London and the Canary Islands, which was to be her winter route for the next twenty years. The unique design of the ship enabled her to carry cruise passengers together with large quantities of fruit and tomatoes.

For the summer, she was renamed *Venus*, her funnel colours were altered, and she operated for Bergen Line on the Tyne-Bergen service. On this service, she carried up to 590 passengers, 180 cars and 200 tons of refrigerated cargo per voyage. The swimming pool, which was popular with cruise passengers, was floored over and used as a lounge during her North Sea crossings.

This system of operation continued for the next twenty years, although from 1982, the ship was chartered by DFDS and then Norway Line during the summer.

In 1986, the joint ownership agreement ended, with each company keeping one ship. Olsens sent *Black Prince* to Wärtsilä in Finland at the end of 1986 for an extensive rebuild and refit for conversion into a full-time cruise ship, from which she emerged as 11,209 grt.

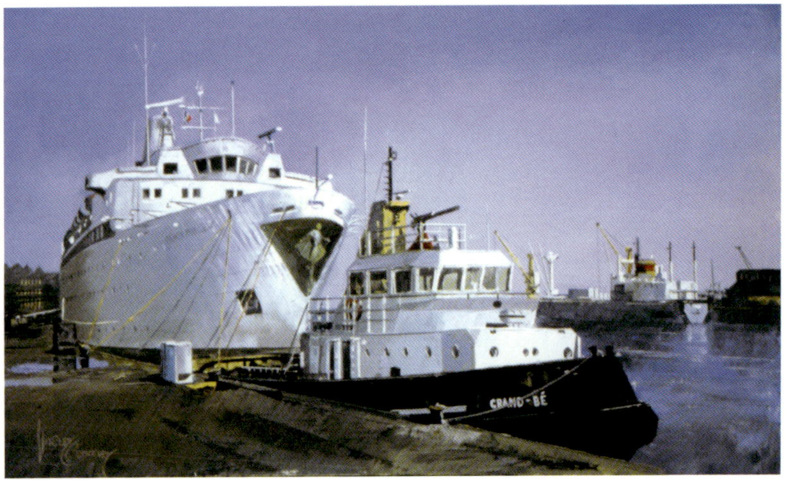

Black Prince at St Malo

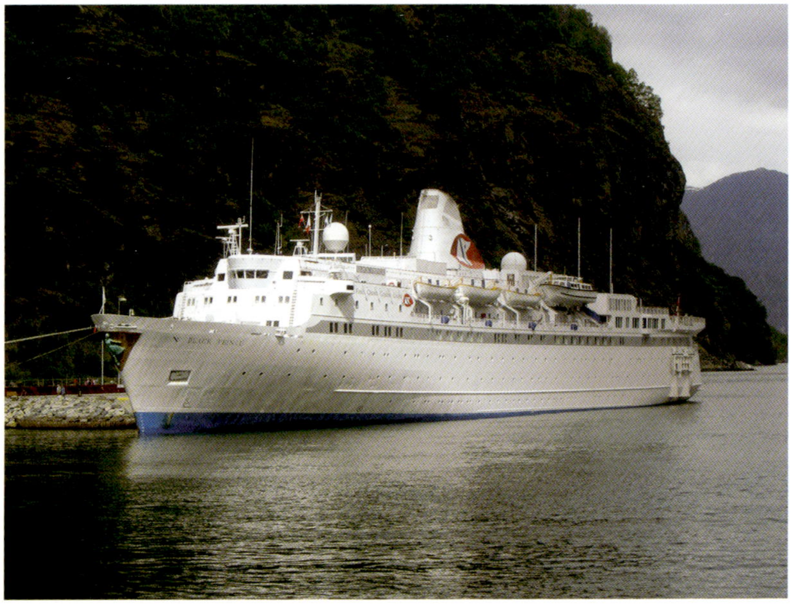

Black Prince at Flamm

Most of the car deck was converted into cabins, and she was fitted with a new lido deck and outdoor swimming pool. A unique Marine Park area was constructed at the stern of the ship, which could be lowered into the sea and used as a water sports area when the ship was anchored, but it was seldom used.

For the next two years, *Black Prince* cruised mainly from the United Kingdom to Europe, building up a loyal following of passengers with a high number of repeat bookings. During 1989, she was relocated for short cruises out of Oslo, but she soon returned to her UK departures from Southampton and Harwich. From 1996, her home port was changed to Dover.

After 2003, she was frequently chartered to leading tour companies, mostly sailing out of Southampton. The ship cruised mainly in European waters until 2009, when the impending 2010 SOLAS regulations made it uneconomic to upgrade her to meet these. *Black Prince* was sold to SAVECA in October 2009 and renamed *Ola Esmeralda* being scheduled for further service in Venezuelan coastal waters from that date. This never materialised, and the ship was left unused until May 2010, when she was chartered by the United Nations for use as accommodation for relief workers in Haiti.

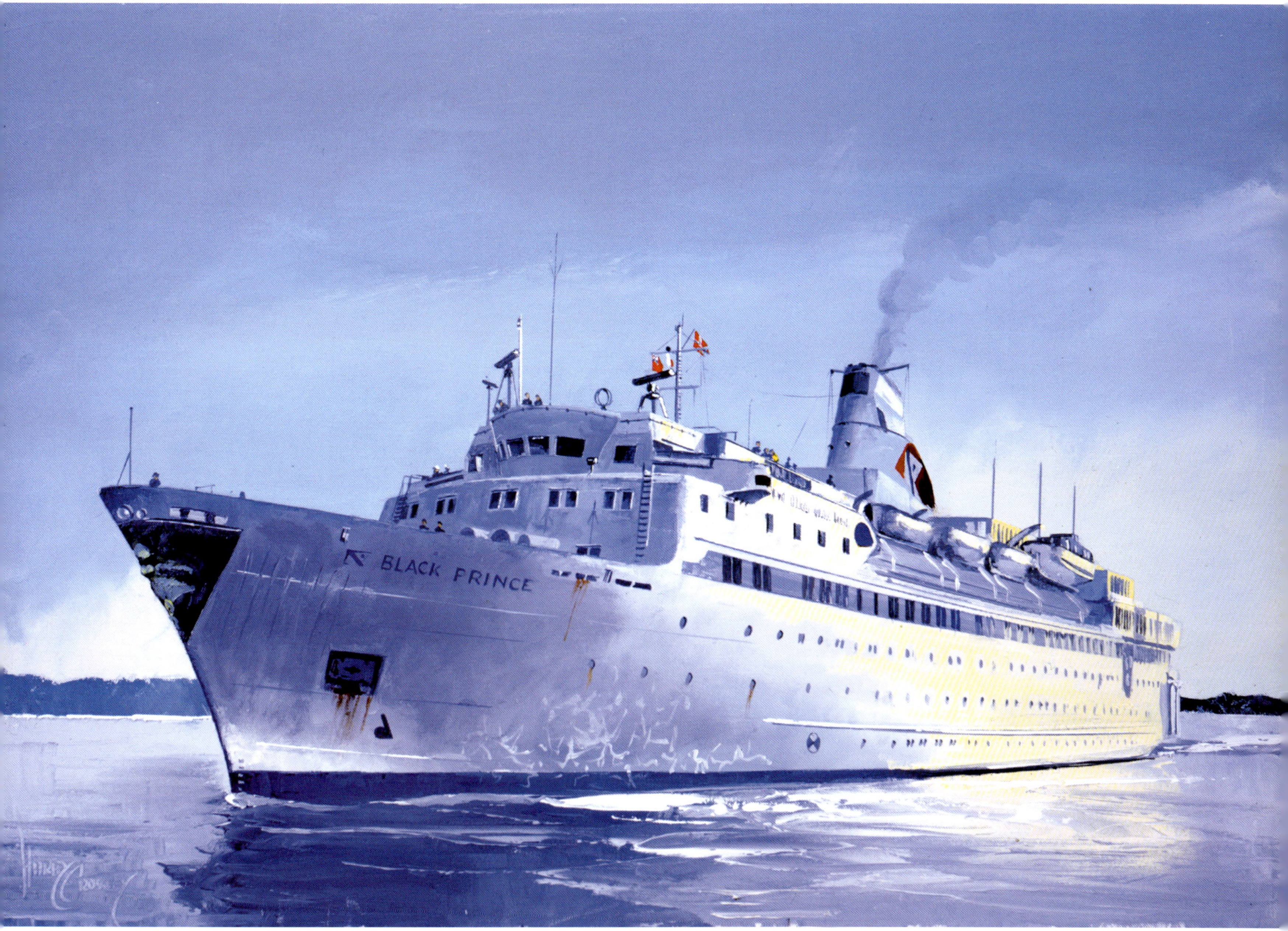

Black Prince

VICTORIA

660 feet x 86 feet 27,670 grt

Originally built as the *Kungsholm* by John Brown & Co., Clydebank, she was the last passenger liner ordered by Swedish America line. Originally due for delivery in October 1965, she was finally delivered in March 1966. This beautifully proportioned two-funnelled ship, the forward one being a dummy, was the first Scandinavian vessel to be fitted with a bulbous bow.

She sailed on her maiden voyage from Gothenburg to New York in April 1966.

Her contracted speed was 21 knots, but on her first crossing of the North Sea, she actually achieved 25 knots. Although used mainly for cruising, she did make the occasional line voyage across the Atlantic.

In 1975, Swedish America Line decided to abandon passenger services, and the ship was sold to Flagship Cruises of Bermuda. After a refit at Swan Hunter on the Tyne, she left for New York, flying the Liberian flag.

Retaining her name of *Kungsholm*, she cruised for the next two years, mainly from New York, and many of the cruises took her back into European waters.

After an expensive salvage operation in 1978 when the ship was aground for five days after leaving the port of Fort de France in Martinique, the ship was eventually sold to P&O cruises.

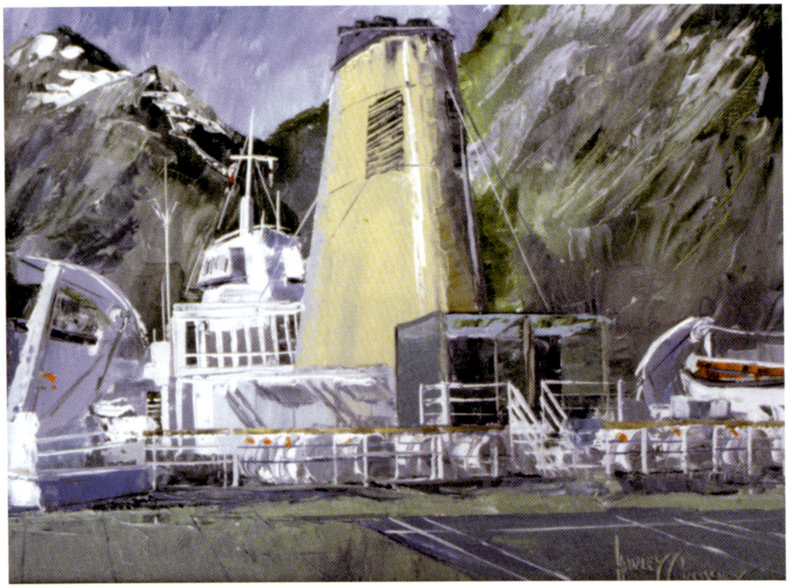

On board view at Geiranger

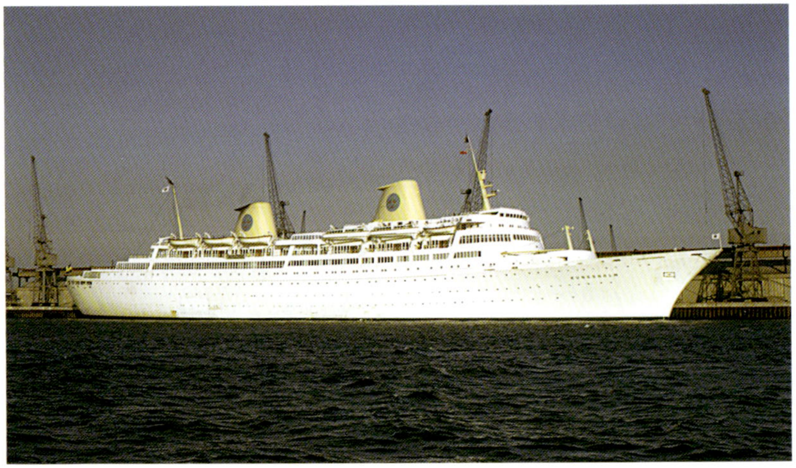

Kungsholm (Mike Lindsay)

During an extensive refit in the Bremer Vulcan shipyard, she lost her classic profile when her forward funnel and main mast were removed. An additional eighty-six cabins were also fitted at the rear of the veranda deck. She re-entered service as the *Sea Princess* for P&O in January 1979, and after her renaming, she sailed for Singapore. Here she took on the passengers from *Arcadia* to complete the remainder of *Arcadia*'s cruise, due to that ship being sent to Taiwan for scrapping. *Sea Princess* arrived in Sydney, her new home port, on 6 March 1979. In her turn, she was replaced in Australian waters by the older but larger *Oriana* in 1982.

She was used for cruises from the UK until 1986, when, after a refit in Malta, she joined the Princess fleet to cruise from the west coast of America in the Pacific.

Eventually returning to the UK in 1991, it wasn't until 1995 that she was renamed *Victoria*. For the next seven years, she cruised out of Southampton as part of the P&O fleet. In 1999-2000, she was chartered for a cruise round Africa to commemorate the centenary of Union Castle Line with her funnel repainted in Union Castle colours.

In 2002, the ship was sold but leased back for a further year's service by P&O. Subsequently operated by Holiday Kreuzfahrten and renamed *Mona Lisa*. In 2006, she was briefly laid up in Piraeus, then used as a hotel in Qatar until chartered by RCCL and renamed *Oceanic II*. Renamed the *Scholar Ship* for two years, she was then called the *Peace Boat*, before reverting to *Mona Lisa* again. Her future is now uncertain, as she does not meet current SOLAS requirements.

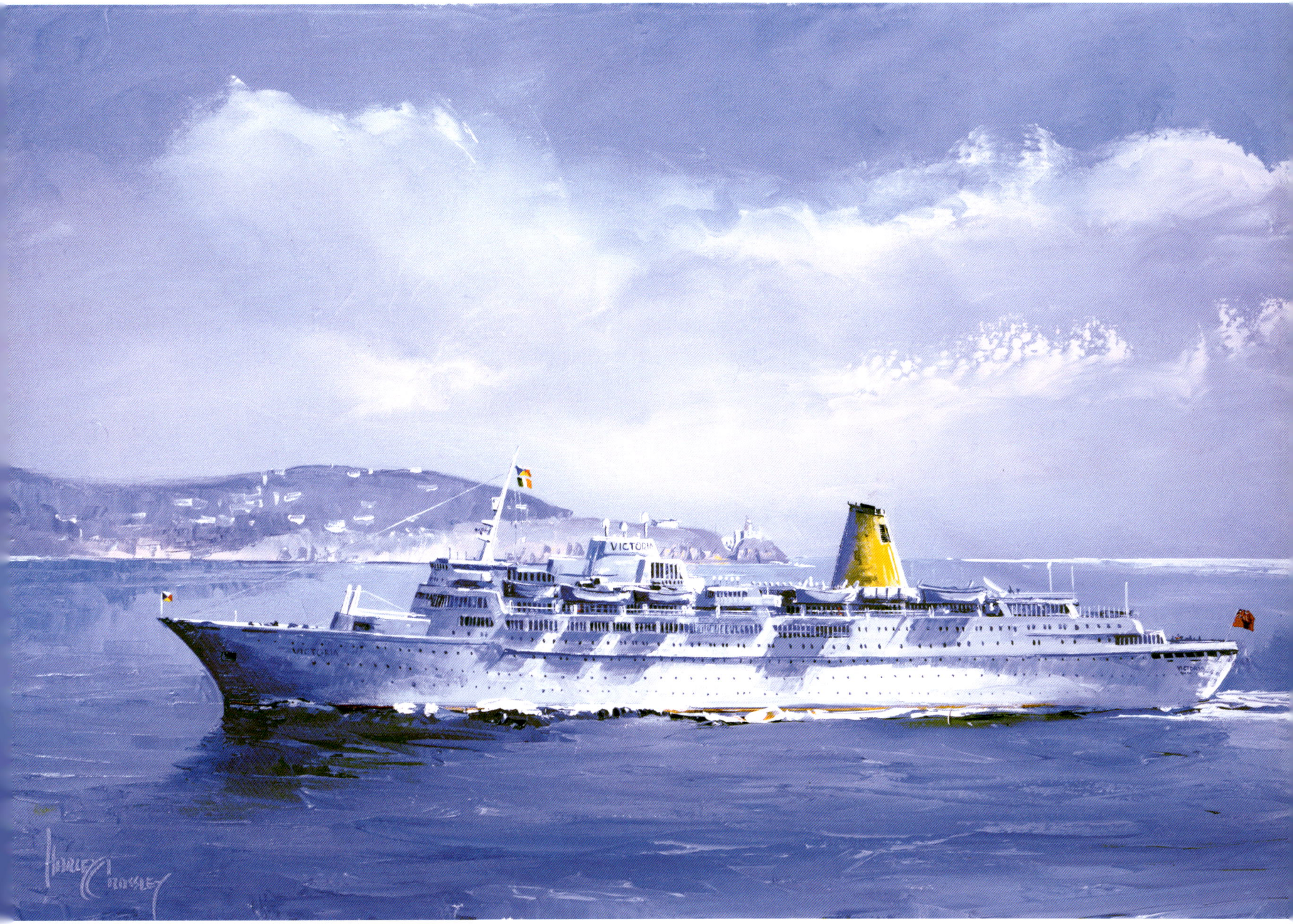

Victoria approaching Dublin

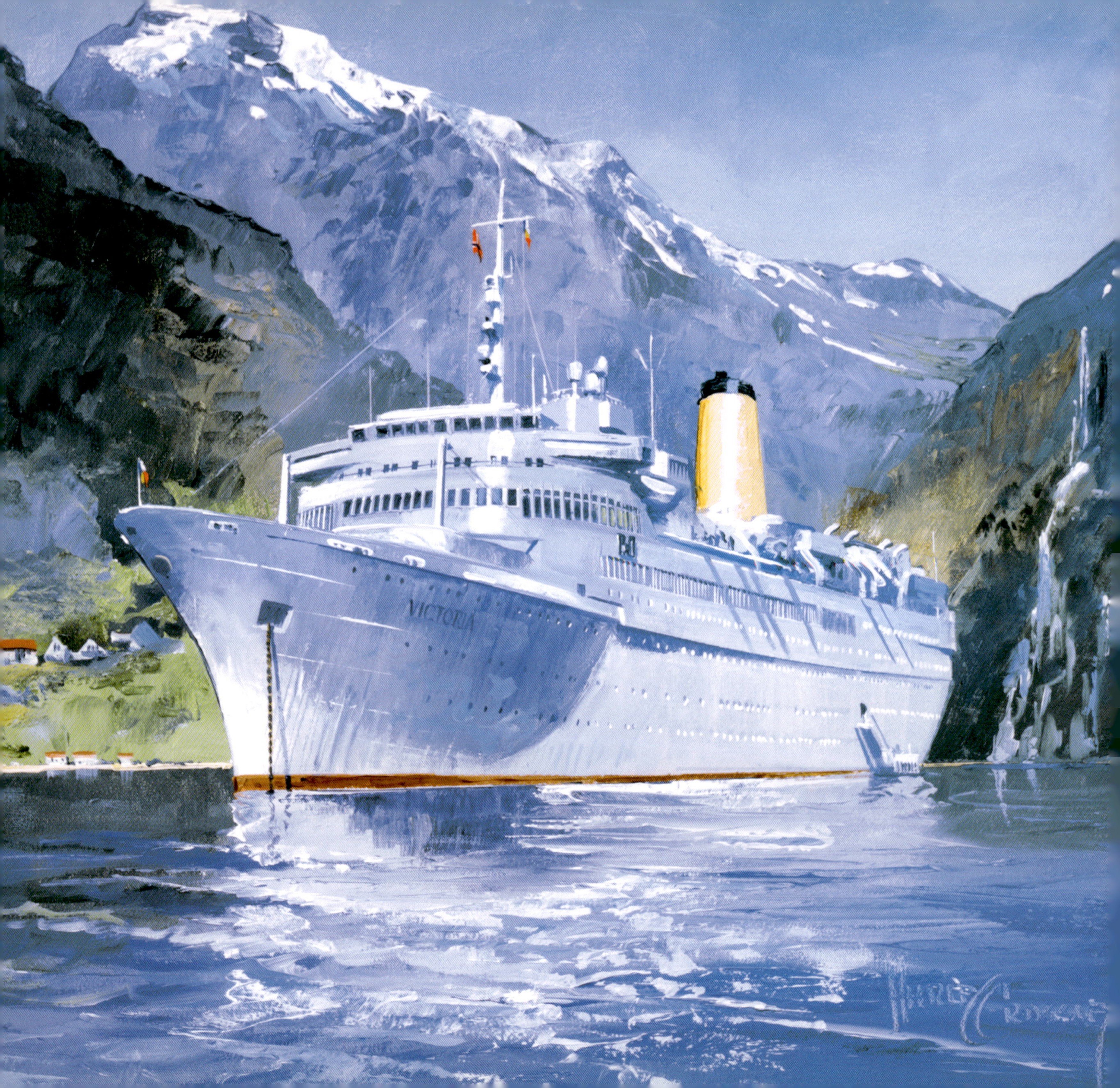
VICTORIA

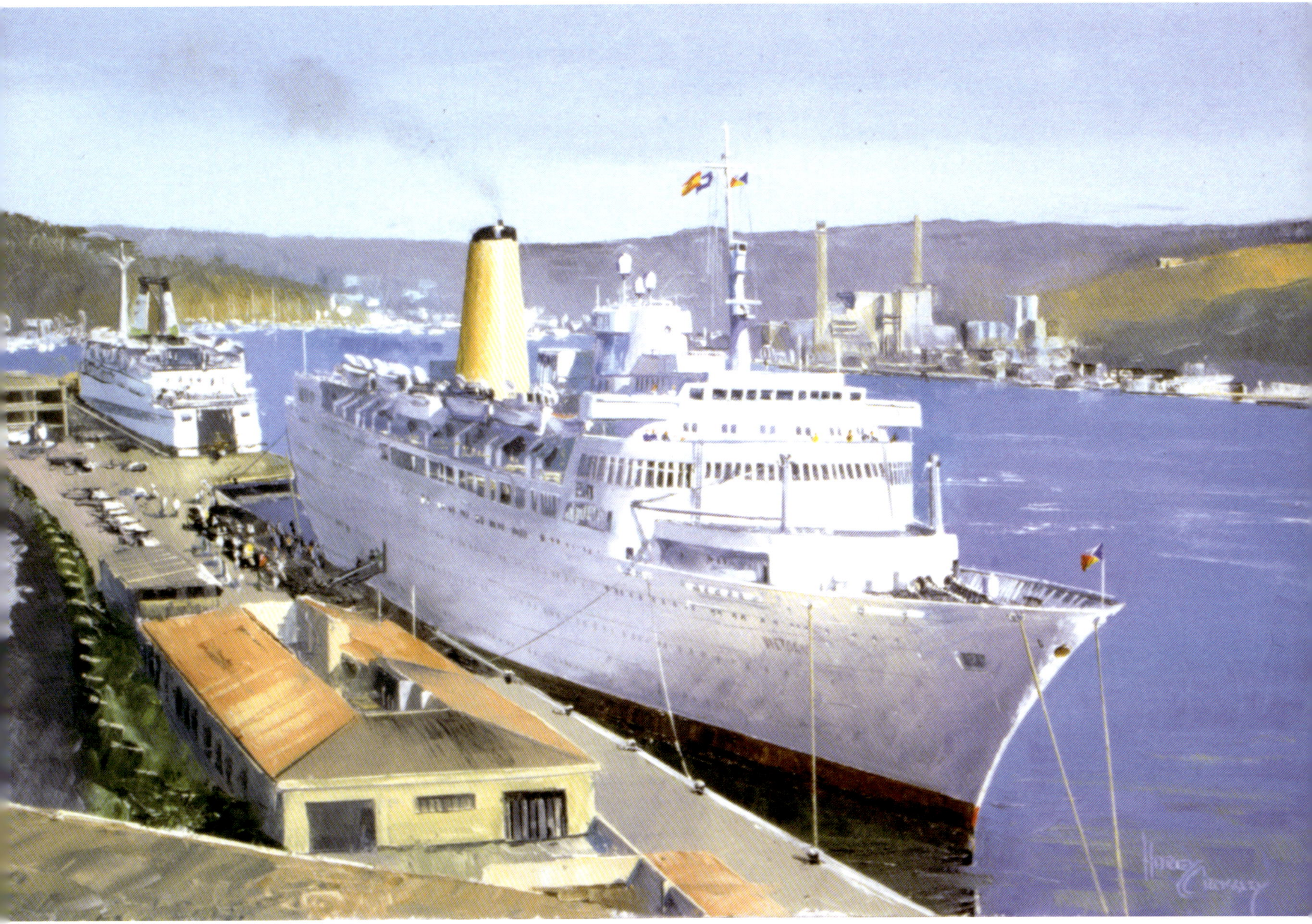

Above: Victoria at Port Mahon

Opposite: Victoria at Geiranger Fjord

QUEEN ELIZABETH 2

963 feet x 105 feet 67,139 grt

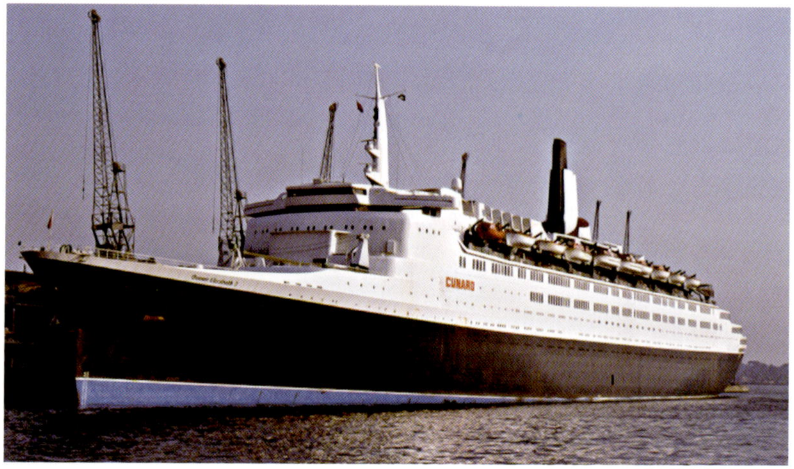

Queen Elizabeth 2 (Mike Lindsay)

Built for Cunard by Upper Clyde Shipbuilders in the John Brown yard at Clydebank, the keel was laid in 1965. Fitted with steam turbines giving a top speed of 32.5 knots, she was designed as a two-class transatlantic liner with one-class cruising during the winter months. She was also able to carry cars, but this facility did not last long.

Launched on 20 September 1967 by Her Majesty Queen Elizabeth II, her sea trials took place in November and December 1968. A 'shake-down' cruise from Greenock to the Canaries was abandoned after turbine damage, and she returned to the builders with Cunard refusing to accept the ship.

After repair and fresh trials, the company finally took delivery on 18 April and *Queen Elizabeth 2* sailed on her maiden voyage from Southampton to New York on 2 May 1969, an immediate success with her passengers.

In 1971, she assisted in the rescue of passengers from *Antilles*, which was on fire near Mustique.

Whilst off Bermuda in April 1974, a damaged fuel pipe necessitated the transfer of 1,654 of her own passengers to the Norwegian cruise ship *Sea Venture* before she was towed to Hamilton for repair. Her much-publicised first world cruise was in 1975.

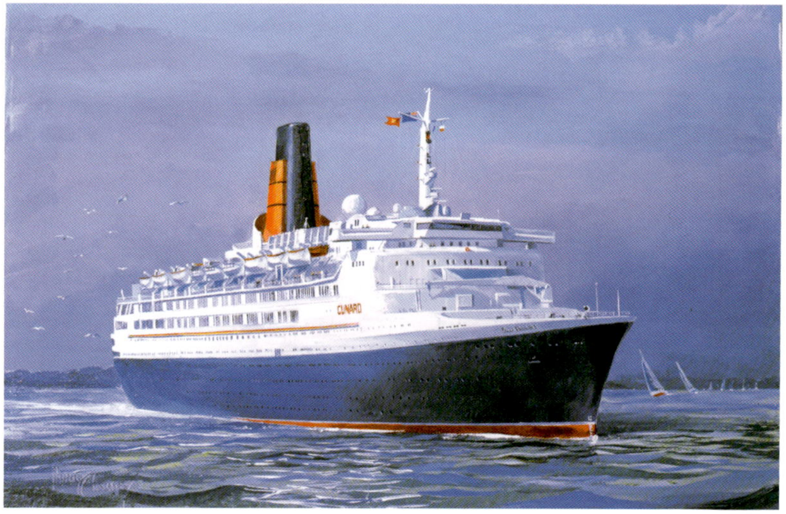

Queen Elizabeth 2 in the Solent

Requisitioned for the Falklands War, *QE2* left Southampton for South Georgia on 12 May 1982 with 3,000 troops on board. Her triumphant return to the port in June was greeted by a flotilla of small vessels, including Her Majesty the Queen Mother on board the Royal Yacht *Britannia*.

After refit, she returned to civilian service on 14 August 1982, her funnel finally painted in Cunard colours and her hull a light grey. Shortly afterwards, the hull reverted to the traditional company colour. During a massive refit at Lloyd Werft, Bremerhaven, in October 1986, the steam turbines were replaced by diesels, and a new funnel fitted. *QE2* resumed service at the end of April 1987.

After hitting rocks off Vineyard Sound on 7 August 1992, sustaining a large gash in her hull, passengers were disembarked at Rhode Island. Temporary repairs were carried out in Boston before the ship sailed to Blohm & Voss in Hamburg for dry-docking.

After a much-publicised crossing of the Atlantic in tandem with the new *Queen Mary 2* in 2004, she reverted mainly to cruising. By now, Cunard company had become part of the massive Carnival Corporation.

Unable to meet the SOLAS regulations of 2010, it was decided to retire the ship in November 2008, when she was handed over to her new owner, Nakheel, part of Dubai World. Plans for her to be permanently berthed in Dubai as a floating hotel did not materialize, and in March 2010, she was still moored at Port Rashid with her future uncertain.

With over thirty-nine years of sailing *Queen Elizabeth 2* was the longest-serving Cunarder of all time.

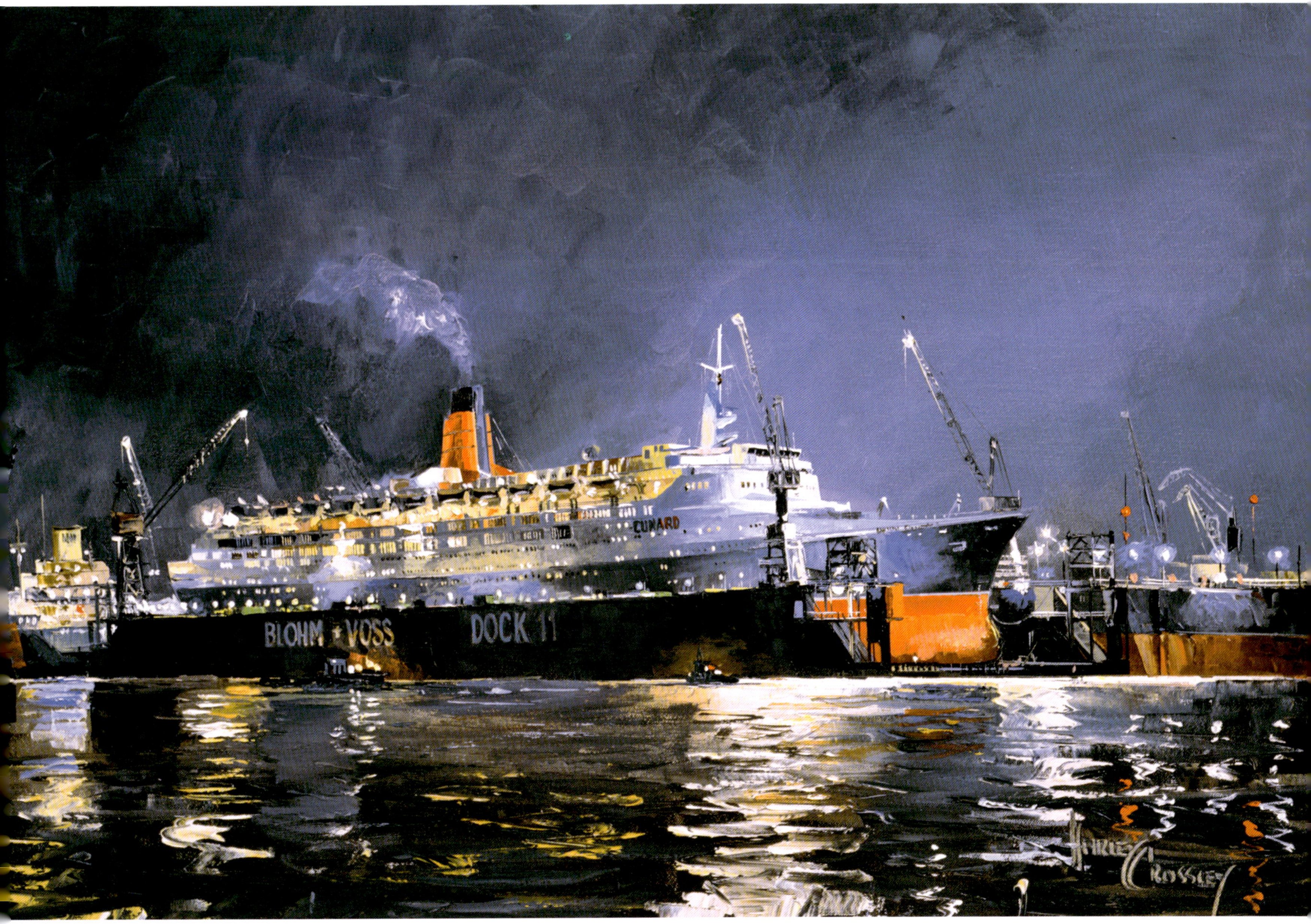

Queen Elizabeth 2 in dry dock at Hamburg

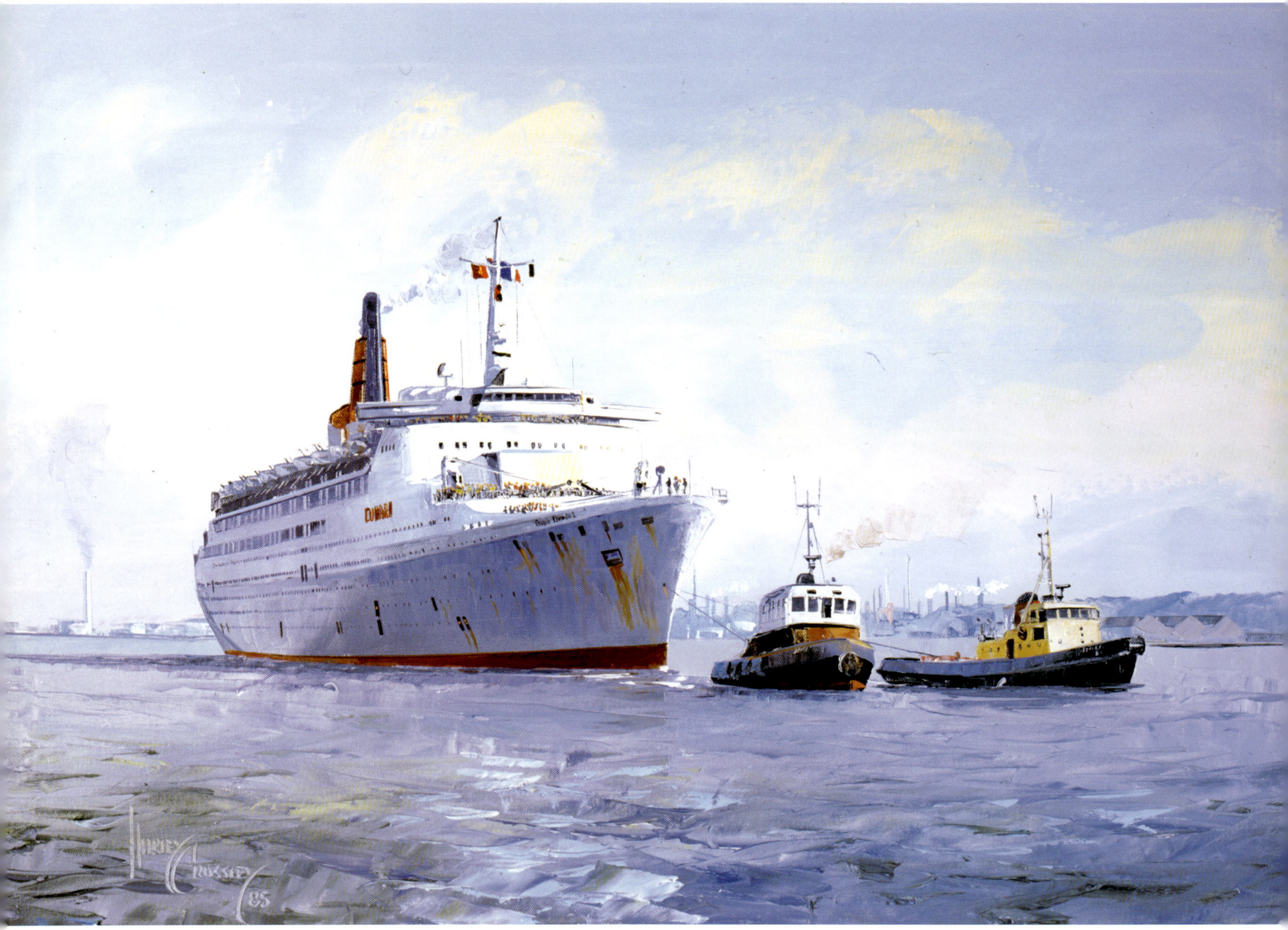

Queen Elizabeth 2 post-Falklands colour scheme

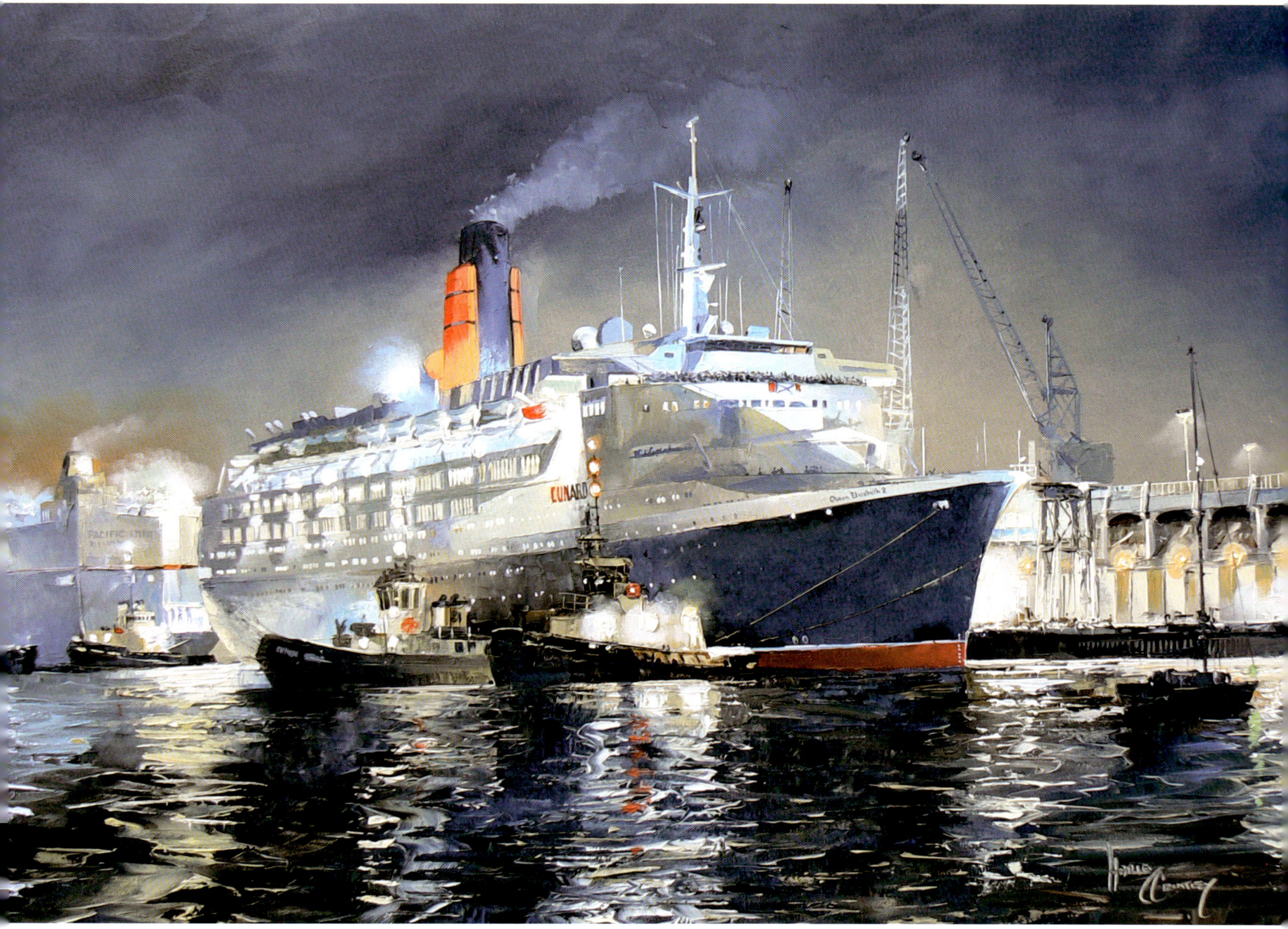

Final home port departure

BLACK WATCH

583 feet x 82 feet 21,847 grt

Built by Wärtsilä in Helsinki for Royal Viking Line, the ship was launched on 12 May 1971 as *Royal Viking Star*, the first of three sister ships. Designed as a one-class ship with nearly all outside cabins, she was one of the top five luxury ships at that time, alongside Norwegian America Line's *Vistafjord* and *Sagafjord*. The ship entered service on 26 June 1972 to begin her successful career in cruising worldwide.

In 1981, she went to Lloyd Werft in Bremerhaven, where she was cut in two and a new midships section of 93 feet was inserted. This increased her passenger capacity from 550 to 758 and her tonnage to 28,221 grt. She was the first of the three sister ships to be lengthened. All three ships were well loved and built up a loyal following with many repeat passengers travelling on them.

The company was taken over in 1984 but continued to operate as Royal Viking Line until the ship was transferred to NCL in April 1991 and renamed *Westward*. Under her new name, she successfully cruised from New York to Bermuda and in the Caribbean.

Three years later, she was transferred to Royal Cruise Line, a subsidiary of NCL, renamed *Star Odyssey* and used for cruising in the Mediterranean as well as further afield to exotic locations such as the Seychelles.

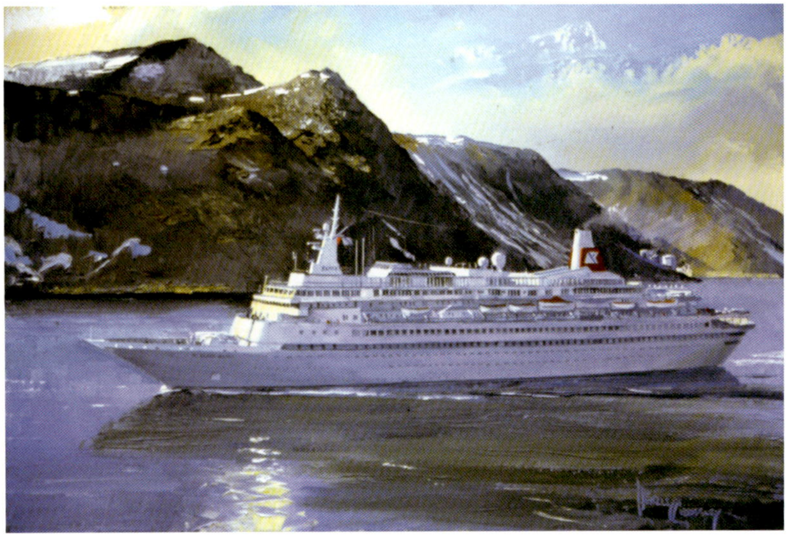

Black Watch at Hammerfest

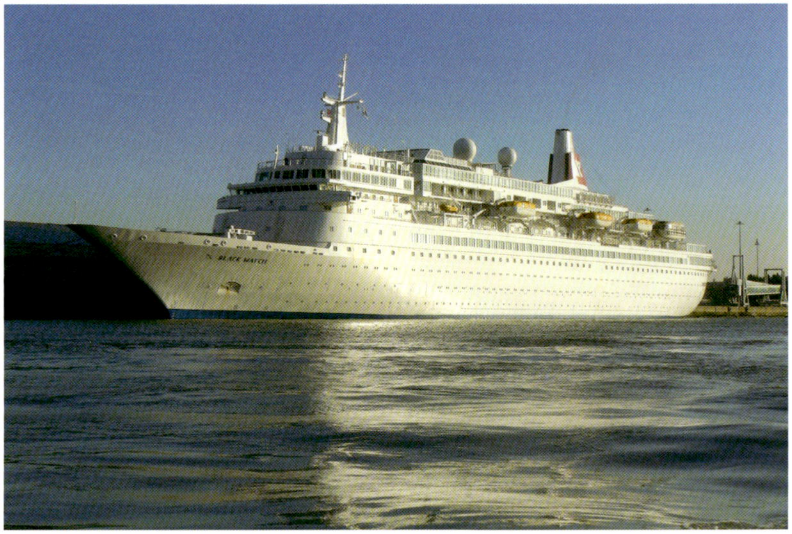

Black Watch at Southampton

The purchase of *Star Odyssey* by Fred Olsen Cruise Line was announced in 1995, but she was chartered back to Royal Cruise Line to complete her 1996 cruise programme for them.

From November 1996, she entered service as *Black Watch* for Fred Olsen. An inauspicious start to her career for the company saw her in dock in Valetta for two weeks in February the following year with engine problems. Aimed primarily at the British market, she had been refurbished with artefacts from previous Olsen ships, including the impressive bronze from the 1950s ferry of the same name, which adorns the Braemar Lounge on board.

During a two-month refit at Blohm & Voss in Hamburg in the spring of 2005, her engines were upgraded, and she underwent a massive refurbishment before returning to her cruising schedule. A well-maintained and happy ship, *Black Watch* has a loyal following of mostly older British passengers. Of particular appeal is the Observatory, a restful lounge located above the bridge, affording splendid views over the bows. Her annual world cruise draws many repeat bookings. It is said that 50 per cent of her bookings are repeats.

In July 2006, she suffered an outbreak of Legionnaires' disease on board, which affected a number of her more elderly passengers.

Although now thirty-eight years old *Black Watch* meets all the current SOLAS regulations and continues to cruise to interesting destinations around the world.

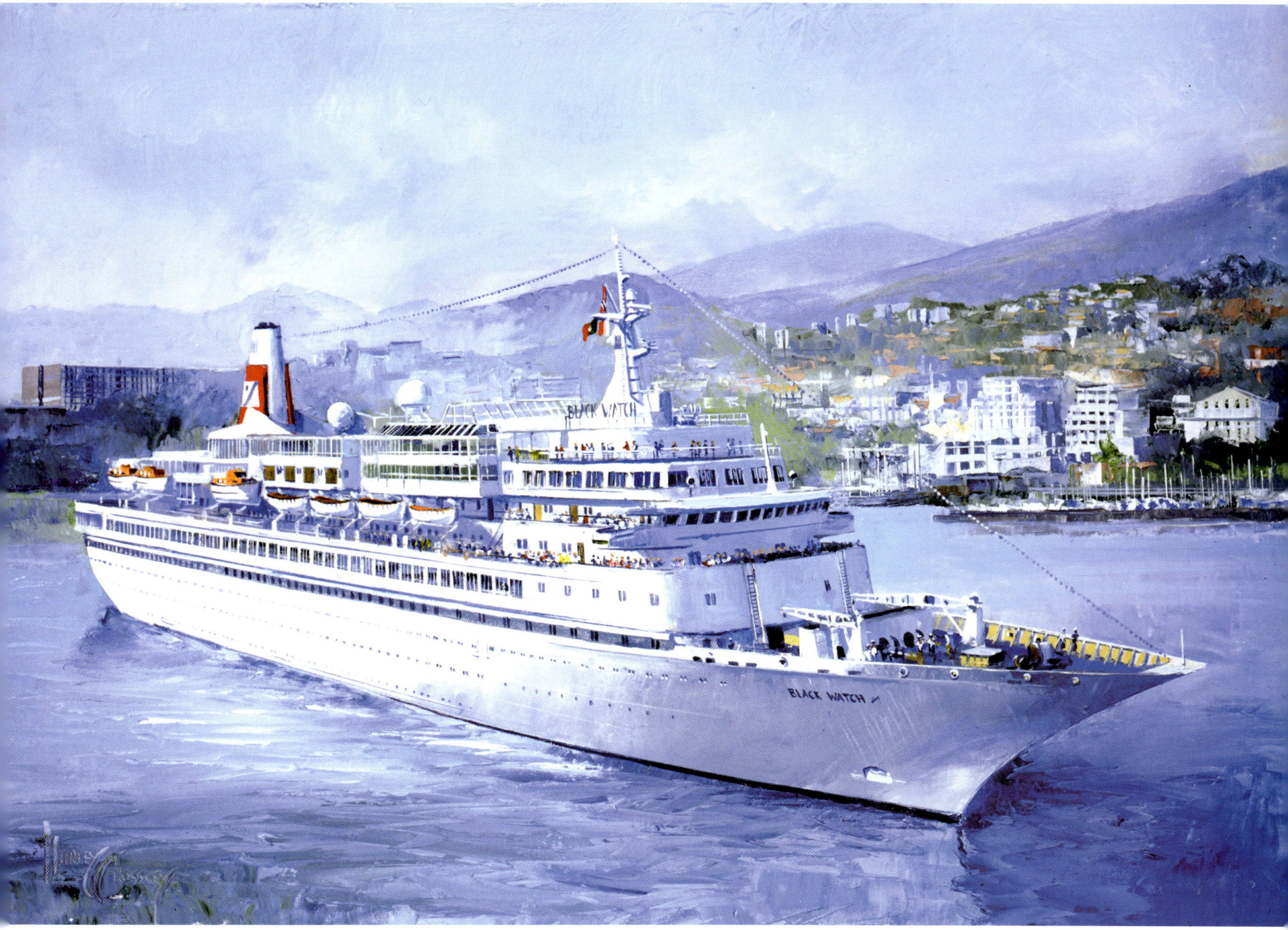

Black Watch at Funchal

SAGA RUBY

627 feet x 80 feet 24,292 grt

Built as the *Vistafjord* for Norwegian America Line by Swan Hunter at Wallsend on the River Tyne, she was very similar to *Sagafjord*, which had been built eight years previously by Forges et Chantiers de la Méditerranée in France. *Vistafjord* was to be the last ship built for the company and was also the last major deep-sea passenger liner with traditional sheer to be built on the River Tyne. Prefabricated cabins were used extensively by the builders, an innovative idea at that time.

Fitted with two nine-cylinder Sulzer diesel engines, she had a cruising speed of 20 knots with a maximum of 23 knots.

Like *Sagafjord*, she was built for transatlantic voyages and cruising at the luxury end of the market, but with only one class. Launched in May 1972, she sailed to Oslo on her delivery voyage a year later.

Departing from Oslo on 22 May 1973 for her maiden voyage to New York, *Vistafjord* soon enjoyed a loyal following of discerning passengers, taking her place as one of the five top luxury cruise ships afloat at that time. Like her fleet sister, her main voyages were luxury cruises with positioning crossings between Europe and the Caribbean.

In 1980, a new company, Norwegian America Cruises, was formed and *Vistafjord* was transferred to them continuing to operate under her original name.

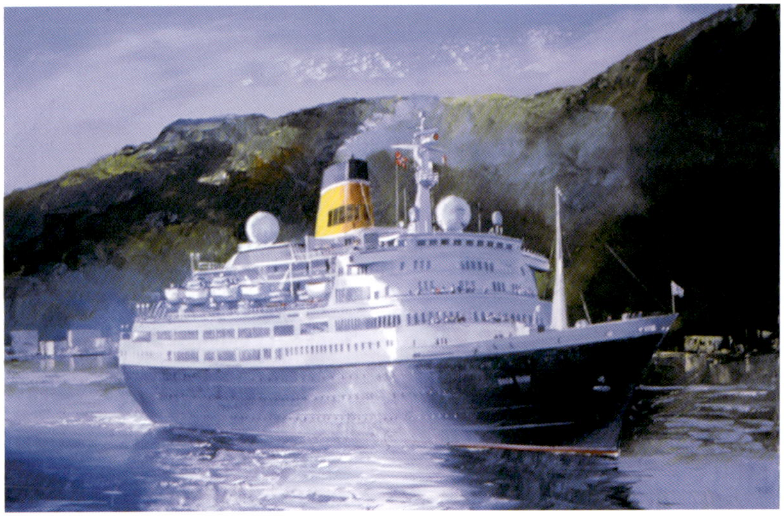

Saga Ruby

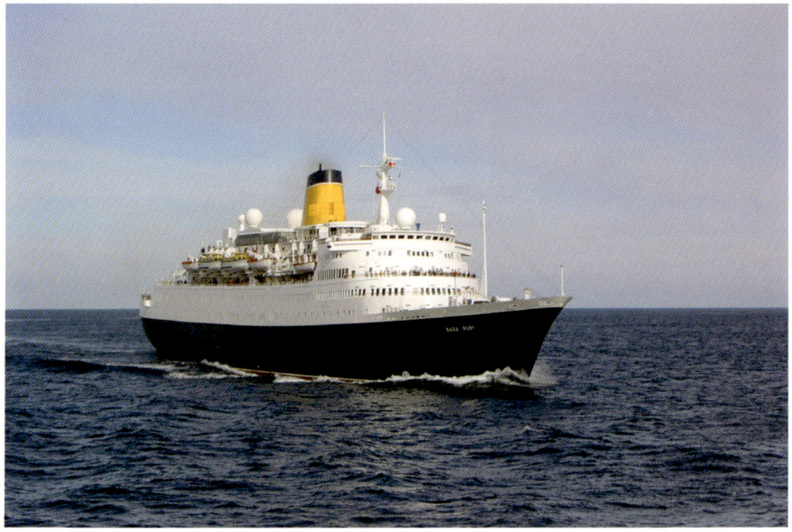

Saga Ruby

Cunard bought the company in 1983 and continued to operate the ship to the same high standard, retaining the mostly Norwegian crew. A year later, the ship had a major refit in Malta, emerging with a new two-level night club, extra cabins, and an enlarged restaurant that could seat all passengers in one sitting. A further major refit in 1994 saw an upgrade of cabin furnishings, more fitted with balconies, and the addition of two new two-level suites on the Bridge deck.

Kvaerner took over Cunard in 1996 and then, two years later, sold it to the Carnival Corporation. After another refit at Lloyd Werft in Bremerhaven, the ship was repainted in traditional Cunard colours with a dark hull and, on 10 December 1999, was renamed *Caronia* at a ceremony in Liverpool.

The ship was sold to Saga Shipping Company in May 2003 with a one-year lease back, at the end of which, the ship went to Malta for refurbishment and refit before sailing under her new owners. Renamed *Saga Ruby*, she sailed from Southampton in March 2005 on her maiden cruise for Saga, a company which specialises in the market for passengers over the age of fifty. Once again, she was sailing with her near sister ship, the ex-*Sagafjord* now renamed *Saga Rose*. Her continued success as a cruise ship is in no small part due to her classic lines and the relaxed atmosphere on board, appealing to older passengers who enjoy going to sea without the frenetic glitz of so many of the larger modern vessels today.

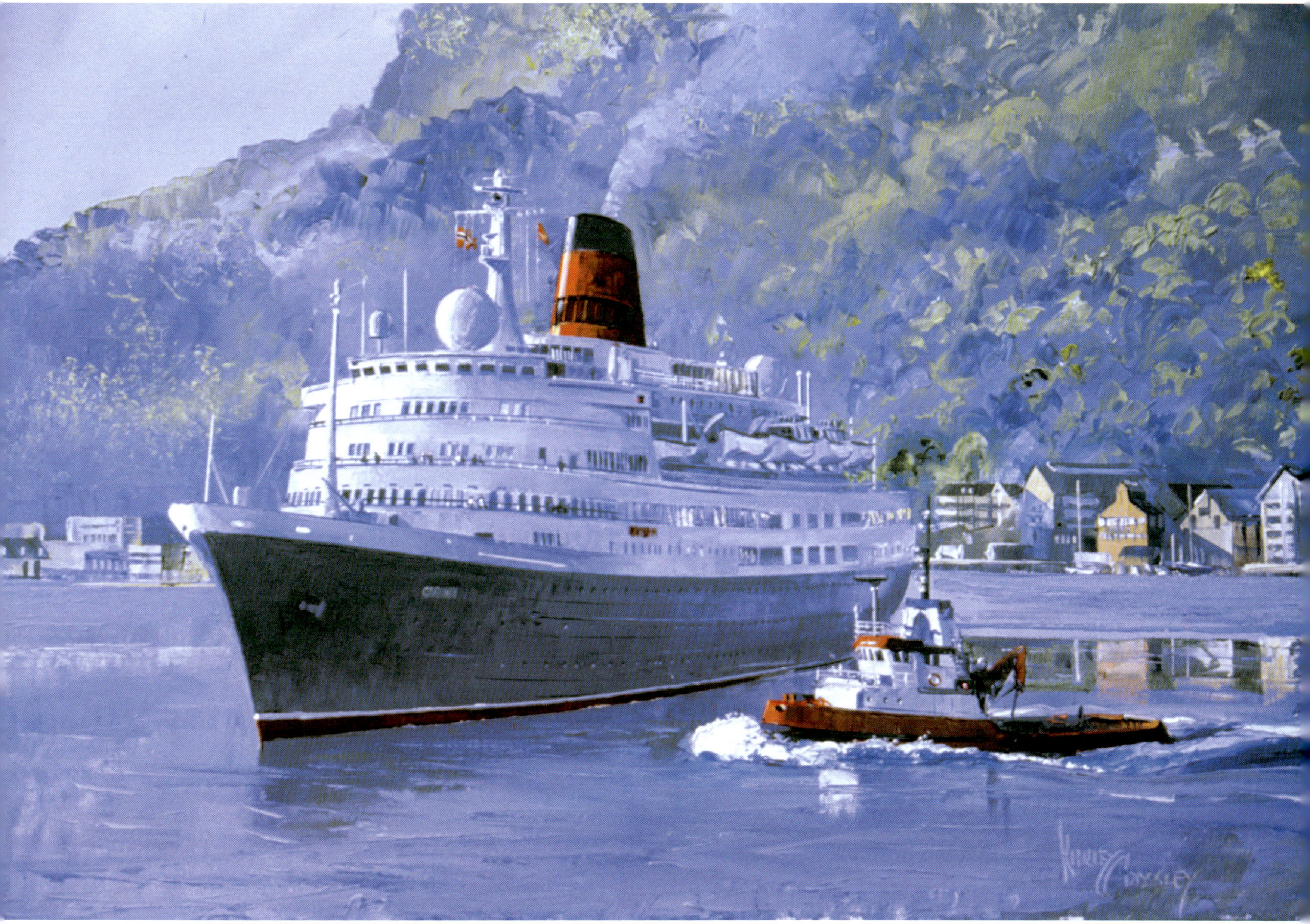

Caronia at Bergen

SOVEREIGN OF THE SEAS

873 ft x 105 ft 73,192 grt

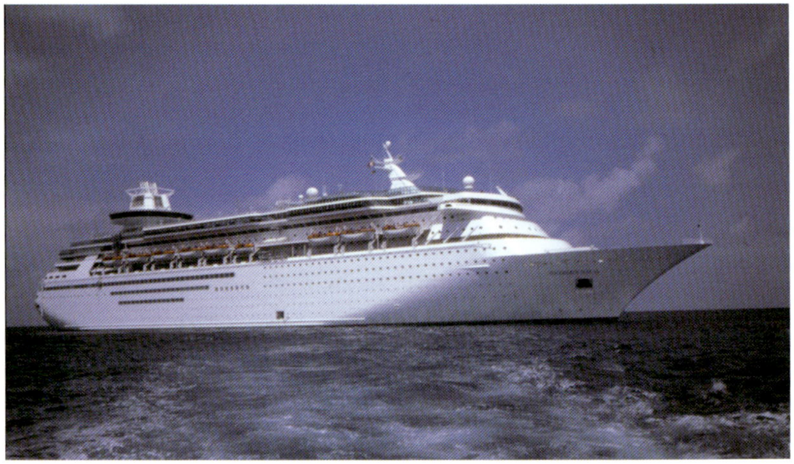

Sovereign of the Seas in the Caribbean

Floated out of her building dock in St Nazaire in April 1987, this was the first of the Sovereign class of ships ordered by Royal Caribbean Cruise Lines from Chantiers de L'Atlantique. Fitted with four Pielstick diesels and twin screws, she had a cruising speed of 19 knots. When launched, she was the largest purpose-built cruise ship afloat, although in length she was shorter than both the *Queen Elizabeth 2* and the *Norway*.

Fourteen decks high with a short but flared bow, *Sovereign of the Seas* was a modern design, with the Viking Crow Lounge wrapped round the funnel giving panoramic views. She was the first ship to have an open atrium area spanning five decks, an immense and impressive space featuring grand staircases and two glass lifts. Surprisingly, none of the cabins had balconies and they were also rather small, particularly when fitted with four berths. Unusually, there were no tables for two in either of the two restaurants.

After fitting out, she sailed in December on a positioning voyage from France to Miami, which was to be her home port. Originally destined to sail under the Liberian flag, this was changed to the Norwegian registry, much to the delight of her Norwegian officers.

Christened on 15 January 1988 by the former First Lady of America, Rosalynn Carter, the ship sailed from Miami the following day on her maiden cruise. The scheduled call at St Thomas had to be abandoned after she was unable to depart on time from San Juan, the Puerto Rican capital, due to a container ship, the *Long Beach*, going aground in the channel. The itinerary was altered and passengers were taken instead to Labadee, the private resort on Haiti leased to RCCL.

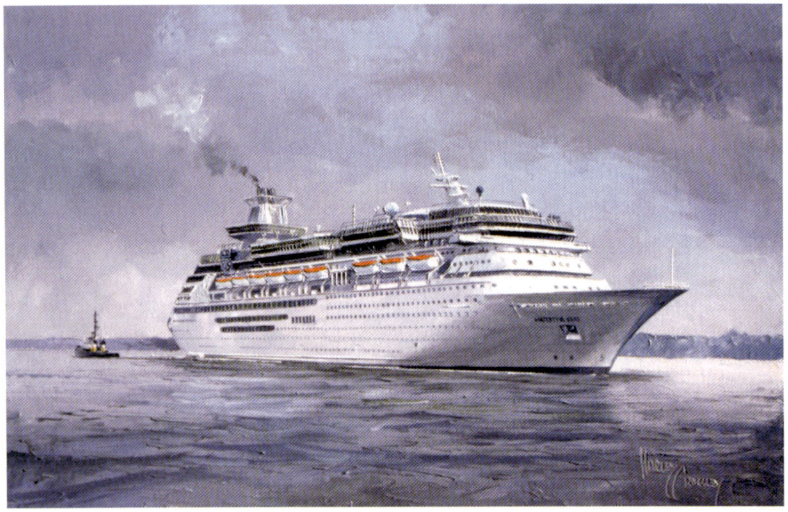

Majesty of the Seas

Sovereign of the Seas proved to be a popular ship with mainly American passengers enjoying short cruises to the Bahamas and Caribbean. Two more Sovereign-class ships followed, *Monarch of the Seas* entering service in 1991 and *Majesty of the Seas* in 1992.

In 1997, the company merged with Celebrity Cruises, and *Sovereign of the Seas* was extensively refurbished with her passenger capacity increased.

Adverse publicity followed during 1998-99 when a court case alleged that *Sovereign of the Seas* had repeatedly dumped oily waste into the sea and then falsified records to cover up the incidents. Although the company argued that being incorporated in Liberia it did not come under the jurisdiction of the US courts, they lost the case and were fined $9 million.

A mini television series featured the major refurbishment of the ship in 2005. Her port of registry was changed to the Bahamas, and the following year saw her relocated to Port Canaveral for three- and four-night cruises to the Bahamas.

Transferred to Pullmantur Cruises two years later and reregistered in Malta, her first cruise under the new name of MS *Sovereign* was in March 2009. She is scheduled to be chartered during the winter of 2010/11 to Viagens CVC, Brazil.

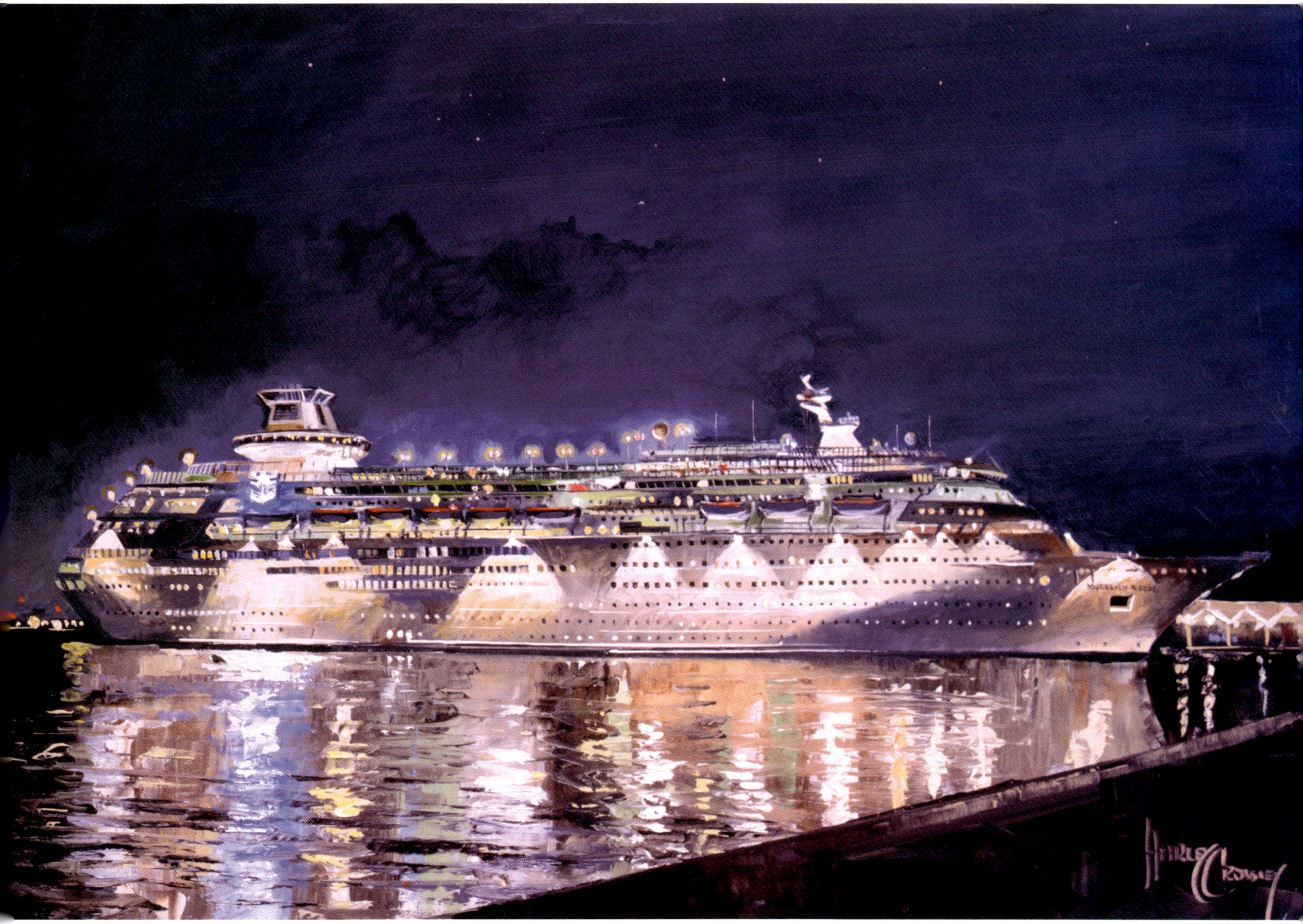

Sovereign of the Seas in Puerto Rico at night

ARCADIA

806 feet x 105 feet 63,524 grt

In 1986, Sitmar Cruises ordered a new 1,600-passenger cruise ship from Chantiers de l'Atlantique in St Nazaire. She was launched as *Sitmar Fairmajesty* on 5 March 1988, but before her completion, Sitmar was taken over by P&O, who assigned the new ship to Princess Cruises.

The first modern cruise ship to be built with diesel-electric propulsion, she had more room per passenger than many similar-sized ships and was destined for use mainly in the American market.

Named *Star Princess* by film star Audrey Hepburn at Port Everglades in March 1989, she sailed from here on her first cruise under the Liberian flag.

The next eight years were spent with a schedule of winter cruises in the Caribbean from Fort Lauderdale and summer on the west coast and Alaska. During the summer of 1992, she cruised in the Mediterranean between Barcelona and Venice.

In June 1995, whilst under the control of the Alaskan pilot, *Star Princess* struck a rock, which damaged the starboard propeller and put a gash in her side. 1,500 passengers were landed by the ships tenders and taken to Juneau, and the ship eventually sailed to Portland, USA, for repairs that took a month to complete.

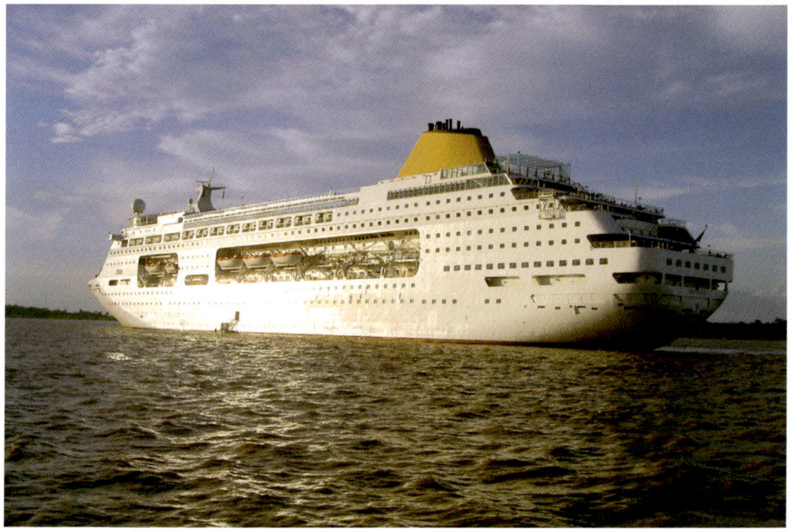

Arcadia in the Amazon

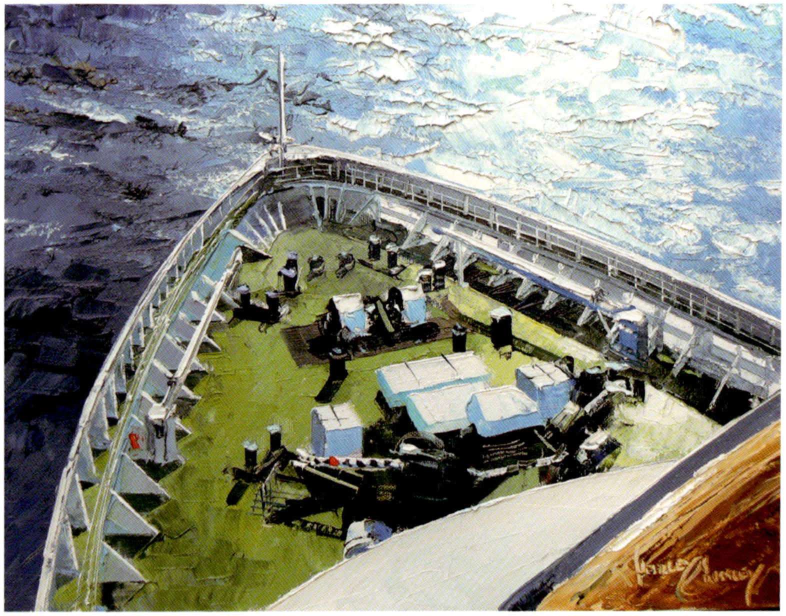

Arcadia – view of bows

At the end of her 1997 season, *Star Princess* sailed from the west coast of America through the Panama Canal to Harland & Wolff shipyard in Belfast. During the refit, her interior was altered to make her more suitable for the British tastes and cruising in the European market. She was to replace *Canberra*, which was being retired from service. At the end of the refit, she sailed to Southampton, where she was renamed *Arcadia* by Betty Boothroyd, the Speaker of the House of Commons, on 19 December 1997. She left on her maiden cruise as *Arcadia* four days later.

In January 1998, *Arcadia* sailed from Southampton on a three-month round-the-world cruise. For the next five years, *Arcadia* regularly sailed from Southampton to European destinations and the Caribbean. In 2001, she was marketed by P&O as an adult-only cruise ship.

Marketing a new concept in cruising for young people and families in 2003, the ship was renamed *Ocean Village*. She sailed on economy cruises in the Mediterranean during the summer and the Caribbean in the winter under the new P&O Ocean Village division and was joined by another ship, *Ocean Village Two*, in 2007.

This was not the success the company had hoped for, and *Ocean Village* is scheduled to be transferred to P&O Australia in the autumn of 2010 and renamed as *Pacific Pearl*.

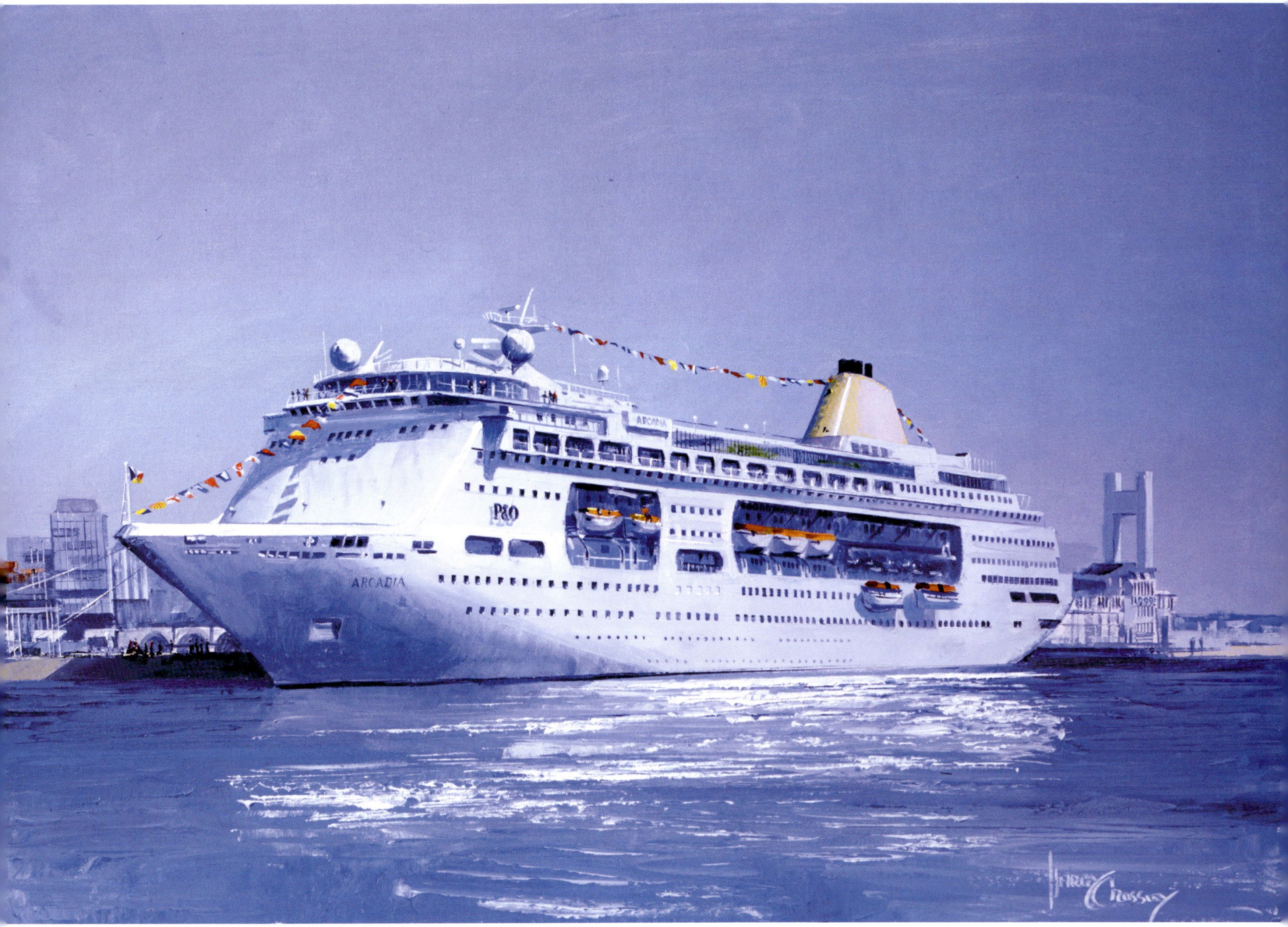

Arcadia at La Coruña

ORIANA

853 feet x 105 feet 69,153 grt

Built at Meyer-Werft in Pappenburg, Germany, in 1995 for P&O Cruises, she was the second ship to bear the name for the company. Fitted with four MAN diesel engines giving a service speed of 24 knots, *Oriana* was the fastest cruise ship to be built for twenty-five years. She was also the first cruise liner custom built for the British market, and the largest ship to be built in Germany since 1914.

Her naming ceremony took place in Southampton on 6 April 1995, when she was christened *Oriana* by Her Majesty Queen Elizabeth II.

When she sailed on her maiden voyage from Southampton on 9 April 1995, she was one of the largest cruise ships in the world, with a maximum capacity of 1,975 passengers, although she usually only carries around 1,800.

Undertaking cruises in the Mediterranean, Canaries and the Baltic, *Oriana* proved popular with the British public, catering as she did for this specific market. She annually undertook a world cruise of around three months duration, which attracted many repeat bookings.

In 1997, *Canberra* was retired from the P&O fleet, and during her final cruise, when both ships were anchored off Cannes, the Golden Cockerel was handed over to *Oriana* as recognition for being the fastest ship in the fleet.

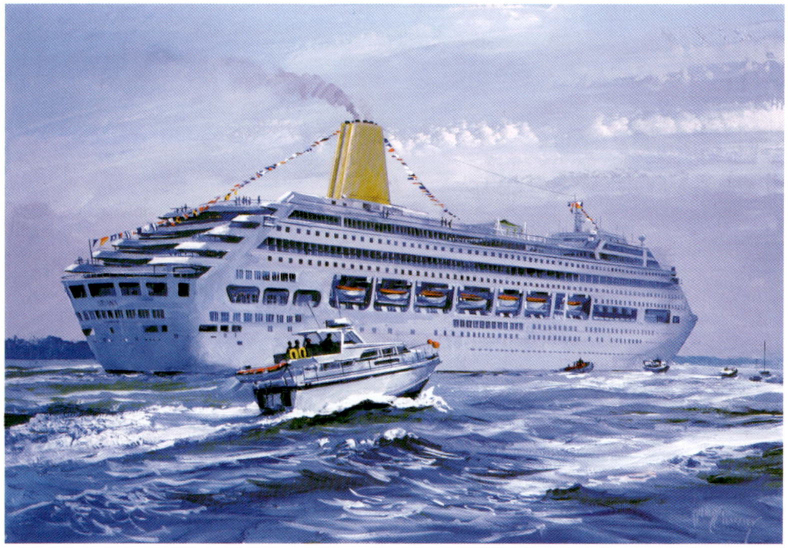

Oriana, maiden departure from Southampton

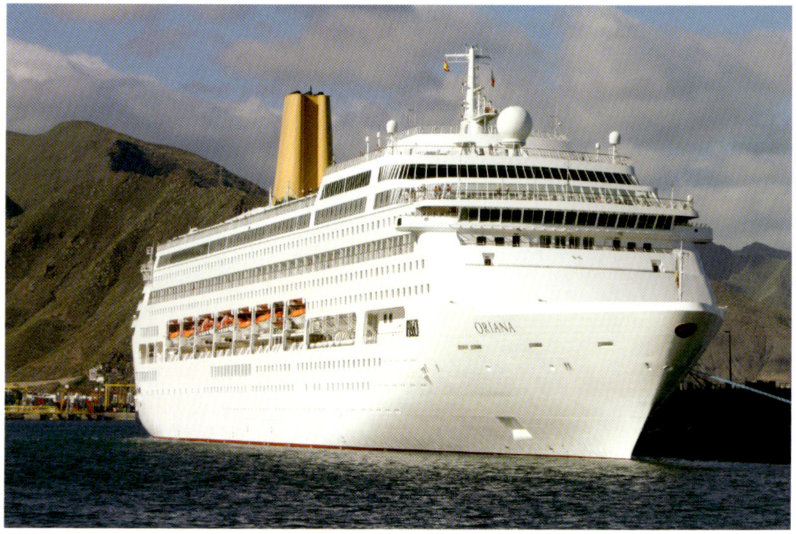

Oriana

Oriana went to Bremerhaven for a massive refit in December 2006, afterwards changing her port of registry from London to Bermuda. This change meant that wedding ceremonies could now be performed on board the ship, which proved to be a popular attraction. During the refit, all the cabins were restyled with new furnishings reflecting a more modern decoration. At the same time, the elegant Curzon Room was replaced with a 'celebrity restaurant' bearing the name of Gary Rhodes, capable of seating ninety-six people.

With her tiered rear decks giving more open deck space than a lot of modern ships, *Oriana* is a popular ship with cruisers of all ages. The open wrap-around promenade deck is particularly popular with passengers when many ships now have partially enclosed promenade areas. Her more traditional décor, which some might say is old fashioned, fills a niche in the current market, where not all passengers are enthusiastic about the glitz of American-style cruising. Indeed, many passengers were unhappy at the removal of the Curzon Room, which was originally used as a quiet, relaxing lounge during the day, and the venue for Classical concerts in the evening. The latter form of entertainment is now relegated to either the theatre or the cinema. The Theatre Royal is an imposing venue, appropriately decorated in rich reds with a revolving stage, orchestra pit and seats with individual air-conditioning.

Oriana continues to cruise from Southampton to Europe and the Mediterranean, also undertaking a grand or world cruise each year.

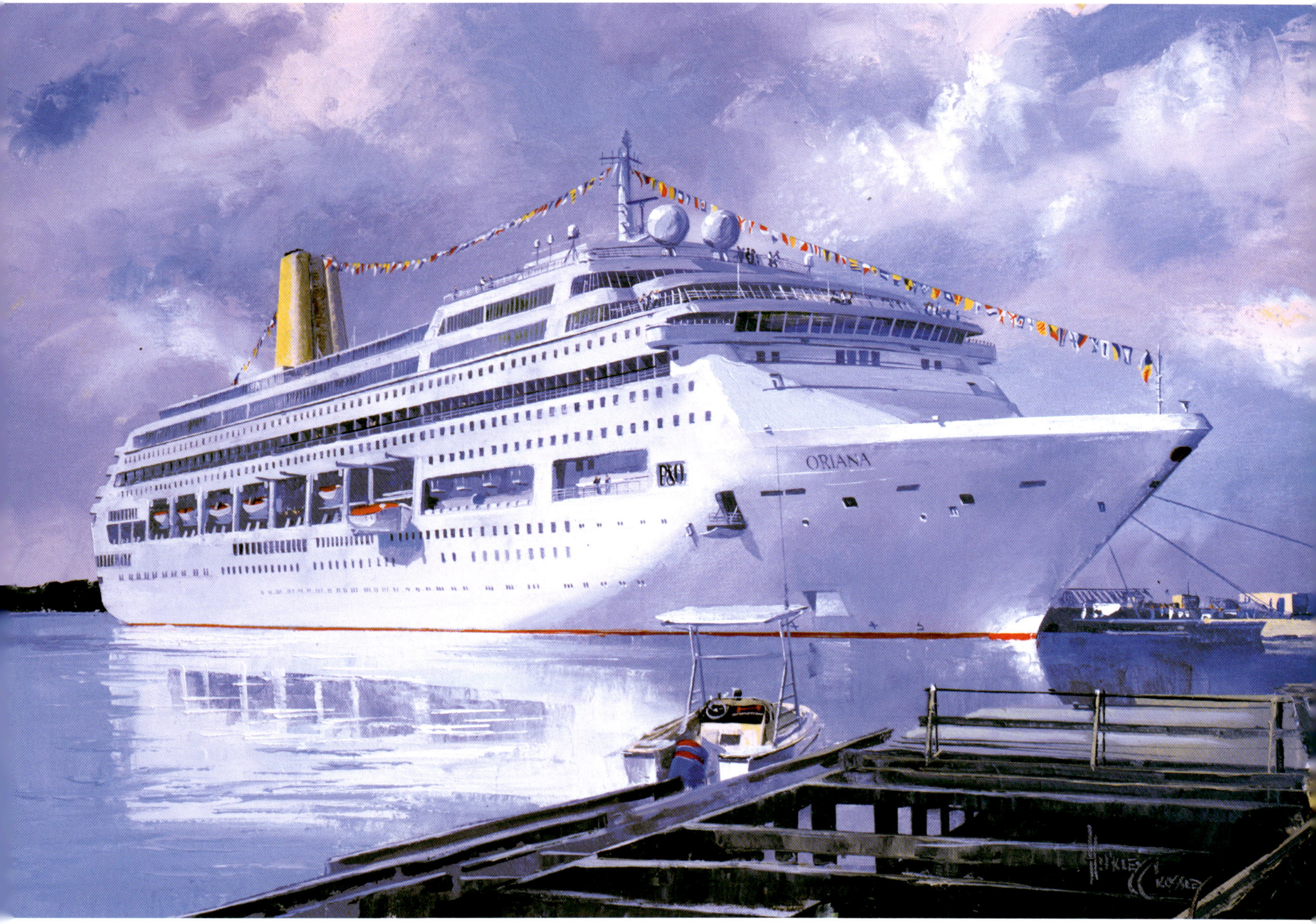

Oriana at Antigua

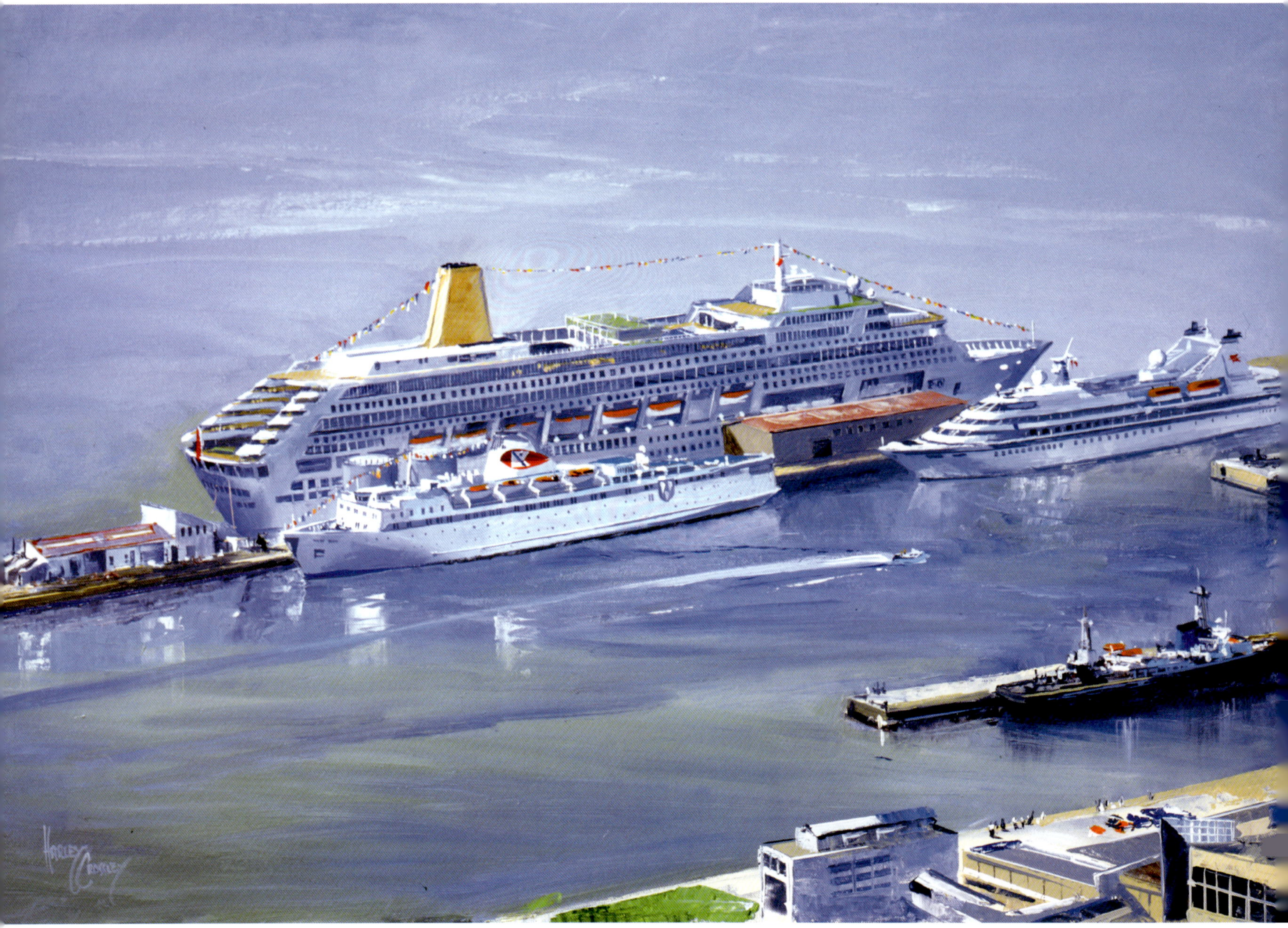

Oriana at Gibraltar

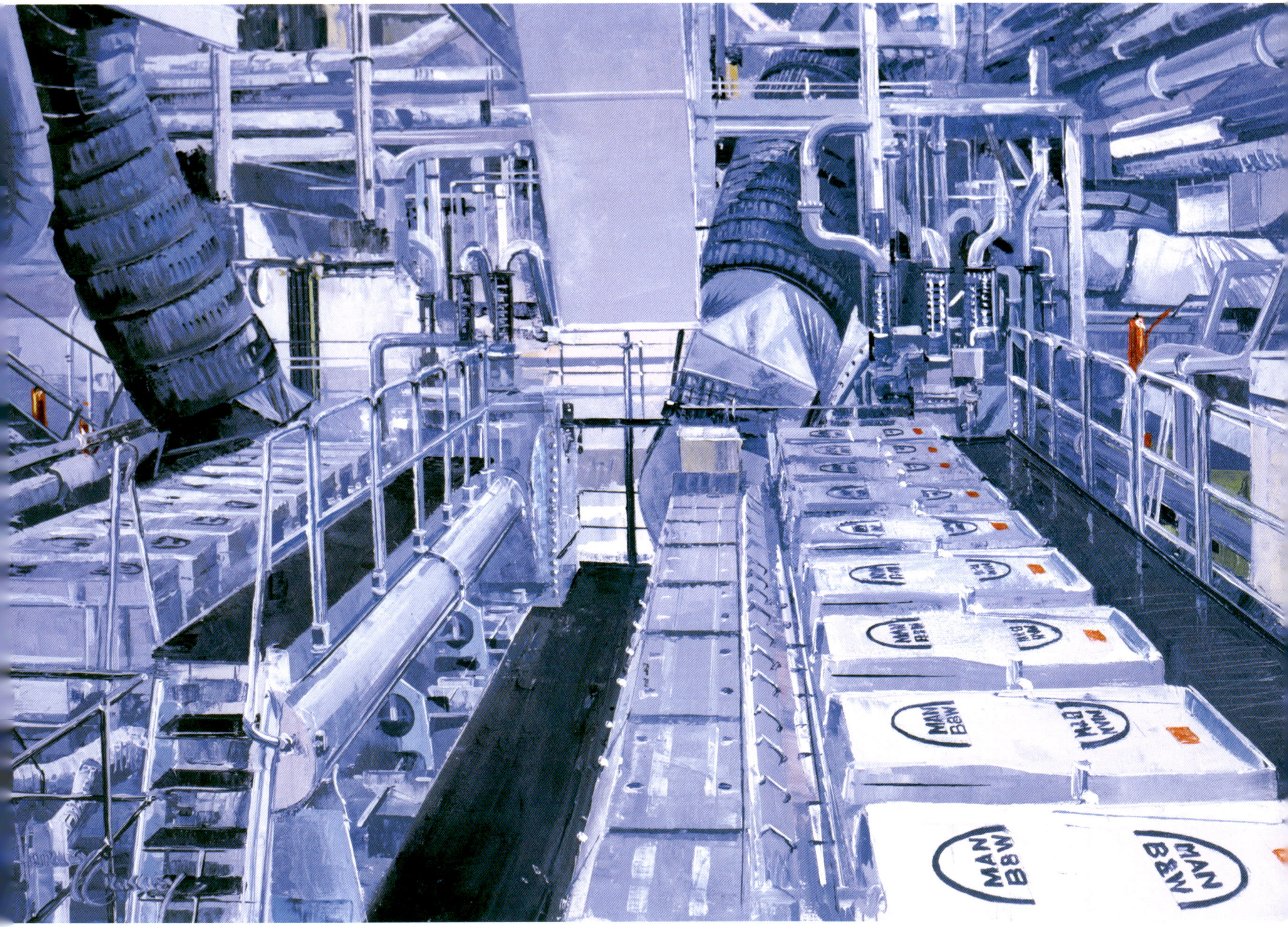

Oriana – part of the engine room

ADONIA

856 feet x 105 feet 77,690 grt

Built by Fincantieri in Italy for Princess Cruises, she entered service in 1998 as *Sea Princess*. She is one of the Sun class of sister ships from the same yard, the first being *Dawn Princess*, launched the previous year. Fitted with diesel-electric engines, each ship had a passenger capacity of 2,250 and sailed under the Liberian flag.

Although large ships at the time of building, they were designed with attractive profiles. The funnel contained a sports court for tennis/volleyball in the base of it. Built with plenty of deck space, they also had numerous small public rooms, which gave an intimate feel to the interior.

Cruising from America in the Caribbean, *Sea Princess* was a successful addition to the growing Princess fleet for the next five years.

When *Arcadia* was transferred and renamed *Ocean Village*, catering for younger passengers, it left a gap in the P&O fleet of cruise ships. This resulted in the transfer of two of the Princess ships to P&O in 2003.

Ocean Princess was renamed *Oceana* and *Sea Princess* became *Adonia*. In the first ever double naming ceremony, the two ships were rechristened in Southampton on 21 May 2003 by HRH the Princess Royal and her daughter Zara Phillips.

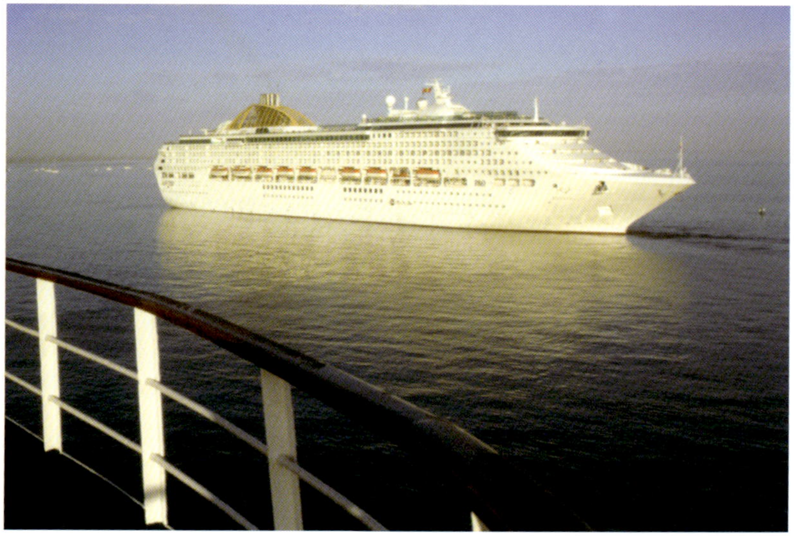

Adonia at Walvis Bay

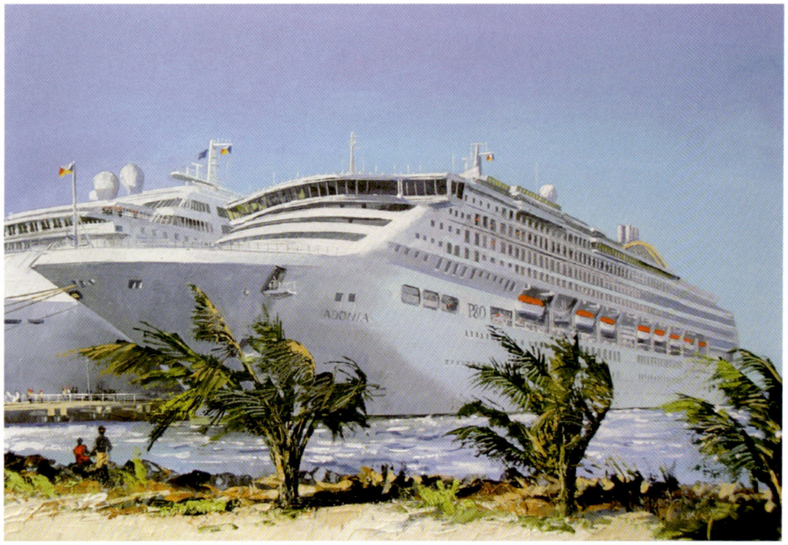

Adonia at Tortola

Adonia was marketed as an adults-only ship for P&O, and many passengers welcomed this restriction. The children's playroom was converted into a quiet lounge with massage chairs, where passengers could relax whilst looking out of the panoramic windows. The children's pool was transformed into a Feng Shui area, a markedly different use from the original one.

However, her service for P&O was only of short duration, lasting just two years.

Designed originally for cruising in the Caribbean, *Adonia* was not ideally suited to sailing in anything other than calm waters, but this did not deter P&O from sending her on a world cruise in 2004. It was not an unmitigated success, as she had trouble keeping to the schedule due to her lack of speed, arriving late at many of the ports and breaking down several times. After repair, she completed the voyage, but many passengers were unhappy about the cruise, and she did not sail on another world cruise for P&O.

In 2005, the new *Arcadia* entered service with P&O, and *Adonia* was transferred back to Princess Cruises. For her new service with them, she reverted to her original name of *Sea Princess*. Aimed at both the American and British market, she cruises out of both the UK and the Caribbean, but the currency on board is now the US dollar.

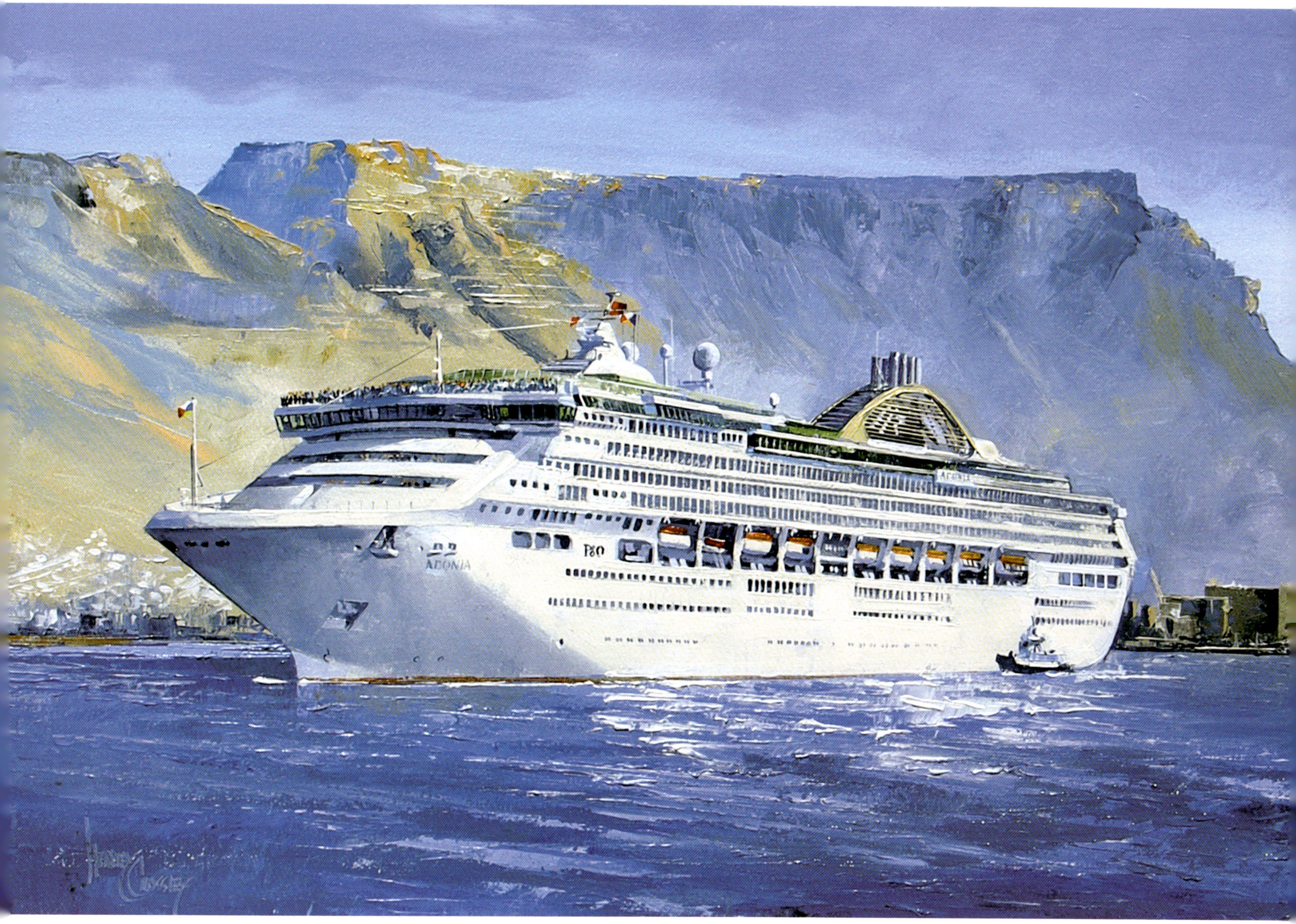

Adonia at Cape Town

AURORA

886 feet x 105 feet 76,152 grt

Built for P&O Cruises Ltd at the privately owned German shipyard of Meyer Werft in Pappenburg, where they have been building ships since 1795, construction of *Aurora* was begun in December 1998. With a similar layout to her near sister ship, *Oriana*, which was built at the same shipyard, *Aurora* was specifically designed for the expanding British market.

Her four MAN B&W diesel engines develop 79,860 shp, giving a maximum speed of 24 knots, although on her trials she achieved 29 knots. The final propulsion is by two 20,000-kw electric motors, driving two 19-foot-diameter fixed-pitch propellers, which turn at 142 rpm.

The ship has the popular curved rear decks first seen on *Royal Princess* and later developed on the *Oriana*. She is also fitted with a Magrodome, which enables one of the three swimming pools to be covered during inclement weather.

Named after the Greek Goddess of Dawn, she was christened *Aurora* on 27 April 2000 at her home port of Southampton by Her Royal Highness the Princess Royal and entered service in May.

Her maiden voyage was curtailed after eighteen hours when a propeller-shaft bearing failed. After disembarking the passengers at Southampton, *Aurora* returned to Hamburg for repairs. Passengers were given a full refund and the choice of another cruise. Repaired, she sailed from Southampton on 15 May 2000 on her first cruise.

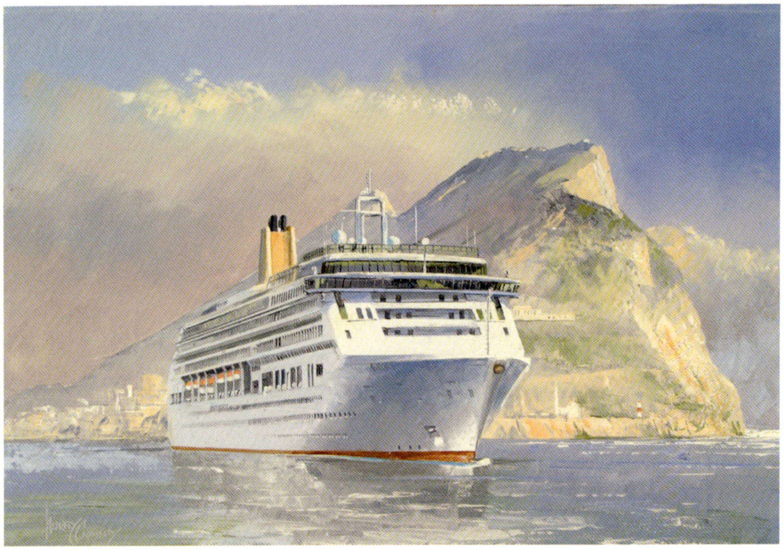

Aurora at Gibraltar

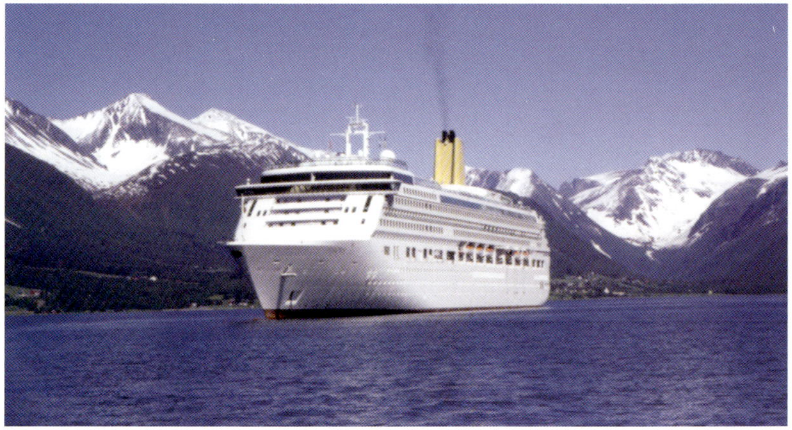

Aurora at Andalsnes

The ship settled into her cruising routine covering Europe from the North Cape to the Canaries and further afield during the summer and autumn, soon proving popular with her mainly British passengers. She left on a three-month cruise around the world starting from Southampton each January with many passengers being repeat bookings each year.

Aurora sustained some damage to one of her propellers in March 2001 when she rescued eleven Russian seamen after their ship sank in the South China Sea.

A major fault was discovered at the start of her 2005 winter Grand Voyage when one of her main electric-propulsion motors failed. After ten days, during which time the ship twice went on trials with her passengers along the south coast of England, the cruise was cancelled, passengers disembarked, and *Aurora* again returned to Blohm & Voss in Hamburg for repairs and a refit, returning to service in April that year. This cruise became known as the Grand Voyage Round the Isle of Wight.

In December 2007, during her refit, all the cabins were refurbished and upgraded. The ship's registry was changed from London, England, to Hamilton, Bermuda.

During the 2009 World Cruise a fault developed in the port-shaft bearing, and the ship sailed from Sydney to Auckland on one propeller. Repairs took five days, and three Pacific ports were missed to enable the ship to regain its schedule. Despite her intermittent problems, *Aurora* remains a firm favourite with British cruise passengers.

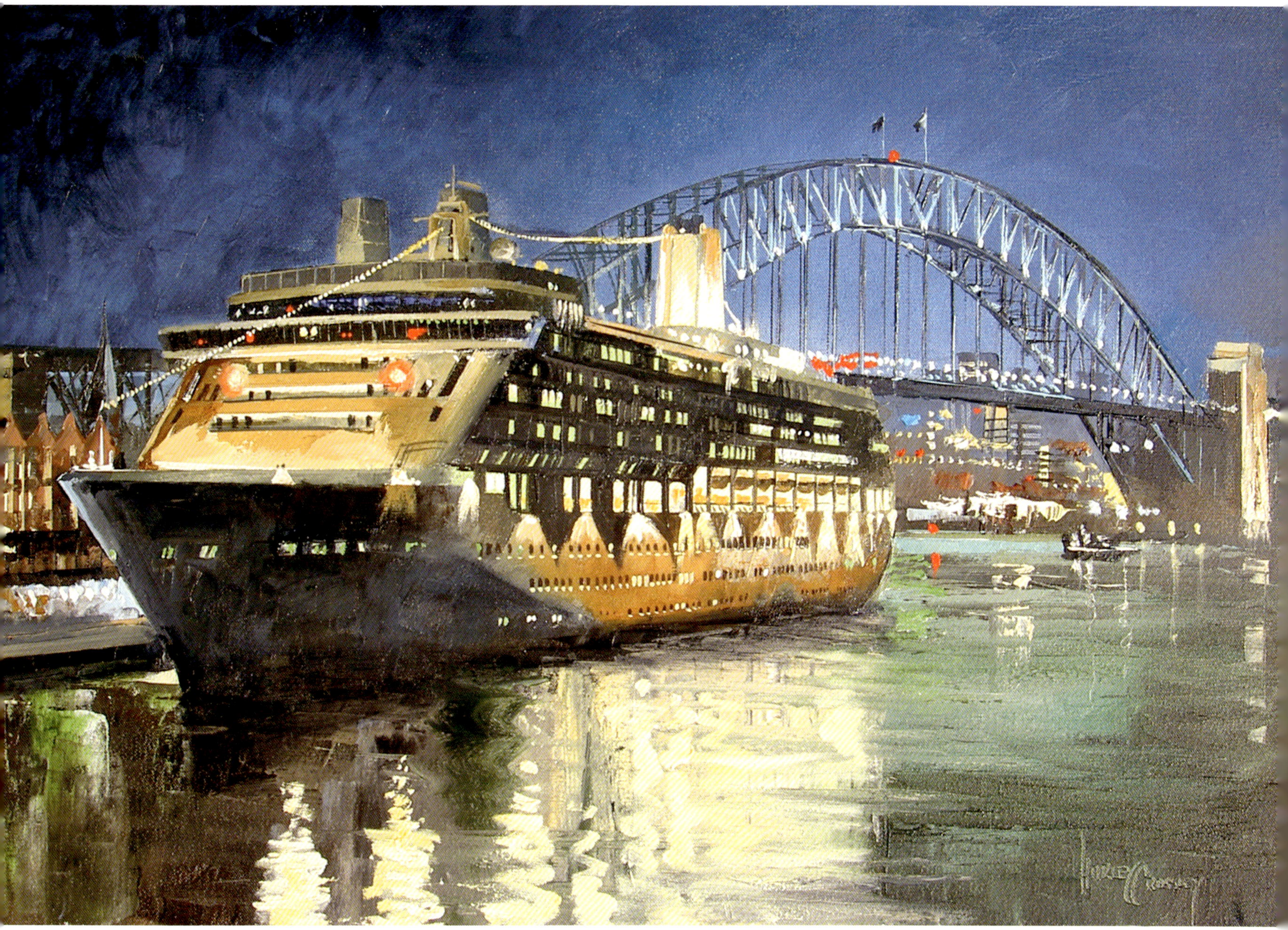

Aurora at Circular Quay, Sydney

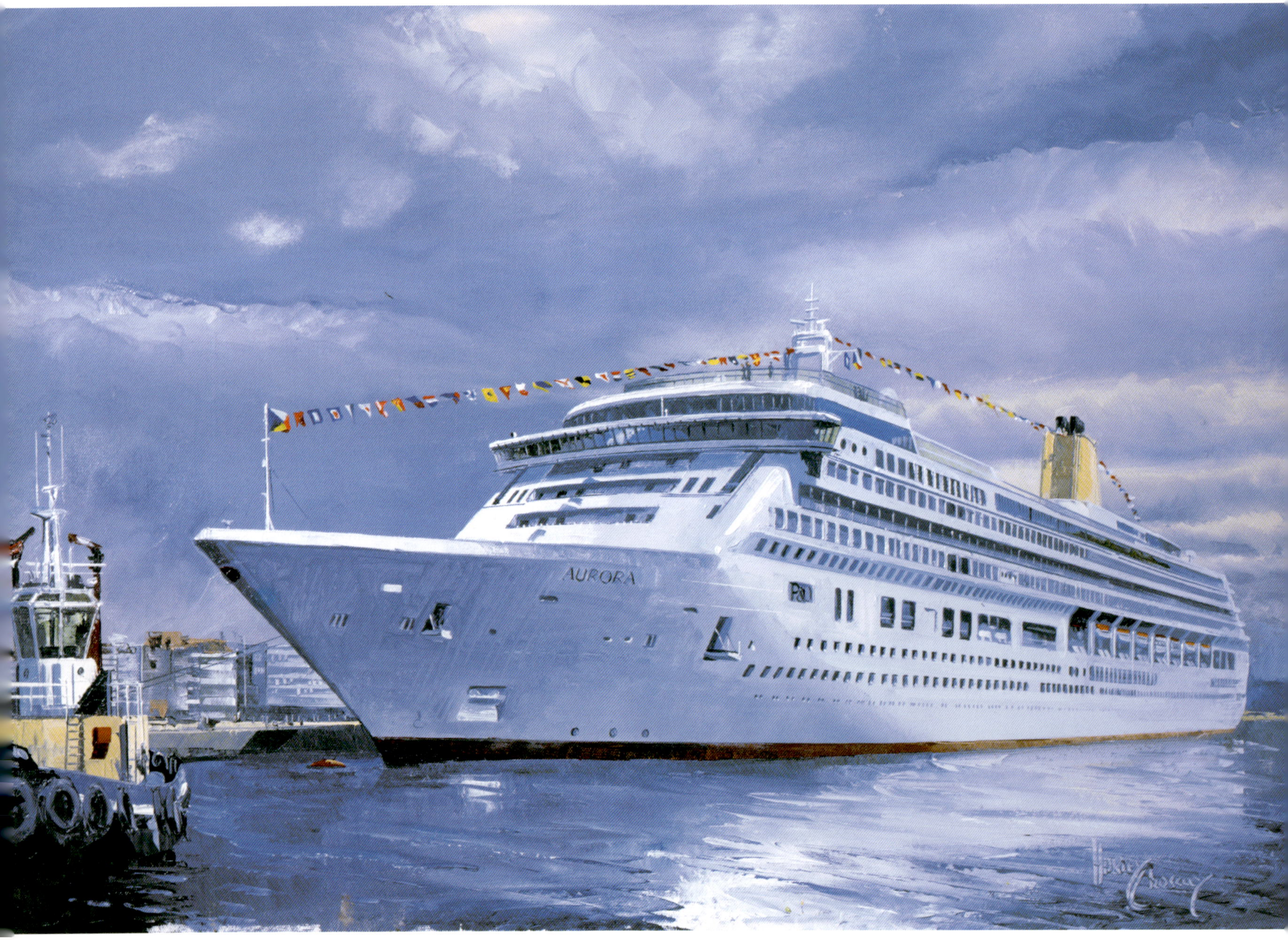

Aurora in La Coruña

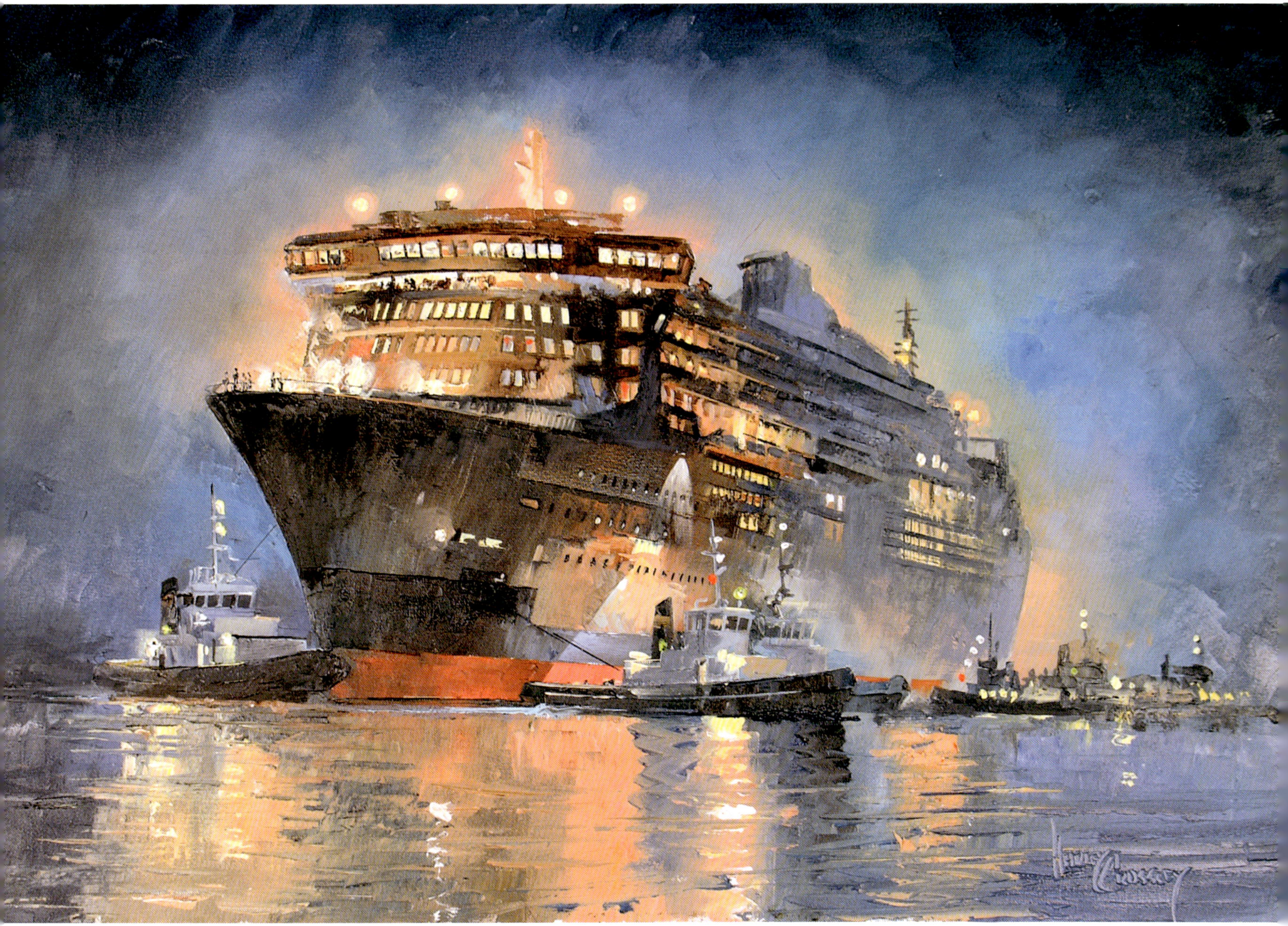

Queen Mary 2 – her first move

QUEEN ELIZABETH

964 feet x 106 feet 90,400 grt

Cunard's latest addition to their fleet is the new *Queen Elizabeth*, which at the time of writing is under construction by Fincantieri in Monfalconi, Italy. With a passenger capacity of 2,092, she is due to enter service on 12 October 2010.

Bookings for this maiden voyage to the Atlantic Isles were completely sold out in 29 minutes, 14 seconds: a record for Cunard.

The following photographs show Harley at work on the official ship's portrait commissioned by Cunard to hang in the Grand Lobby of *Queen Elizabeth*.

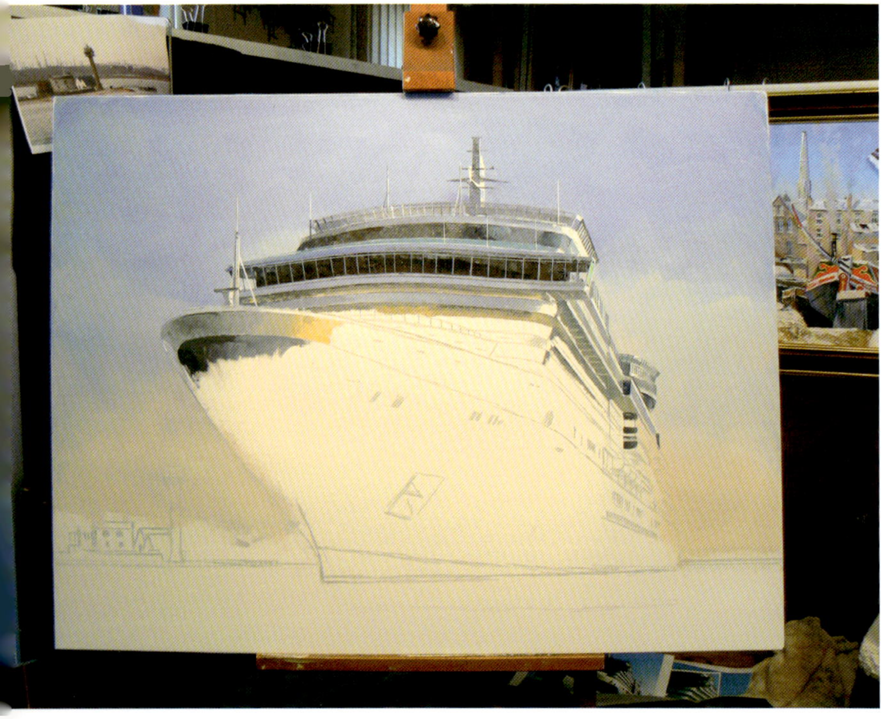

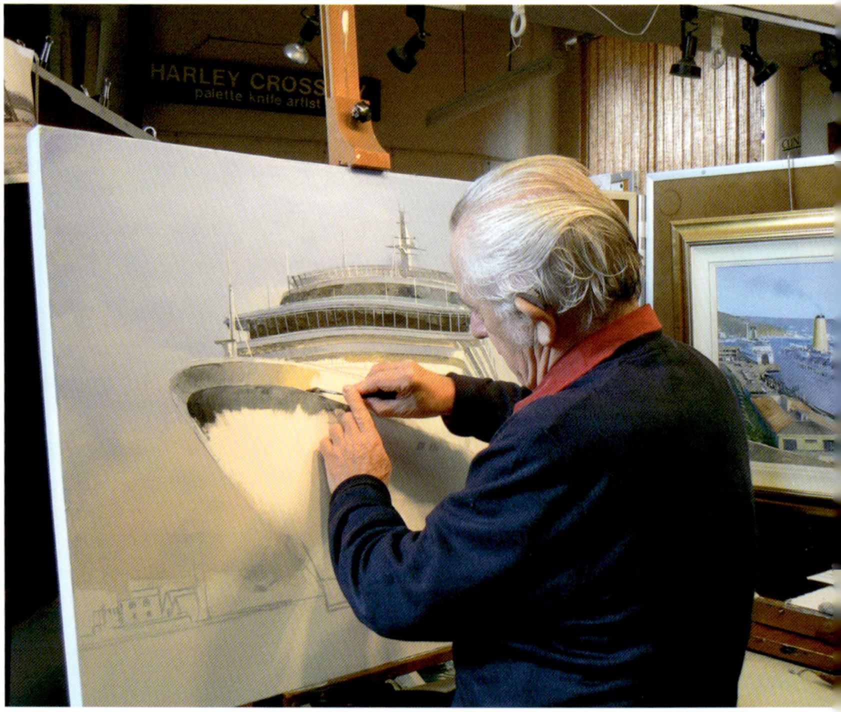

Above: Painting in progress

Opposite: *Queen Elizabeth* passing *Calshot*, Southampton Water

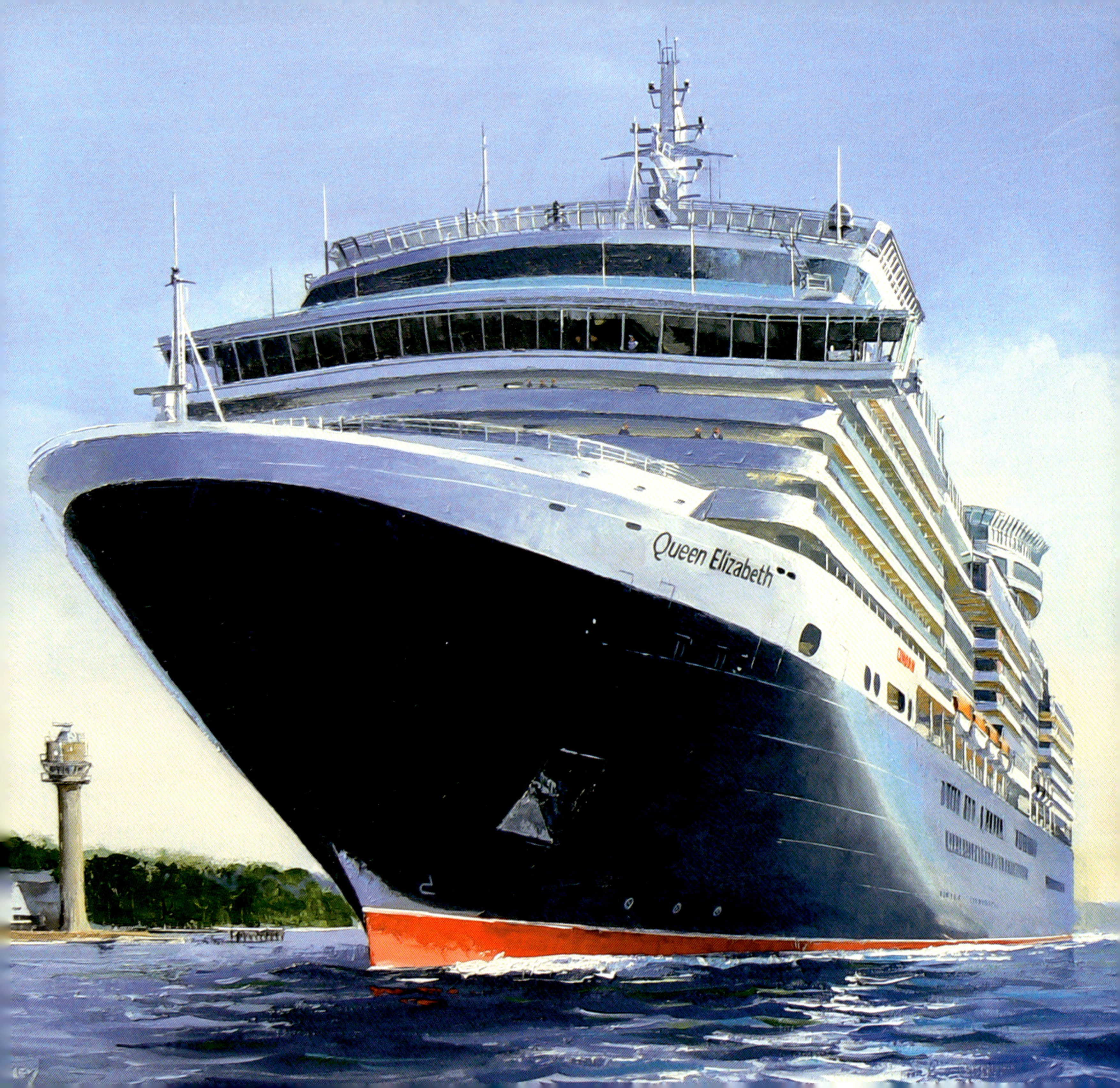
Queen Elizabeth

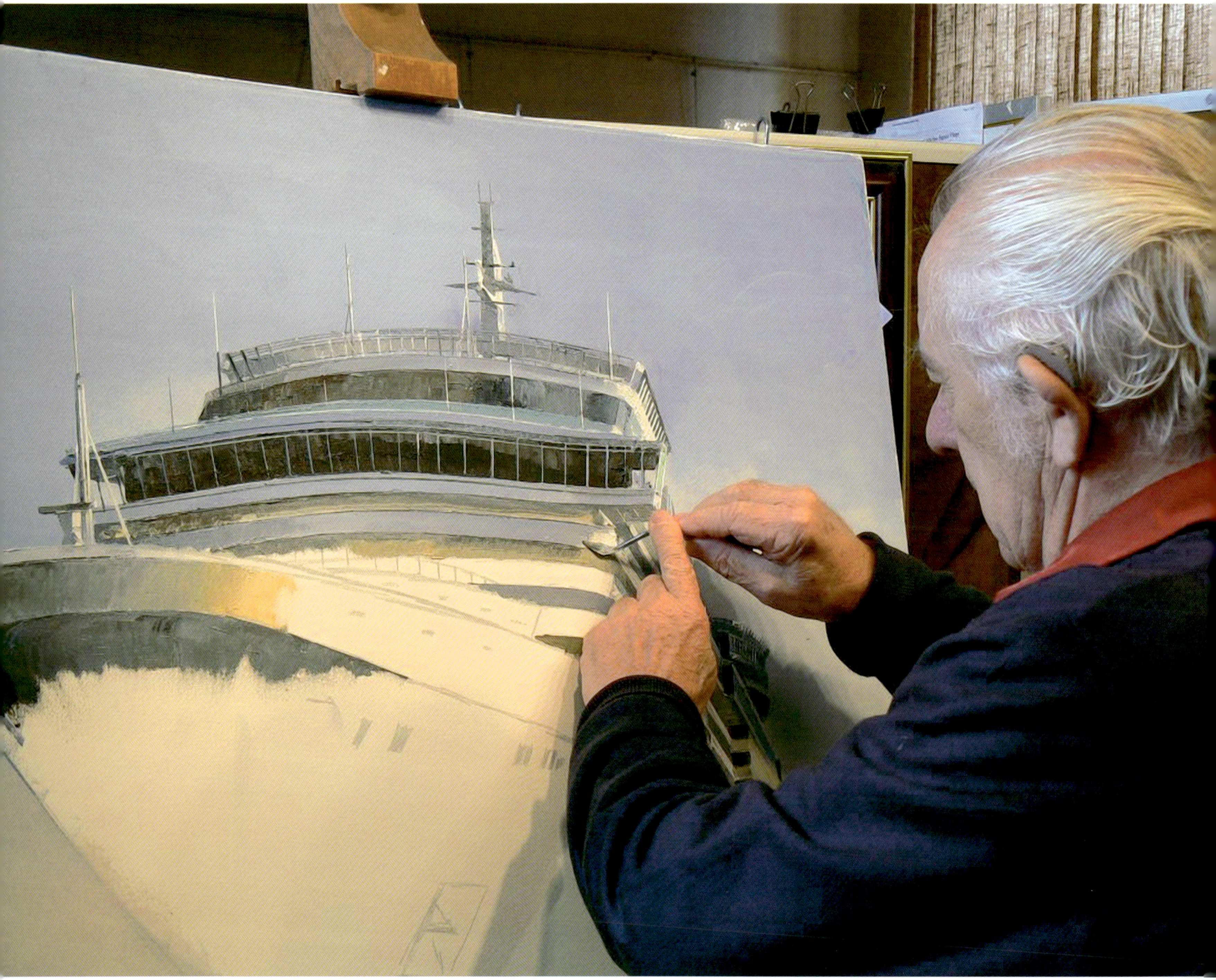

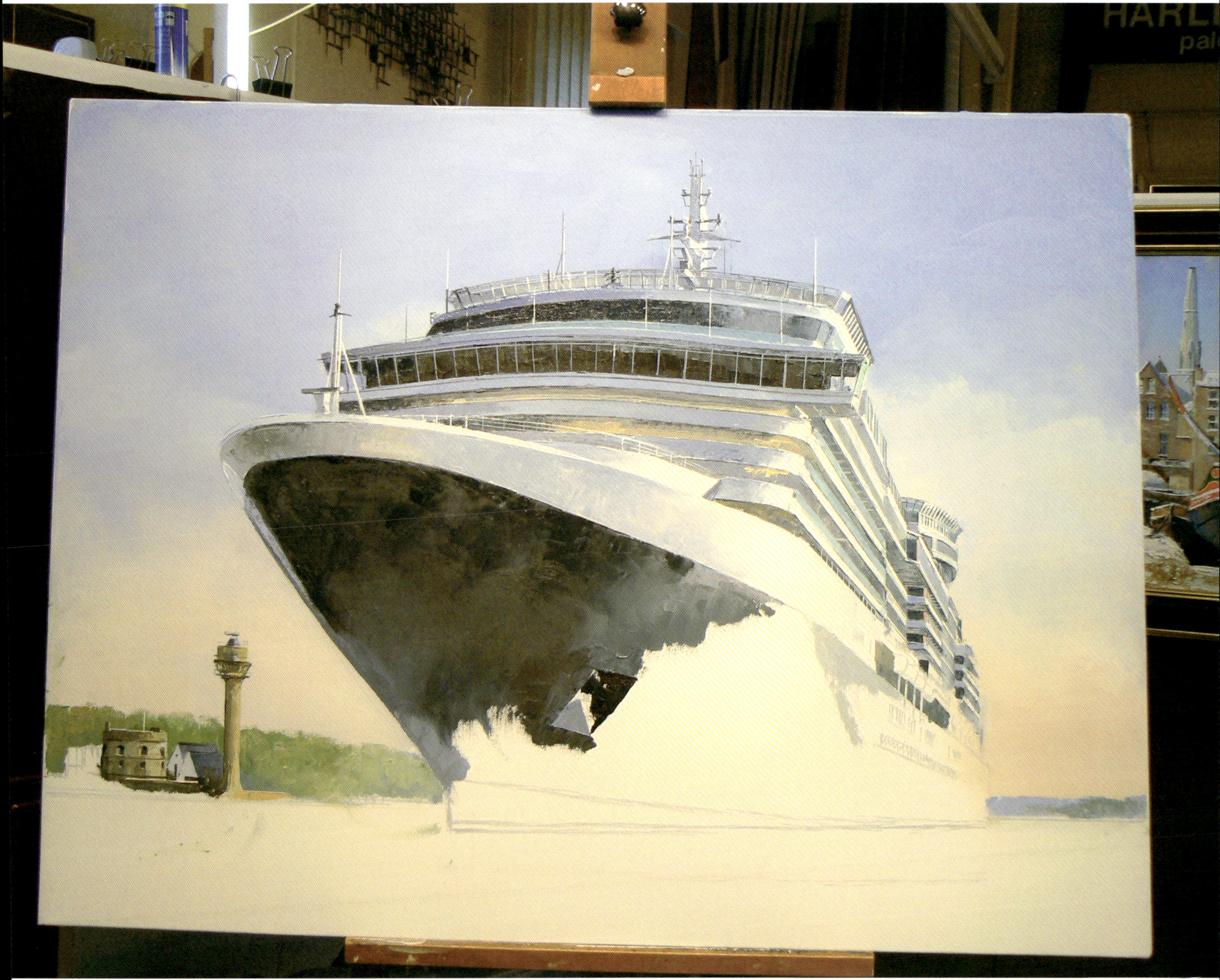

INDEX